M000158630

ROTH FAMILY FOUNDATION

Imprint in Music

Michael P. Roth

and Sukey Garcetti

have endowed this

imprint to honor the

memory of their parents,

Julia and Harry Roth,

whose deep love of music

they wish to share

with others.

The publisher and the University of California Press Foundation gratefully acknowledge the generous support of the Roth Family Foundation Imprint in Music, established by a major gift from Sukey and Gil Garcetti and Michael P. Roth.

Support for this book was generously provided by the AMS 75 PAYS Endowment of the American Musicological Society, supported in part by the National Endowment for the Humanities and the Andrew W. Mellon Foundation.

The Operetta Empire

The Operetta Empire

Music Theater in Early Twentieth-Century Vienna

Micaela Baranello

UNIVERSITY OF CALIFORNIA PRESS

University of California Press
Oakland, California

© 2021 by Micaela Baranello

Library of Congress Cataloging-in-Publication Data

Names: Baranello, Micaela, 1985– author.
Title: The operetta empire : music theater in early twentieth-century
Vienna / Micaela Baranello.
Identifiers: LCCN 2020046916 (print) | LCCN 2020046917 (ebook) |
ISBN 9780520379121 (cloth) | ISBN 9780520976542 (ebook)
Subjects: LCSH: Operetta—Austria—Vienna—20th century.
Classification: LCC ML1723.8.V6 B18 2021 (print) | LCC ML1723.8.V6
(ebook) | DDC 782.109436/13—dc23
LC record available at https://lccn.loc.gov/2020046916
LC ebook record available at https://lccn.loc.gov/2020046917

Manufactured in the United States of America

29 28 27 26 25 24 23 22 21
10 9 8 7 6 5 4 3 2 1

CONTENTS

CONTENTS

I was first attracted to operetta because of its optimism. Amid the thickets of Schoenberg and Mahler, the works of Lehár and Kálmán seemed to suggest a world in which men and, most crucially, women could find happiness, if only onstage. Of course, the relationship between that onstage happiness and the real world is a tricky thing. When I tell people, particularly if I'm in Austria or Germany, that I study operetta, the reactions vary wildly. To many, operetta represents the culture of their parents or grandparents, the world of postwar West German TV movies starring Rudolf Schock, a kitschy style still evident in the conservative performance practice of some specialist theaters. Operetta's promise of historical continuity and an unchanging world of Old Vienna has, for many contemporary audience members, political implications. When the far-right Austrian politician Heinz-Christian Strache's Freedom Party adopted the motto *Mehr Mut für unser 'Wiener Blut'* (More courage for our "Viennese blood") in 2010, the Green Party condemned the phrase as a revival of Nazi sloganeering; the motto also alludes to "Wiener Blut," a waltz by Johann Strauss II that in 1899 became the title of an operetta based on his music.[1]

To another audience, however, operetta promises a kind of progressive liberation. As of this writing, the Komische Oper Berlin is still in the midst of a series of productions of works by composers like Oscar Straus and Ralph Benatzky that argue for operetta as a theater of anarchic pleasure capable of dissolving divisions between time periods, sexualities, and genres. Writing in early 2020, at a time when the forces of H.C. Strache (though not Strache himself) are ascendant, I understand and share the longing to find in operetta a subversive rather than conservative utopia. This seems particularly salient because much of Vienna's operetta world was later persecuted by the Third Reich, which co-opted operetta even as it murdered many of its artists. Strache himself is likely unaware that the librettists of *Wiener Blut* were both Jews and that the operetta concludes that Viennese blood is not determined by race but rather flows in the veins of whoever adopts an appropriately suave lifestyle.

Neither the traditional nor the radical vision has an exclusive claim to validity. In this book, I argue that both discourses—operetta as comfortable conservative bourgeois entertainment, and operetta as space for satire and experimentation—have deep historical roots. The history of operetta in Vienna has been defined by the pull between the two, and the divisions do not fall along clear lines of politics or ethnicity. I have attempted to locate some of what audiences saw in operetta in the early twentieth century, which both is and is not what they seek today. In particular, I am fascinated by operetta's playful self-reflexivity and intertextuality, which are invisible when two or three works stand in for the whole genre. Understanding the roots of these still-popular works not only helps us hear more in them but also uncovers some lesser-known conversations about entertainment, art, and the role of art in everyday life in this most famous world of early twentieth-century Vienna.

ACKNOWLEDGMENTS

This book would not have been possible without the generous help and support of many colleagues and friends, as well as significant institutional support. It originated in my Princeton University musicology dissertation, and I am grateful above all for the generous support I received from the Princeton Department of Music and my primary adviser, Wendy Heller, who not only tirelessly commented on my very long drafts but also convinced me that operetta has more in common with seventeenth-century Venetian opera than either of us initially suspected. I also benefited from the wisdom of my committee members Scott Burnham and Mary Ann Smart.

I am thankful to Raina Polivka at the University of California Press for her guidance and encouragement, the generous readers of the manuscript for helping me make it better, Madison Wetzell for answering my many questions, and Heidi Fritschel for meticulous copy editing. This book would not be what it is today if it weren't for the friends and colleagues who read and commented on it throughout the process, including Ellen Lockhart, Jonathan Neufeld, Saraswathi Shukla, David Schneider, Kim Teal, William Robin, Douglas Shadle, Bibiana Vergine, Barbara Milewski, Jacek Blaszkiewicz, Kate Steiner, Laurie McManus, Steve Waksman, Jamie Reuland, and Zoe Lang. My writing groups at Smith College and the University of Arkansas have proved a vital support system, and I am particularly grateful to my Arkansas colleagues Kim Teal, Wing Lau, and Joon Park for their encouragement and company. At conferences, including meetings of the Austrian Studies Association, the American Musicological Society, and the Biennial Conference on Nineteenth-Century Music as well as the University of Leeds's operetta conference and Berkeley's EZ Music conference, I benefited from input from numerous generous scholars but would particularly like to thank Derek B. Scott and

Lynn Hooker. The German Studies Association's "Liberalism and Its Discontents" seminar, organized by Benjamin Korstvedt, Karen Leistra-Jones, and Jonathan Gentry, helped me develop the larger context of this work. Zachary Woolfe at the *New York Times* is a generous editor and sent me to interview Barrie Kosky. I am also grateful to Pieter Judson and Morten Solvik for first introducing me to the Austro-Hungarian Empire and its music in their undergraduate classes, Mike Jennings and Tom Levin for offering a critical theory class at exactly the right time, and Barbara Milewski and the entire Swarthmore Music Department for getting me into this field in the first place.

I am grateful to the American Musicological Society for its generous subvention to fund the images and examples in this book. At Arkansas, I have benefited from support from my department chair, Ronda Mains, as well as guidance from Jim Gigantino, Jeannie Hulen, and Melody Herr and funding from the Provost's Research Enhancement Fund and the Fulbright College Humanities Research Stipend. Graduate student Matthew Magerkurth polished the notation of the music examples. During my two years as a postdoc at Smith College, I was generously supported with a light teaching load and generous research funding. I also am grateful to the Fulbright Commission, which supported a yearlong study trip to Vienna, as well as the support of the Andrew W. Mellon Foundation, which through the American Council of Learned Societies Dissertation Completion Fellowship funded my final year of graduate school. While I was at Princeton, my research was also supported by a generous grant from the Center for Arts and Cultural Policy Studies.

At every step I have benefited from the support of libraries. In particular, I am in debt to the indefatigable staff of the University of Arkansas Interlibrary Loan Department, who can track down anything. In Austria, the staff of nearly every single branch of the Austrian National Library helped me with innumerable queries (no matter how sweltering the reading room at the Theater Collection got), as did the staff of the Wienbibliothek am Rathaus, especially the keepers of the microfilms. Michael and Nan Miller introduced me to their invaluable Operetta Archive in Los Angeles, Maria Sams was helpful with the elusive Lehár Archive in Bad Ischl, and the staff of the Niederösterreichisches Landesarchiv in St. Pölten patiently explained their collections to me. I am also thankful to the staff of the Theatermuseum archive in Vienna, the Houghton Library at Harvard, and the Billy Rose Theatre Division at the New York Public Library. I am also thankful to T+T Fotographie and the Opernhaus Zürich for granting permission to reproduce their image.

I also send all my love and gratitude to my friends (Nora, Mark K., Lucy, and Tammy), to my Vienna people (especially Radmila and Manu), to all the Fayettevillians, and finally to my parents.

Music examples are from *Ein Herbstmanöver, Der Zigeunerprimas, Die Csárdás- fürstin*, and *Die Rose von Stambul* © Musikverlag Josef Weinberger GmbH, Frank- furt am Main.

An earlier version of chapter 1 was published as "*Die lustige Witwe* and the Creation of the Silver Age of Viennese Operetta" in *Cambridge Opera Journal* 26, no. 2 (July 2014), 175–202. © 2014 Cambridge University Press. Reprinted with permission.

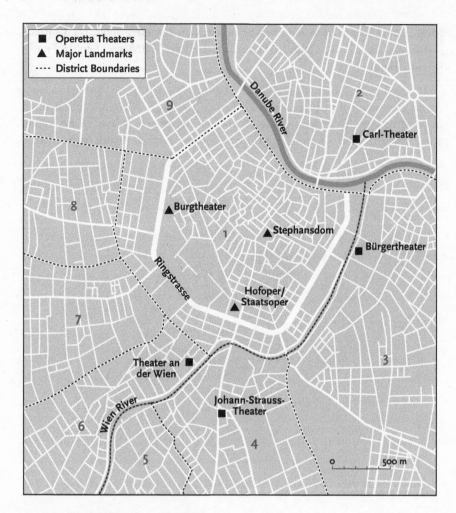

Map of Viennese landmarks and theaters

Introduction

Operetta in Vienna

At the beginning of Ivan Cankar's 1901 short story "Before the Goal," Karl Jereb, a Slovenian immigrant in Vienna, takes himself to the theater.[1] He leaves home at six in the evening, passing workers leaving factories, seamstresses, servants, and drunks. Eventually he reaches the grand streets of tall buildings and elegant people. As the city stares back at him, his head begins to sink in shame. When he reaches the theater, he pauses to watch the wealthy arrive in their carriages before slipping through the crowd and climbing to the third gallery, the highest and cheapest level of the theater.[2]

When the performance begins, he does not hear precisely what is being said onstage, nor does he care. He simply enjoys the singing and the sound of the actors' voices and is enthralled when the sound of the violins soars out of the orchestra pit. An idle, sweet sensation envelops him. It is as if he were "submerged up to his face in pure, lukewarm water, somnolent."[3]

Karl Jereb had gone to the operetta.

For the fictional Karl Jereb, like many of the residents of the time and place now enshrined as "fin de siècle Vienna," operetta was the most popular, most glamorous, most exciting, and most novel entertainment in the city. Its beauty promised respite from the toil of manual, clerical, or domestic labor. It offered a vision of a better world, one familiar enough to seem—if only for a few hours—possible.

1

What has become known as operetta's Silver Age began in 1905 and extended through Austria's post–World War I First Republic.[4] It was multinational, multiethnic, and embedded in the empire's own internal conflicts. Like the convoluted bureaucracy that bound the empire itself, operetta achieved mass popularity through negotiation and hybridization. Operetta mixes songs and other musical numbers with spoken dialogue and dance, a structure it shares with its predecessors the *Singspiel* and *opéra comique* as well as the later Broadway musical. And while opera in Vienna was at this time primarily the domain of subsidized state theaters, operetta was performed in commercial theaters for profit. Drawing on a rich vocabulary of influences and conventions, it stood in an uneasy zone between art and entertainment, central but liminal, encompassing both vaudeville and Wagner, alternating quasi-operatic arias with the latest international dance styles, and drawing on national traditions ranging from its progenitors of French *opérette* and German *Volksstück* to Hungarian "Gypsy music." Some of its composers and performers hailed from conservatories and opera houses, others from nightclubs and army bands—and many from all of them. They went to the Café Griensteidl and they went to the circus. To write operetta was to stand in the middle of things, to understand high and low and the spaces in between at this confluence of industrialization and early high modernism. While composers of the so-called Golden Age of the nineteenth century—Johann Strauss II, Carl Millöcker, Franz von Suppé, and Carl Zeller—sought to create traditionally Viennese works, twentieth-century operettas embraced cosmopolitanism, modernity, and sentiment alongside the usual waltzes. They were central to a growing international network of mass entertainment.

This pluralism is the subject of the present study. Operetta was both a distillation of fin de siècle Viennese life and one of its most contested genres. Its unstable fusion of styles and cultural registers enabled its ubiquity and fueled controversy; among scholars working in the crowded field of fin de siècle Viennese art, it has often been judged too commercial to be accorded the sustained attention that has invigorated English-language opera studies in the past three decades. But to subject it to this attention is to participate in current disciplinary conversations regarding hybridity, the popular, and the middlebrow—and to bring the too-rarified world of fin-de-siècle Vienna into this arena. Operetta's liminal status makes it an important lens through which to see Viennese music and theater in the early twentieth century. Even as musicologists have considered an increasingly wide range of musical practices, the study of Vienna has remained a conservative realm associated with a high-art canon. This study challenges musicology to move beyond the conventional view of Vienna as a modernist "temple of art" to consider wider audiences and works usually deemed aesthetically disposable.

Operetta's transgressive status served to define discourses of art and commerce, popular and middlebrow, in an era when musical autonomy was becoming increasingly prized. Operetta's twentieth-century shift into sentimental romanticism, decried by critics who favored a nineteenth-century Offenbachian ideal of detachment, catered to the needs not of an elite musical culture but of a rapidly industrializing city. The emergence around 1905 of "Silver Age operetta"—a periodic designation not without problems—as a genre was founded on composers' and librettists' close engagement with the changing demographics and theatrical audiences of industrializing bourgeois and lower-middle-class Vienna. Even as their operettas perpetuated earlier myths of Vienna and Austria-Hungary, they revised them for a changing city and an international market. Operetta and its reception were shaped by this emerging discourse of a classical canon, as creators both were defined against it and sometimes aspired to its prestige. Many operettas are self-reflexive texts, inscribing these very conversations into their librettos and scores.

While operetta's multifaceted identity allowed it to speak to a wide audience, this identity also caused enormous instability in its composition and reception. Its hybridity has been a disadvantage in a critical discourse that has, since operetta's own day, privileged aesthetic purity and a purportedly objective construction of aesthetic quality. For Carl Dahlhaus, it is "trivial music," important on a sociological level but insignificant on the larger musicological continuum of "compositional history" owing to its perceived lack of technical innovation and influence beyond its own boundaries of genre.[5] Since its canonization, operetta has generated its own internal debates over performance practice and style, and a quest for a "real" or "authentic" operetta is still evident in very recent scholarship.[6] But in Vienna, operetta was always synthetic. It was contentious because it attempted to cross between art and entertainment at a time when such boundaries were increasingly strictly policed, a stratification studied by scholars such as William Weber, Lawrence Levine, and Andreas Huyssen.[7] In the German-speaking realm, this divide is often described as a distinction between E- (*Ernste*, serious) and U- (*Unterhaltung*, entertainment) music, the latter referring mostly to the products of the industrialized popular music industry, which emerged over the course of the nineteenth century. Derek B. Scott has termed the rise of this new industry the "popular music revolution," a transformation that "brought forth musical idioms whose difference in both style and meaning from the classical repertoire created insuperable problems for those who were unfamiliar with the new conventions and lacked the particular skills demanded by the new styles."[8] Operetta was one such industry that was, by the twentieth century, professionalized and specialized.

Yet for Viennese operetta it was unclear whether works should be measured by the standards—or written or performed accorded to the ideals—of opera or of popular music, particularly after Johann Strauss's ambitious *Der Zigeunerbaron* (The Gypsy Baron) premiered in 1885. Even as scores' well-publicized compositional ambition assumed the mantle of serious music, operetta's commercial nature doomed it to remain forever entertainment, making it an early example of the middlebrow.[9] Ultimately, it was the porosity of the *U/E* boundary that made operetta so provocative. For some fin-de-siècle critics, operetta represented an ennoblement of the public taste, a stepping stone toward proper opera; to others it was a dangerously hypnotic form of escapism. For Adam Müller-Guttenbrunn, an anti-Semitic theatrical impresario, it was "an artistic bastard, which might have been conceived by a stock exchange jobber and a Parisian cocotte."[10]

According to high-art practitioners and critics such as Karl Kraus, Theodor Adorno, Ernst Krenek, and many others, Viennese operetta was uppity, with pretensions to an artistic value not applicable to art with such blatantly capitalistic intentions and so broad an audience. For the more politically minded, operetta was sentimental, materialistically capitalist, and, ultimately, part of the culture industry. To these critics, Jacques Offenbach's nineteenth-century satiric operettas represented a medium of social commentary delivered with ironic detachment, unhappily supplanted in the twentieth century by sentimental identification and mass-produced pathos.[11] Beyond politics, Offenbach allowed space for what Carolyn Abbate has termed "ethical frivolity," encouraging us to "make peace with impermanence and insouciance,"[12] but twentieth-century Vienna created an operetta with a canon of classic, would-be immortal works. Compared with the anarchy of Offenbach, twentieth-century operetta was redolent of the rationality of bourgeois liberalism. Both its formulas and the steady production of new works marked it as industrialized commercial art for a society that increasingly devalued individual craft.[13] (For some of those liberals themselves, however, its category-crossing offended. Operetta could not win, except at the box office.)

When the time and place immortalized by Hermann Broch and Carl Schorske as "fin de siècle Vienna" is celebrated by scholars as a cultural paradise, operetta is rarely included among its achievements. (Broch refers to it as a "vacuum-product."[14]) In surveys of fin de siècle Viennese culture, the grand achievements of Freud, Mahler, Klimt, and Schoenberg are given modernist purpose while operetta is mentioned in passing as a racy curiosity low in nutrition and high in calories. But its status as a historical footnote belies its tremendous ubiquity and broad appeal, as well as its role as a nexus for a variety of anxieties of the period, both those explicitly thematized on the operetta stage and those projected by fans and critics.

This ubiquity was central to operetta's identity. Vienna's wide world of theater included different venues for different social and economic classes—a defining feature of post–Industrial Revolution mass entertainment.[15] But operetta needed to appeal to as wide an audience as possible to remain economically sustainable: it was one of the most expensive and complex forms of commercial culture in the city (playing in large theaters with a sizable cast, chorus, dancers, and orchestra, plus elaborate sets and costumes) and lacked the security of a patron system or the imperial subventions which kept the Hofoper and Burgtheater afloat. While its audience was primarily middle class, it spanned the working and high bourgeoisies, even the occasional aristocrat. Each operetta was created to be as popular as possible with everyone, wrote influential librettist Victor Léon (1858–1940). Operetta audiences contained both *Kenner* (expert) and *Liebhaber* (amateur), but the writer must compromise between the two:

> What suits the aristocrat in the orchestra will not always suit the cook in the gallery, but what suits the cook in the gallery will always also suit the aristocrats. Therefore one works first and foremost for the cook, for the gallery, for the popular success. But nonetheless: constant cries for better, for quality.[16]

Operetta, Léon wrote with the deference of one who has read his Schopenhauer, never aspired to be "the pure product of the will of an artist, of what moves him, forced into form through psychic propulsion." Or, in the similar words of Pierre Bourdieu,

> Middle-brow art is the product of a productive system dominated by the quest for investment profitability; this creates the need for the widest possible public. It cannot, moreover, content itself with seeking to intensify consumption within a determinate social class; it is obliged to orient itself towards a generalization of the social and cultural composition of this public.[17]

Bourdieu argues for "generalization," but Léon's description contains an element of unresolved tension indicative of the issues facing operetta in his time. Operetta creators themselves struggled to reconcile art and commerce. For some, such as Franz Lehár, this dual mission could serve an explicitly didactic purpose, sneaking in musical sophistication to gradually "elevate the public taste."[18] (But would it be elevated to Wagner or to more Lehár?)

As Léon suggested, the shape of a twentieth-century operetta is predictable. The *Liebhaber* can enjoy the entertainment, the *Kenner* can appreciate the finer details of execution, such as an unusually clever third act or an unusually convincing connection between the primary and secondary plot. The plot typically concerns the romantic travails of two men and two women, ending with a double engagement. Conventionally, the first couple, who receive more songs, are more experienced in life and love, and their scenes take on a somewhat more serious tone; the second couple's romance is a subplot loosely linked with the main couple, and they are younger, more comic, and more inclined to dance numbers. The overall trajectory of plots was described dismissively by Franz Hadamowsky and Heinz Otte in their 1947 history, which contains the first prominent use of the term "Silver Age":

> The plot's construction almost always reveals the same template: two young, pretty people, seemingly or in actuality from two opposing social spheres, fall in love with each other in the first act, are separated in Act 2 through all sorts of real or contrived misunderstandings, which could be remedied all at once with one honest word; the

obstacles become insurmountable in a grandiose Act 2 finale, which quakes with false sentimentality; nevertheless the lovers find a happy end in Act 3.[19]

Theodor Adorno identified a similar standardization and classified operetta as a capitalist product that had displaced folk cultures.[20] Yet the repetition of operetta plots was more than the necessity of an assembly line. This predictability, in fact, enabled operetta to become remarkably self-reflexive and self-critical, commenting on its own plots, allegorizing its own musical histories, and acknowledging its own clichés, even alongside the sentimental romanticism long recognized as a defining feature of twentieth-century operetta. In 1948 Arthur Maria Rabenalt suggested that the mismatched couples of so many operetta plots were an externalization of operetta's own internal conflicts:

> It is notable that the storytelling invention of operetta goes almost entirely in one direction: namely toward rectifying its own illegitimacy, to rehabilitate itself in society. The only theme of operetta is misalliance, the only conflict is social difference. So thus operetta, in the false tragedy of its plot, reflects back the problem of its heritage.[21]

But reflexivity, prominent in many of the works considered in this volume (most notably *Die lustige Witwe*, *Die Csárdásfürstin*, and *Die Bajadere*), has been frequently overlooked by high culture critics, who were far from operetta's insular cultures and who registered only formula.[22]

The warmly conciliatory plots of operettas often imagined a utopia of a unified, multiethnic Austria-Hungary. The industry itself was diverse. As the most lucrative and prestigious market in the Austro-Hungarian Empire, Vienna was a magnet for composers, writers, and actors, and their mix of ethnicities mirrored that of their audience—with the exception that they were much more likely to be Jewish. In a city already split not only by class but also nationality, ethnicity, religion, and education, operetta served as cultural glue. It gave the shaky coalition of the city and even the Austro-Hungarian Empire a common song, and its identity became tightly bound with the coalition of the empire. After the empire's disappearance after World War I, operetta's conventional subjects took on a whole new meaning. In the unstable First Republic, operetta became nostalgic, reimagining the empire in ever-sunnier terms. In the face of competition from film and eventual Nazi persecution of Jewish artists, Viennese operetta fragmented. Since 1950 operetta programs have consisted almost entirely of canonized classic works.[23]

Twentieth-century operetta's dramaturgical language strengthened its function as a refuge and dream space for its audiences. In Offenbach's day, operetta had traded in exaggerated, commedia dell'arte-like types strictly estranged from reality; in the twentieth century, characters became figures of sentimental identification for the audience. Operetta echoed high art's turn to interiority, though it stopped well short of expressionism. While it still contained spoken dialogue and emphasized dance, twentieth-century operetta's use of more complex musical forms, increasingly chromatic harmony, and more demanding singing roles marked it as comparatively operatic. Operetta shed the dry, rhythmically driven scores of the nineteenth century, and characters declaimed their inner emotional lives in a lyrical, quasi-Wagnerian style of song. Nearly every operetta plot of the Silver Age concentrates on a romantic relationship threatened by pragmatic concerns. There are rarely any villains; only misunderstandings and social conventions threaten their relationships. Men and women fall in and out of love, worry about the impressions they make, and voice their desires in song.

Operetta librettos balance social reality and romantic idealism. Like the actors themselves, operetta characters provided fantasies for their audiences. The characters onstage were glamorous, rich, and happy in ways inaccessible to many of their audience members (as seen in Karl Jereb's journey from grim outer suburb to the glamorous theater), and yet the problems the libretto made them face spoke—absolutely intentionally—to their daily concerns. Audiences watched the beautiful people struggle with their finances, toil at boring jobs, attempt to negotiate convoluted love lives, and experience the rapid changes of fortune common both to modern city life and farcical plot mechanics.

For Marxist critics, twentieth-century operetta was a textbook example of false consciousness. In the happy ending that concludes most operettas, barriers are overcome and the ideal of a romantic marriage that is also economically advantageous always triumphs.[24] These sunny endings led to frequent charges of sentimentality and escapism that carried a reflexively negative judgment. These accusations would intensify as the genre became more and more grandiose in the 1920s.

WHY VIENNA?

Considering operetta's hybridity also forces us to consider a wider swathe of Viennese society, including populations and concerns not directly related to Brahms or Bruckner. As David Broadbeck points out in his study of the "Czech question" in Vienna, "much in this field remains to be done."[25] In particular, operetta invites a focus on the city's belated modernization and immense population growth. Emperor Franz Joseph I had sat on the imperial throne since 1848, but while the empire itself attempted to stop time, the city was technologically and demographically transformed. Between the *Gründerzeit* (literally, founding period) of the 1860s and the early twentieth century, the city developed from a small, relatively homogenous German-speaking political and cultural center into a cosmopolitan metropolis. Yet industrialization in Vienna was modest compared with the larger European cities of Paris and London, and the modern industrial world coexisted with the stubborn traditional one in an uneasy alliance between old and new. The city was geographically stratified such that the lower echelons were invisible to the upper—a division that has been replicated in much scholarship—but operetta's physical and symbolic location in between the upper and lower zones is a rare point of contact.[26]

Most important for popular entertainment, the rising demand for unskilled labor was accommodated by a major demographic shift. Between 1860 and 1910, Vienna experienced enormous population growth and diversification. The city grew from 476,000 inhabitants in 1857 to 1,675,000 in 1900, thanks partly to the incorporation of outlying suburbs into the official city limits. In 1910 the Viennese numbered 2,031,000.[27] The new inhabitants came largely from within the empire, especially the less industrialized areas of Bohemia and Moravia, and the majority were unskilled laborers.[28] The previously homogenous, often provincial Viennese were now in the most literal sense surrounded by strangers with new languages, new food, and new traditions.

Vienna's most illustrious residents lived in the city's core, known as the *innere Stadt* (inner city), officially numbered as 1, which was circled by the *Ringstrasse* (see the 1905 city map on page xii). Surrounding the inner city was the *Vorstadt*, numbered as districts 2 through 9 and home to the bourgeoisie. The *Vorstadt* was the site of most of the city's operetta and other commercial theaters (only the exalted, state-supported Burgtheater and Hofoper were located in the *innere Stadt* on the inner edge of the Ring). It was in the outer districts beyond the *Vorstadt* (on the other side of a second ring road, the *Gürtel*) that the new migrants congregated, prompting a construction boom in the last decades of the nineteenth century. These districts were incorporated into the city by 1890.[29]

This topography created a clear hierarchy, tidier than those found in London and Paris. An 1859 ordinance had recommended that the rapidly developing outer suburbs be built in a geometrical grid pattern, contrary to the irregular streets of the older districts. The rigid urban plan—the straight lines of the streets filled with poor-quality tenement housing and the hierarchal organization of the city itself—created an impersonal, alienating experience for populations already in shock as a result of their relocation from rural to city environments, particularly when combined with the strictly regulated labor schedules associated with industrialization. The geographic compartmentalization also made the outer suburbs easy for the more privileged classes to ignore.

In scholarship, the dubious charms of Viennese operetta hover at the margins of a magnificent historiographical construct: the cultural paradise of "fin-de-siècle Vienna." In his study *Fin-de-siècle Vienna: Politics and Culture* (1979), still popular and influential among musicologists today, Carl Schorske argued that the conservative atmosphere of a decrepit Austro-Hungarian Empire created the conditions that would nurture the Modernist movement. According to his thesis, in the face of their political decline in the late nineteenth century, the Austrian liberal elite retreated from public life and politics to explore the psyche. While Schorske's work, along with William McGrath's *Dionysian Art and Populist Politics in Austria* and Allan Janik and Stephen Toulmin's *Wittgenstein's Vienna*, did much to bring Vienna to the forefront of English-speaking scholarship on modernism, his concentration on elite cultural circles has often led to the fetishization of a narrow slice of Vienna's culture and population as "a treasure chest of high culture's most precious objects," as historians Wolfgang Maderthaner and Lutz Musner write in their study of Vienna's lower classes.[30] Similarly, historians such as John Boyer and Pieter Judson have argued that the liberals considered by Schorske were not alienated from public life at all.[31]

It is here that operetta provides a particularly informative lens: Vienna was socially compartmentalized to a greater degree than most cities, and operetta was one of the few cultural forms that bridged gaps between cultural groups and economic classes. But operetta's wide appeal did not correspond to the mass political movements of the early twentieth century—particularly because it was written primarily by Jews at a time when Viennese politics were turning increasingly anti-Semitic. (Nor can it be securely classified a protest against anti-Semitism, an issue that will be examined in more detail in chapter 2.)

Indeed, operetta's in-betweenness is an ideal example of the middlebrow, an artistic category that has been largely ignored when it comes to this time and place. As argued by Christopher Chowrimootoo in his recent study *Middlebrow Modernism*, the label "middlebrow" was often wielded to "shore up the great divide by discrediting those who fell 'in between.' Yet, evidently, it also had the opposite effect, calling attention to those institutions, artists, critics, and audiences that—more or less consciously—sought to mediate its supposedly irreconcilable oppositions."[32] Chowrimootoo dates the term itself to 1920s England, a time and place later than and geographically distant from the balance of this study. Yet such an aesthetic category, initially wielded as an insult, is apt for many of the sentiments expressed by critics of operetta, who often found operetta's transgression of aesthetic categories offensive. In his consideration of Eduard Hanslick's nineteenth-century criticism of Johann Strauss II, Dana Gooley describes the critic's desire that "works clearly invoke the genres to which they belong, because without such reference points, aesthetic judgment is impossible," a demand that composers "respect their natural boundaries and behave in a way 'true' to their given constitution and temperament." This preference for rational order and categorization is typical of liberal thought.[33] Viennese critical discourse, wedded to the binary lens of E- and U- music, did not recognize the middlebrow as a legitimate category—not even as one of dubious merit—but operetta nonetheless embodied it.

By the twentieth century, Viennese operetta was fully congruent with Scott's "popular music revolution," a professionalized industry with a well-developed community of theaters, performers, composers and librettists, critics, publishers, and audiences, as well as a larger network of provincial theaters that extended across the Austro-Hungarian Empire and eventually were linked with musical theater enterprises of various sorts around the world. But despite this clearly defined ecosystem, its role within the larger artistic world remained unstable. Operetta has never shed its reputation as an arriviste. Indeed, this pull toward "high art" is as much a feature of its criticism and subsequent historiography as its history to date. As operetta became increasingly canonically conscious, histories began to proliferate. Like early critical writing, most early histories were preoccupied with the legitimization of operetta as an art form, concentrating on the training and accomplishments of composers and the glorification of their accomplishments. The first such study, written by Otto Keller in 1926, described a two-pronged genealogy based on Mozartean *Singspiel* and *Volksstück*. One of operetta's parents is artistic, the other popular; neither carry the stigma of commercialism and mass production that afflicted operetta in the 1920s.[34] Keller's history was followed by Karl Westermeyer's *Die Operette im Wandel des Zeitgeistes: von Offenbach bis zur Gegenwart* in 1931 and Franz Hadamowsky's *Die Wiener Operette* in 1947. More recently, Richard Traubner's *Operetta: A Theatrical History*—the only comprehensive history of the operetta genre in English—practices a similar art of legitimation, sorting worthy works from dross to prove that the genre as a whole is worthwhile.[35]

More recent historians, however, have reevaluated both the research and the assumptions behind these older histories. In fact, in the past ten years there has been something of a boom in operetta studies (as well as performance projects). Marion Linhardt's work in theater history has illuminated the complex topographies of Viennese theaters, Stefan Frey's series of well-researched biographies has solidified the historical record, and Camille Crittenden's critical study of Johann Strauss brought unprecedented attention to operetta among anglophone scholars.[36] Even more recently, Ulrike Petersen's dissertation and Kevin Clarke's multiple studies have supplied in-depth studies of largely forgotten interwar works, Mattias Kauffmann has written the first comprehensive study of operetta during the Third Reich, and Barbara Denscher has offered an unusual large-scale study of a librettist in her work on Victor Léon.[37] Laurence Senelick has also offered an illuminating, often revisionist biography of Offenbach through his works.[38] They make a strong case for operetta's importance as a topic of study, and a recent collection issued alongside an exhibit at the Austrian Theater Museum demonstrated the diversity of recent approaches to operetta.[39]

This book continues this work by examining several works of operetta—some well known, some obscure—through the aesthetic conversations and social issues that defined their meaning. I consider operetta's dependency on market forces, conventionally considered a liability, a central feature of the genre. Most of the operettas I examine were exceptionally successful, and their subsequent performance histories in opera houses, on film, and in a million recital encores are not typical. Despite their fame—many are still staged in Central Europe and beyond—they have been subjected to virtually no scholarly scrutiny in English. In addition, popularity means that their composition and premieres were unusually well documented in the Viennese press, making them rich texts for study. Their success also made them immediate subjects of imitation by other composers and librettists.

Rather than separating the works and their reception, I consider both simultaneously. Close readings of operettas reveal that these works contain nuances, intertextuality, and allegorical readings that cannot be appreciated in a more generalized study. These readings reveal a theatrical culture in which reception and composition were closely linked: issues frequently discussed in the press wound their way into operetta plots, sometimes in stealthy fashion. At the same time, the reception of operetta, including by figures who were not themselves part of operetta culture, most importantly Karl Kraus, can reveal aspects of operetta's meaning not evident in the texts themselves. Many studies have either narrowly considered operetta texts or broadly examined their entire culture; this study argues that the two are best considered together.

Many of these operettas were also successful internationally, and these transnational histories have recently become of great interest to historians, for example in studies by Kevin Clarke, Tobias Becker, and Derek Scott as well as a recent collection of essays centered in the interaction between London and Berlin.[40] The fame and fortune that could be gained through a success in London or New York became an incentive for composers and librettists to tailor their works to more generic rather than specifically Viennese tastes or to heavily adapt (or have others adapt) their works for a foreign audience. This book, however, locates Viennese operetta within the orbit of Austro-Hungarian and Viennese studies and makes a case for the specific theatrical culture of the city of Vienna, a discrete culture of composers, librettists, actors, critics, audiences, and cultural expectations. I argue that Viennese world of operetta constituted a particular habitus in Bourdieu's sense—that is, "a structuring structure, which organizes practices and the perception of practices."[41] For this reason, I only rarely shift my focus to Berlin and largely do not discuss other cities of the Austro-Hungarian Empire, such as Prague, Budapest, and Graz, which had their own theatrical traditions. The international reception and adaptation of these works in other urban centers—what might be called operetta's international networks—can be understood only when we have acquired a more vivid sense of their origins.

SCOPE AND STRUCTURE

In this study I trace the history of Silver Age operetta and its reception through key works by the four of its most important composers: Franz Lehár, Oscar Straus,

Leo Fall, and Emmerich Kálmán. My scope is from the beginning of the Silver Age, around 1900, to around 1930, when operetta's decline in the face of economic depression and competition from sound film rendered it increasingly irrelevant. My goal is to explore not only the genre and the works themselves but also their role as a nexus in Vienna's cultural ecosystem and how they reacted to and were shaped by criticism, current events, and social concerns.

The first chapter considers the watershed of *Die lustige Witwe* (The Merry Widow, 1905), usually credited for beginning operetta's twentieth-century Silver Age. This work was mythologized as a once-in-a-century success, and fact and fiction often mix freely in accounts of its origins. But it was less a fluke than a coalescing of many musical and dramatic trends that had been unfolding in the operetta world for the previous few years. Those conversations, in fact, form the operetta's subject: viewed in the context of early twentieth-century operetta, *Die lustige Witwe* is a story about operetta's future, contrasting a frivolous Paris with a more soulful, folk-inspired homeland. Simultaneously, its portrayal of homesick immigrants and lazy workers spoke directly to its ethnically diverse middle- and lower-class audience.

Twentieth-century operetta's portrayal of labor and escape are the subject of my second chapter. Operetta depicted itself as a respite from a newly industrialized city, but only within limits. Oscar Straus's 1907 hit *Ein Walzertraum* (A Waltz Dream) provides a particularly interesting example. The operetta portrays a *Damenkapelle*, an all-woman orchestra, who bring the sounds of a pastoral vision of Vienna to a remote principality and its homesick prince. Yet despite the sentimentality of much of the music, it ultimately affirms that this world of pure pleasure is an unattainable fantasy. In contrast, Franz Lehár's 1911 *Eva* purports to show social reality, but despite its gritty factory setting, its Cinderella-like tale never achieves plausibility, particularly for a city in the midst of worker protests. Lehár's music shows an increasing grandeur befitting a fairy-tale subject matter.

Chapter 3 concerns the portrayal of the Hungarian half of the empire in Viennese operetta. While Budapest was only a few hours away from Vienna, the Viennese image of Hungary, particularly of its music, depended more on the stereotype of the temperamental "Gypsy" than it did on any lived experience. "Gypsy music" provided a vocabulary for composers to represent Romantic subjectivity, something found in works from *Die Fledermaus* (The Bat) to Franz Lehár's *Zigeunerliebe* (Gypsy Love). This is vividly demonstrated in the early career of Hungarian composer Emmerich Kálmán. While his early works lack some of the stereotypical traits the Viennese expected from Hungarian music, when Kálmán moved to Vienna he found a way to market his Hungarian-ness to the Viennese. In *Der Zigeunerprimas* (The Gypsy Band Leader, 1912, later produced in English as *Sari*), he set up another musical dualism between Hungarian and Viennese music.

The operettas of World War I are the subject of chapter 4. Near the start of the war, Kálmán and Victor Léon produced *Gold gab ich für Eisen* (I Gave Gold for Iron, 1914), a rustic *Singspiel* written as war propaganda. But despite its patriotism, its endorsement of the war is hardly unequivocal. I argue that it reproduced the view of the war frequently modeled by the media as suitable for Austrian women: open to expressions of grief and suspicious of patriotism. Simultaneously, it creates a historical background for a confusing war, quoting folk songs and drawing on history to link it with the Napoleonic conflict with the French. *Gold gab ich für Eisen*, along with operetta in general, came under considerable criticism from journalist Karl Kraus, who called operetta a tool of the powerful to instill blind patriotism among the common citizens. Kálmán's 1915 operetta *Die Csárdásfürstin* (The Csárdás Duchess, performed in English as *The Gipsy Princess* in London and *The Riviera Girl* on Broadway) is a test case for Kraus's critique, and this chapter argues that Kálmán's dualism between an outdated and hypocritical Viennese society and a nihilistic Hungarian cabaret represents a greater independence of perspective than Kraus suggested.

The fifth chapter examines a series of exotic operettas dating from 1916 to 1929 that portray crises of succession and a confrontation with the unknown. In most of these works, a romance between a European and an exotic foreigner is threatened by social norms. These works defy many conventions of exoticism, often undercutting their own attempts to portray a foreign land and reflecting the anxieties of a city suddenly dethroned from its imperial status. These operettas include *Die Rose von Stambul* (The Rose of Istanbul), an operetta by Leo Fall about Turkish feminists, Kálmán's *Die Bajadere* (The Bayadere, performed as *The Yankee Princess* on Broadway), a purposefully inauthentic operetta about an operetta about India, and Lehár's *Das Land des Lächelns* (The Land of Smiles), in which the forces of China crush an international romance. The exotic is repeatedly revealed to be only a titillating surface feature that conceals universal human characteristics. The only villains are the societies that keep the international couples apart. (This perspective gains particular force in *Das Land des Lächelns*, written by Jewish librettists in 1929, a period of rapidly increasing anti-Semitism.) Increasingly over-the-top scores help these characters retreat ever further into themselves and further from society.

As operetta was threatened by competition from revues and film, it increasingly adopted their conventions, including looser plots and greater visual spectacle. Simultaneously, operetta commemorated the departed empire with which it still maintained a special relationship. Such nostalgia and appropriation could take on surreal form, seen in chapter 6 in an analysis of Kálmán's *Die Herzogin von Chicago* (The Duchess of Chicago, 1929). While this operetta uses the old device of the tinpot kingdom to contrast old Habsburg music with a visiting American millionairess's jazz band to spectacular musical effect, the kingdom's prince is a despot and needs to learn generosity and open-mindedness from the American. She, in turn, needs to learn respect for tradition. Finally, the book concludes with a consideration of how these very questions—tradition and transgression, familiarity and novelty—are translated into contemporary productions in European theaters and festivals. Despite historic ruptures, the relationship between operetta and society is still defined by debates over satire, sentimentality, and artistic register. Around a century after Viennese operetta's heyday, its meanings remain contested.

Die lustige Witwe and the Creation of Silver Age Viennese Operetta

When Wilhelm Karczag first heard Franz Lehár's score to *Die lustige Witwe*, he supposedly exclaimed, "Das is ka Musik!" (That ain't music!). The setting was Lehár's own apartment on the Mariahilferstrasse in Vienna in the summer of 1905, half a year before the operetta was to premiere at Karczag's Theater an der Wien. This anecdote, not celebrated in print until 1924 and disputed by several of those who claim to have been present, makes Karczag the butt of a joke, for *Die lustige Witwe* was the music that would rule operetta for the next two and a half decades.[1] Karczag's Hungarian accent—he had moved from Budapest only four years earlier—is rendered phonetically, marking him as an outsider who could not hear what the rest of the Vienna later recognized.

Lehár's audition for Karczag became an iconic event in *Die lustige Witwe*'s origin myth as an underdog success. The operetta's purportedly hostile initial reception, which included not only the resistance of the theatrical management but also its ostensibly lukewarm opening night, positions it as a *Naturkind*, so radically different in tone from Karczag's operetta habits that he was unable to recognize it as music. Against all odds, it emerged to conquer the theatrical world and launch what would become known as the Silver Age of Viennese operetta. This story was told over and over again in Viennese newspapers.[2] The anecdote's constantly shifting details were, in large part, reflective of a dispute over ownership. Everyone—composer, librettists, impresarios, and actors—was eager to claim credit for (and preferably also some of the profits from) the greatest theatrical success of the time. *Die lustige Witwe* racked up 483 performances in its initial run in Vienna and 8,338 performances on all German-speaking stages by 1921.[3] At one point Karczag's co-director, Karl Wallner, even claimed to have conceived the third act of the operetta himself. Librettist Victor Léon vehemently refuted this and denied that Wallner had heard the operetta at the fateful audition at all.[4]

The "Das is ka Musik" anecdote was popularized in the 1920s and recirculated through the early 1930s, just as Viennese operetta was beginning its inexorable decline. Mythmaking attempted to rescue this most successful work from anachronism by transforming it into an autonomous classic, worthy of lasting esteem. Indeed, *Die lustige Witwe* is one of the few Viennese operettas still to be regularly performed today—and not in its original commercial environs but in the sanctified space of modern opera houses. But this development occludes the very different circumstances under which the operetta was conceived. The energetic self-advocacy of the operetta's creators helped to conceal the fact that *Die lustige Witwe* was created not with high-art aims nor with thoughts of how it would play decades later, but rather to please, and to please immediately.

The popular operetta literature has tended to describe *Die lustige Witwe* in the same superlative terms used by its creators, positioning it as a work whose inherent qualities and immense success elevated it from its colleagues in fundamental yet vaguely defined ways. Richard Traubner introduces his discussion of *Die lustige Witwe* with a generalized paean to its fantastic success: the operetta is "ravishing," "as good or better than any other of its day," "exciting," "fragrant," and "fabulously effective."[5] In Traubner's teleology, *Die lustige Witwe* is described as extraordinary before it is put in the context in which it began: as an ordinary operetta. In fact, in contrast to the conventional narrative of *Die lustige Witwe* as a work that transcended its era, a look at the world of operetta of 1905 reveals it as an encapsulation of its time—and an instance in which the hybridized musical style of operetta is integral to the dramatic action.

Die lustige Witwe was created while operetta was in crisis, following the deaths of Johann Strauss II and several other major composers, at a point when the genre's direction and purpose were uncertain. Set to a plot about a group of hapless "Pontevedrans" playing matchmaker in the midst of Parisian society, the operetta's music embodies and utilizes this instability. *Die lustige Witwe* dramatizes the contrast between Paris and the imaginary Balkan principality as a contrast between Parisian (and English) and Austro-Hungarian operetta styles. Its score presents a binary division between these styles, and its drama is generated by the friction between the two. This allegorical deployment of stylistic juxtaposition is a defining feature of the Silver Age.[6]

The operetta was also created for a particular audience. The true geographical home of *Die lustige Witwe* is not Paris nor Pontevedro, but 1905 Vienna. *Die lustige Witwe* captures the experience of a city of immigrants in the throes of modernization. The Austro-Hungarian Empire's belated industrialization was transforming the city's demographics, bringing an influx of new citizens, new models of social organization, and new technology. The Pontevedrans of the operetta are ethnic outsiders, planted in the center of a dazzling urban metropolis, forced to balance the boredom of wage labor and the pull of urban temptation against the weight and value of their indigenous traditions. Like many operettas, *Die lustige Witwe* is wish fulfillment, displaying an opulently staged, romantic solution to problems found in its audience's everyday lives.

I begin this chapter by surveying the world of operetta in Vienna up to 1905, considering its French heritage and quickly acquired Germanic identity. The passing of the nineteenth century's "Golden Age" composers resulted in both an identity crisis, endlessly debated in the contemporary press, and a richly experimental period for a new generation of composers and librettists. This led directly to the allegorical character of *Die lustige Witwe*, which emerges as a meta-operetta dramatizing the polemics of this unstable era. It can also hint, perhaps, at some of its resonances. Describing *Die lustige Witwe*, Felix Salten wrote, "All that resonates and hums in our daily lives, what we read, write, think, praise, and the new, modern clothes our expressions wear, all these are intoned in this operetta."[7] Quotidian entertainment engaged with its audiences' most urgent concerns, and the polemics of newspaper critics extended into operettas themselves. Despite its current status as the rare operetta to withstand the test of time, *Die lustige Witwe* is inseparable from the aesthetic and social concerns that surrounded its creation.

THE "GOLDEN AGE"

Viennese operetta scavenged from many other genres. Containing elements of French *opérette* and *opéra comique* and German *Singspiel* and *komische Oper*, it also borrowed from Viennese theater genres like the *Lustspiel, Schwank,* and *Posse*; the traditional Germanic *Volksstück*; the French boulevard theater that bequeathed the Viennese so many librettos; and even Italian opera. Operetta was an urban genre, but one that often incorporated elements of older folk traditions.[8] Critics perennially dismissed it as the banal bastard of one of its more artistic or more ancient progenitors.[9] But it was the breadth of this family tree that allowed operetta to build its rich vocabulary of conventions and codes with remarkable speed, and it was the diversity of its city, theaters, and audiences that made these codes intelligible. Many operettas wear their hybrid character proudly, using stylistic variation allegorically for dramatic effect and characterization. Serious characters sing with operatic breadth, modern ones dance the cakewalk, and Balkan ones do Balkan dances. Folk song in general connotes sincerity and interiority, quasi-French music the intrigues and debauchery of a night at the Folies Bergère. The talents and personas of the leading actors were written into their roles. If anything did not make sense in a revival, it was simply adjusted to fit new circumstances.[10]

Operetta arrived in Vienna in the form of *opérettes* by Offenbach, which first gained popularity in commercial Viennese theaters in the late 1850s. What in

Vienna was considered an Offenbachian style would continue to be a building block of operetta. Offenbach's musical language was based on the *opéra comique* template of Boieldieu, Auber, and others. The songs are cast in a few predictable and simple forms, the most important being the *couplet*, in this context meaning a comic number in strophic form, often including a chorus echoing the soloist and sometimes improvised texts.[11] The melodic construction is similarly regular. The music makes a kind of anxious chatter, unfolding in short motives of straight eighth or sixteenth notes in scalar motion. Text and music are often juxtaposed for comic effect.

An example of both Offenbach's musical syntax and this characteristically acerbic relationship between music and text can be found near the start of his satiric *Orphée aux enfers*, whose title characters are not the lovebirds depicted in classical mythology. In their Act 1 duet, they debate the appeal of Orphée's music: he loves it, she hates it (ex. 1.1). The music is brisk and patter-like; Eurydice's vocal line repeats a compact melodic turn cell while Orphée's stays on the same pitch, providing additional rhythmic propulsion. The obsessive repetition of short motivic cells, usually with short note values in conjunct motion in a narrow range is Offenbach's melodic signature: phrases are not forward directed or expansive, and they avoid significant harmonic development. Instead they have a formulaic, relentlessly predictable cadence.

The music's mundane but manic energy is enhanced by its relation to the text. Orphée and Eurydice both string together adjectives describing Orphée's violin solo. Their words rhyme, but her descriptions are entirely negative (deplorable, dreadful, boring, irritating) and his entirely positive (adorable, delectable, ravishing, catchy). These directly conflicting sentiments are set to exactly the same music. Eventually, Eurydice seems to run out of words, and her language breaks down into a series of "ah"s, as Orphée switches from singing to playing his violin. They make an ironic statement regarding the expressive possibilities of music itself: the two have differing opinions of the same music, and their expressions of those differing opinions are set to identical music. Just as Orphée's violin solo lacks a single definitive expressive message, the music of their reactions lends itself to two directly opposing messages. The music does not reveal the inner thoughts of Orphée or Eurydice; indeed it seems to negate the ability of music to communicate a psychological state. Such a juxtaposition became, for operetta critics, Offenbach's trademark.

Yet Viennese composers would quickly develop their own operetta style as well. Johann Strauss II, the "Waltz King," entered operetta in 1871, and the progress of his operettas, beginning with *Indigo und die vierzig Räuber* in 1871, mirrored the development of the genre itself. At first Strauss maintained the satire and farce of the French model (as in *Die Fledermaus*, 1874), while his later efforts, beginning in 1885 with *Der Zigeunerbaron*, turned serious and more conventionally operatic.[12]

EXAMPLE 1.1. Jacques Offenbach, *Orpheée aux enfers*, No. 2, Duo, refrain

By the end of the nineteenth century, Viennese operettas generally featured romantically driven plots with sympathetic characters (with the comic relief and grotesque confined to supporting roles) and often included plots or music inspired by folk culture. The integration of the waltz into operetta had made operettas composed in Vienna, for the first time, fully Viennese in spirit, drawing their music from (and incorporating it into) a preexisting sound world. As Eduard Hanslick described Strauss's *Apfelfest*, "What is the setting? The libretto doesn't say. But the music tells us without any doubt: it's an Austrian setting, a good Viennese work."[13] Operetta was seen by Hanslick and many of his contemporaries as filling the need for a quasi–folk art within an urban space. (In 1905, the Viennese critic Max Graf went even further, describing preindustrial Viennese theatrical life as hyperlocal, a characteristic he viewed as having vanished with the advent of the streetcar system.[14])

In the late nineteenth century, the pressures for composers to create "good Viennese work" grew, along with what Carl Schorske termed "politics in a new key."[15] Political developments in the 1870s, from the unification of Germany to the Franco-Prussian War, simultaneously fueled a precipitous increase in Germanic nationalism and a turn against all things French, including Offenbach. (While critics often identified Offenbach's German heritage, his works were classified as French.) In the Viennese theatrical world, the charge was led by journalist-turned-impresario Adam Müller-Guttenbrunn, whose 1885 pamphlet *Wien war eine Theaterstadt* (Vienna used to be a city of theater) argued that the city's theaters had abandoned the morally upright German tradition—a call to arms whose xenophobic and anti-Semitic elements were obvious.[16] What was once French, modern, and racy was now decadent and lascivious. When the alternative was French "frivolity" and willful strangeness, the familiar appeals of the new Viennese operettas—waltzes, Hungarian color, and sentimentality—seemed only more attractive. Three new theaters, the Deutsches Volkstheater, the Raimundtheater, and the Kaiserjubiläums-Stadttheater, were founded with explicit German nationalist agendas, with the latter two directed by Müller-Guttenbrunn himself. While these theaters concentrated on spoken theater, the discourse had ramifications for operetta as well. Already in 1875, an anonymous critic wrote of Johann Strauss's *Cagliostro in Wien*:

> The Viennese composer Johann Strauss has sustained a new victory over the French.... Above all, the libretto by Genée and Zell is a rational one, free from the idiocy that the French take for fun. It isn't set in a fool's land where the people wear impossible hats and robes and speak and act like lunatics; rather the events take place here in the fatherland, in the city of Vienna.[17]

The crux of this move toward localism was a return to the subjects of the old *Volksstück*: homespun, deliberately naive, and "anti-decadent," a label often connoting xenophobia and anti-Semitism.

But by the later 1890s the fervor for German nationalist theater had already ebbed. For Viennese operetta, there loomed another problem, this time not ideological: a lack of major composers. Johann Strauss II and Carl Millöcker—both had already retired earlier in the decade—died in 1899; Franz von Suppé in 1895. Their works continued to be the most popular draws at Viennese operetta theaters. Commentators began looking back to Strauss's and even Offenbach's eras with nostalgia and wondering whether the genre had a future.

Among many, one more reason for concern was a brief but important fad for imported English operettas, translated into German like their Offenbachian predecessors. The D'Oyly Carte Opera Company first visited the Carl-Theater in 1886, but the real breakthrough came in the mid-1890s with the works of the English music hall composer Sidney Jones (1861–1946). Jones's works grew out of the burlesque tradition of London, such as that of the Gaiety Theatre, but in the German press they would come to be known as dance operettas (*Tanzoperetten*).[18] Jones's *The Geisha (A Story of a Tea House)* was first performed in Vienna in October 1897 and became the most popular operetta in some time. It was not particularly novel (the *Fremden-Blatt* referred to "once again the *Mikado* décor," possibly meaning that the sets and costumes were literally borrowed from the previous production[19]), but *The Geisha* was a sensation thanks to its energetic dancing and exotic setting. It lacked Gilbert and Sullivan's satirical edge, thus requiring no knowledge of British society, which perhaps explains why its success in Vienna was exponentially greater than that of *The Mikado*.

The Geisha's most lasting contribution to Viennese culture was its popularization of a physically strenuous style of choreography known as "grotesque dance" or "parody dance" (later known as "eccentric dance"), a series of contortions that tested the performers' elasticity.[20] One of its most famous early proponents was the actor Louis Treumann, who would eventually find himself in the leading male role of *Die lustige Witwe*. Of his dance in Jones's follow-up work, *San Toy*, he said:

> I can modestly say that I laid the foundations for eccentric dance onstage.... [In *San Toy*] because something grotesque was required, I pushed myself so far onstage as to do a "salto mortadella" [*sic!*] in the dance after my couplet ("The Chinese Soldier"). This sparked such a frenetic ovation in the audience that I often had to encore it. Many came to the theater just to see if I would make it through unscathed. The desire for thrills and stimulation![21]

The dance numbers did not advance the operetta's drama but rather stood apart from it. (The same can be said of some of the musical numbers entire, which are often directed at the audience rather than the other characters.) The spectator is aware of the spectacle; there is no mimesis or opportunity for identification with the performer. In this respect, as well as in the general buffo character of the music, dance operetta extended Offenbachian style. But while the works, and even the numbers themselves, are described as "parodic," it is never clear what is being parodied other than a more conventionally graceful aesthetic or more recognizably human motion. It has none of the pointed critique of satire.

English operettas would become an important stylistic reference point in the Silver Age, but, according to most Austrian and German critics, the English craze was a fad without lasting importance, and operetta's central lineage resided on the Continent. What a new age of operetta required was new Viennese composers to reclaim what they considered rightfully theirs. But too often critics were disappointed with the post–Golden Age offerings of local composers and librettists. (The lack of works enjoying long runs during this period suggests that audiences were not overly enchanted either.) As conductor Hans Stieber wrote in 1903,

> Every day we receive another memo about the health condition of operetta. Then Herr X or Herr Y appears with the muse-consecrated work on the plans—we mean the calendar of a Viennese theater—there's a rustling in the leaves of the newspaper: "No, the operetta isn't dead, Herr X has revived it. Charming melodies, a sparkling mood, stirring rhythms, etc." But that doesn't prevent the fact that eight days later at the same place there follows the revival of a Strauss operetta.[22]

Stieber's negative tone is typical of the critical discourse of the era. The struggles of the Theater an der Wien, the oldest and most important of operetta theaters, were symptomatic.[23] Of that theater's premieres in the 1890s, only Richard Heuberger's first operetta, *Der Opernball*, had seemed to point the way to the future and to achieve lasting success, playing 152 performances, around three times as many as an average hit of those years.[24] Its sophisticated yet conventional score, while prefiguring the eroticism of twentieth-century scores, failed to lead to any successors. By 1900 the Theater an der Wien hosted few premieres, the performances were provincial in quality, and the programming lacked focus. In 1901, in financial doldrums under the direction of Karl Langkammer, it was closed and put up for sale. Critic Ernst Decsey, writing in 1924, when he was one of the most important journalists writing about operetta, describes Vienna "around 1900 to 1905" as the era of Mahler and *Salome*, but "as a young critic, I refused to go to operetta, I found it beneath my dignity. In light music I saw only old laziness and unbearable musical blandness."[25]

CRITICISM AND REVIVAL

The periodization of operetta, particularly the idea of a break around 1900, dates from the earliest histories of the genre. Otto Keller's *Die Operette in ihrer Geschichtlichen Entwicklung* (The Historical Development of Operetta) in 1926, the first major history of operetta, was published around the same time that *Die lustige Witwe's* origin story was becoming myth. (He has little to say about the operetta's premiere.) Keller charts operetta's Viennese history in three parts: the *Glanzzeit* (heyday) of the nineteenth century, a period of decay (the later nineteenth-century crisis), and *Die Wiener Tanzoperette* (Viennese dance operettas, covering the turn of the twentieth century to the 1920s).[26] The next major history, Karl Westermeyer's *Die Operette im Wandel des Zeitgeistes* (Operetta in the Changing Spirit of the Age, 1931), simplifies this to a two-part periodization consisting of nineteenth-century "classical operettas" and twentieth-century "romantic operettas."[27]

The frequently invoked labels "Gold" (to refer to the nineteenth century) and "Silver" (for the twentieth) became attached somewhat later. They are in some ways informative and in others, particularly in their implications of decline, problematic. Kevin Clarke and Hans-Jörg Koch have both argued that they originated in the Third Reich, particularly in consideration of the many Jewish operetta composers and librettists. The evidence for this, however, is not definitive.[28] The label "silver" made its first prominent appearance in print in Franz Hadamowsky and Heinz Otte's 1947 history *Die Wiener Operette: Ihre Theater- und Wirkungsgeschichte* (Operetta: Its Theatrical History and Impact), whose periodization encompasses "The Golden Age of Viennese Operetta (1871–1885)," "Decline of Viennese Operetta (1885–1901)," and "The Silver Age of Viennese Operetta (1901–1920)." The authors intended the label as a bit of an insult to the later era, during which, they claimed, "theater lost its ethical mission."[29]

One consistent feature of these histories is the location of a crisis beginning around 1890 (coinciding with the decline of Johann Strauss II's career). This crisis had been identified by critics as it was occurring and discussed in similar terms. Granted, crisis was in some ways integral to operetta culture: To the less favorably disposed, the very popularity and centrality of operetta in cultural life was the crisis. To those more enamored of the genre, the problem was a perceived decline in quality as well as the sudden disappearance of the established Golden Age composers. Most critics believed that operetta served a purpose distinct from that of opera: while opera could and even should challenge its audience, operetta must divert without taxing the audience's understanding. Berlin theater critic Erich Urban described operetta's virtue as its "likable superficiality" and "cheerful, easygoing essence."[30] Critic Ferdinand Scherber wrote in the *Neue Musik-Zeitung* that it should be effortless, "music that goes into our ears without pain, and without exertion brings new excitement to our nerves." This entertainment, Scherber wrote, should be accessible to everyone and offer relief from the toil of modern life (neatly prefiguring Danilo's entrance song in *Die lustige Witwe*): "music that accompanies people in the workshop and office, that makes bearable the monotony of division of labor, that makes bleak minutes fly by."[31] Similarly, the pre-*Witwe* Franz Lehár wrote in a feuilleton essay (the likes of which many composers wrote on occasion to propagate their views) that many critics condemned operetta music as lacking worth; however, he believed that, while most people lacked the privilege to enjoy and understand difficult music, anyone could enjoy operetta as aiding "recuperation after the day's trouble and toil."[32]

Critics condemned Vienna's tendency toward sentimental and romantic operettas—a tendency that would become more and more prominent over the course of the Silver Age—as inferior to the sharper wit of Offenbach. Berlin-based critic Erich Urban went so far as to proclaim: "Offenbach began, fulfilled, and completed operetta. He is simultaneously its beginning, apex, and end."[33] Like Urban, Eugen Thari found the true purpose of operetta to be merry parody and political satire, exemplified by Offenbach, and argued that current composers had abandoned their purpose for mere business concerns.[34]

After arriving in Vienna, critics suggested, operetta gave way to three temptations: the waltz, and dance music in general; an aspiration to achieve the emotional and musical scale of full-blown opera (though this accusation seemingly contradicts the first, it indicates how varied both operetta and criticism could be); and dramatic cliché. Urban blames Johann Strauss II for dance and cliché, arguing that the Waltz King brought the closed forms of dance music into music theater, to its detriment. (Considering Strauss's late-career operatic experiments, in retrospect this charge seems misplaced.) Operetta, Theodor Antropp wrote in the Viennese paper Die Zeit, was not dramatic: it had "no self-contained lyric-dramatic plot that requires the music to serve as an expressive or atmospheric medium, but rather a wild potpourri of low folk theater scenes, inserted songs, and spectacular processions; words and music aren't positioned to signify together and interact but rather are rendered individually for their own purposes."[35] These criticisms would never really go away.

Those who thought operetta salvageable proposed various solutions. Thari wrote that operetta should return fully to its Offenbachian roots, a model of a "satyr play" that would seduce with "human, artistic, and political humor."[36] Urban thought that the solution was to look to the artists of his city, Berlin, for a fresh "jovial, brash, satirical spirit." (Indeed, Berlin composers produced many lighthearted, irreverent works in the early twentieth century, and the Berlin milieu was an important influence on Viennese composers Leo Fall and Oscar Straus.[37]) The "Silver Age" is easily demarcated by this period of instability and the complete replacement of operetta's major composers by a new group. But many of the criticisms that would later be leveled against twentieth-century operetta had already been clearly stated around 1900, before the Silver Age even began: namely, a perceived conflict between the satire of Offenbach and the increasing tendencies of Viennese composers to reach toward sentiment and musical grandeur.[38]

The theatrical seeds of the Silver Age concept were planted by Hungarian writer Wilhelm Karczag (1857–1923), who was appointed director of the Theater an der Wien in 1901 by its new consortium of owners.[39] Karczag revolutionized the program almost overnight, assembling an ensemble of operetta actors (starring his wife, soubrette Julie Kopasci), and in November the theater presented its first new operetta production under his direction: a staging of Der Zigeunerbaron with the by then legendary Alexander Girardi. This choice signaled, above all, Girardi's popularity in the role of pig farmer Kálmán Zsupán, but it also proclaimed the theater's central place in the lineage of Viennese operetta (the operetta had premiered in the same space). The revival's reception revealed among critics a growing historical consciousness, an understanding of the still relatively new genre of operetta as a genre with a canon of classic works, a pantheon in which *Der Zigeunerbaron* took pride of place and most operettas since the 1890s were not often programmed. Crucially, Karczag embarked on a mission to discover a new generation of operetta composers, aggressively taking on new works by unknowns. By 1905 Karczag's theater had produced the first operettas of Leo Ascher, Leo Fall, and Franz Lehár; Oscar Straus and Edmund Eylser made their debuts at rival theaters in the same period.

Already in 1904 journalist and composer Albert Kauders had written that he put his hopes "with even greater happiness in Franz Léhar [*sic*], who through all the popular hash can't hide a superior musical education."[40] Indeed, unlike the composers of the Golden Age, Lehár was formally trained in classical music, having attended the Prague Conservatory, and he subsequently served as a military bandmaster.[41] (Having studied violin, he was not highly trained as a composer, but he entered operetta with a much more academic pedigree than his predecessors.) He wrote an unsuccessful opera and some successful salon music and after leaving the military took conducting positions at various theaters, eventually as an assistant *Kapellmeister* at the Theater an der Wien. Such formal training, highly unusual in the Golden Age, would become commonplace in the twentieth century.

Lehár's position at the Theater an der Wien and the four operettas he composed before *Die lustige Witwe* amounted to a crash course in a genre with which he had little prior familiarity; Stefan Frey goes so far as to characterize the young Lehár as a Parsifal of operetta, lost in a magic garden and remaking a genre whose rules he did not know.[42] Lehár's first operetta, *Wiener Frauen* (1902), starred the most important of all nineteenth-century operetta actors, the aging Alexander Girardi.[43] Girardi adopted his customarily folksy Viennese persona, and Lehár's music similarly summoned an earlier era. But while *Wiener Frauen* followed tradition, Lehár's second operetta, *Der Rastelbinder* (1902), was unconventional: written to a libretto by Victor Léon (the most doggedly experimental of operetta librettists), it takes place primarily in Vienna, but the characters are mostly Slovakian immigrants struggling to adjust to city life, and the action jumps between disparate places and times. Lehár's score mixes Slovakian folk music with more typically Viennese sounds (an obvious antecedent to *Witwe*), exploring issues of integration and homesickness. A box office success, *Der Rastelbinder* featured a theme that resonated with contemporary Vienna, presenting something closer to everyday life than the romanticized "Gypsies" and aristocrats of *Der Zigeunerbaron*.

In 1904, before *Die lustige Witwe*, the prolific Lehár wrote two more operettas, both of which demonstrated his ability to write fluently in multiple styles. *Die Göttergatte* is an Offenbach throwback, a domestic adventure among Greek gods set to light, French-style music with none of the regional color of either of Lehár's previous works. It was not particularly successful, but its successor, *Die Juxheirat,* failed even more quickly, despite another star performance by Girardi. Shortly after *Die Juxheirat,* Girardi announced his retirement from the stage, a move that would complete the generational shift that had begun with the departure of Johann Strauss and the other Golden Age composers.

The theater's autumn 1905 season began on October 10 with Leo Ascher's new operetta *Vergelt'sgott!,* featuring a "modern" New York setting and starring two actors new to the theater, Louis Treumann and Mizzi Günther (whom Karczag had lured away from the rival Carl-Theater[44]). It ran a successful 69 performances. Karczag's November 29 premiere was an even bigger risk: the debut operetta of composer Leo Fall and new librettists, Rudolf Bernauer and Ernst Welisch, *Der Rebell,* an experimental piece that attempted to graft grand opera ensembles onto the absurd plot of an Offenbach operetta. Had it been successful, it could have heralded an alternative future for operetta, one of satire and absurdity rather than romanticism. But while Fall received encouraging notices and critics were intrigued by the work's originality, by all accounts it was a muddle. *Der Rebell* closed after only five performances, when the creators withdrew the work for revision.[45] Karczag rushed to open his next production—*Die lustige Witwe*—and planned to return the revised *Der Rebell* to the stage after *Witwe* ran its course. *Witwe's* expedited production schedule, as well as Karczag's doubt about the work's prospects, led to a hastily assembled premiere, which took place on December 30, 1905, furnished with stock scenery and costumes. To this extent, *Witwe's* great success was, as myth later had it, indeed unplanned and unexpected.

DIE LUSTIGE WITWE:
CONCEPTION AND COMPOSITION

Die lustige Witwe was conceived by librettists Victor Léon and Leo Stein. Léon was one of the most adventurous and influential figures in operetta, the creator of Johann Strauss II's opera *Simplicius,* Lehár's *Der Rastelbinder,* and many other librettos. Léon's works often defied operetta conventions in both subject matter and dramaturgy.[46] Sometimes he worked alone and sometimes with collaborators; like many operetta librettists, he did not have an exclusive collaborator relationship but worked with many other writers. With Stein, he had written *Wiener Blut* in 1898 and *Die Göttergatte* in 1904, the latter composed by Lehár. In the case of *Die lustige Witwe,* Stein wrote the song texts while Léon planned the work's overall shape and wrote the spoken dialogue.

The operetta is, crucially, set in Paris. The heroine is Hanna Glawari, a down-to-earth Pontevedran peasant girl raised to exalted status after catching the eye of and marrying Pontevedro's richest man, who, before the operetta begins, promptly dies and leaves her all his money. Hanna then relocates to France, where she is a hot commodity on the Parisian marriage market, but the Pontevedrans are intent on keeping her wealth in Pontevedro to prop up their national bank—so she must marry a fellow Pontevedran. At the operetta's start, the embassy staff is desperately trying to play matchmaker. They identify the lazy diplomat Count Danilo Danilowitsch as the most eligible Pontevedran bachelor in Paris (and indeed he and Hanna had had a romance years before, foiled by her then low social standing). But Valencienne, the wife of the Pontevedran ambassador Baron Zeta, wants Hanna to marry her own French would-be lover, Camille de Rosillon. Danilo and Hanna love each other, but he cannot face proposing to her, believing that she would think his motivations are solely financial. After this exposition, the plot largely concerns itself with Hanna and Danilo cautiously circling each other and Camille and Valencienne interfering. After a dramatic falling-out at the end of Act 2, Danilo and Hanna finally successfully declare their mutual love in the third act.

Léon and Stein described the libretto as "partly based on a foreign basic idea," without naming the specific source But Henri Meilhac's L'attaché d'ambassade, first performed at the Théâtre du Vaudeville on October 12, 1861, was a known quantity in Vienna and was still produced on occasion.[47] The librettists probably avoided crediting it so they would not be obliged to pay royalties to Meilhac's estate; indeed the lack of attribution would lead to legal action in 1909.[48] Léon and Stein changed many details of Meilhac's setting and plot, but most critics noted, as Leopold Jacobson dryly put it in the Neues Wiener Journal, that "the basic idea is, however, not entirely foreign."[49] But Jacobson thought the old comedy made a fine operetta libretto: "The authors have lifted from [translator] Hackländer's comedy Der Attaché and made a very entertaining, well-built libretto."[50] Similarly, Julius Stern wrote in the Fremden-Blatt, "Already after the introductory scenes of the exposition it comes to one: 'Pretty mask, but I recognize you!' It is in fact Der Attaché—a beloved comedy, created as if for a proper operetta."[51]

But critical changes were made from Meilhac's play, ones that would have significant importance for the operetta's musical style. The operetta, like the play, takes place in Paris, but the key location of the imaginary bankrupt state has changed. Meilhac's small Germanic state made less sense in the wake of a unified Germany, and the shift to the imaginary "Pontevedro" relocated the cast of characters to within the Austro-Hungarian Empire's orbit. Moreover, Pontevedro was an obvious stand-in for the actual state of Montenegro. (In fact, Léon and Stein had originally named the setting as Montenegro, but the censor, extremely sensitive on matters of nationality, had disallowed its use.[52]) The male lead is called Danilo (the name of the crown prince of Montenegro at the time as well as Montenegro's first secular ruler) and Baron Zeta's name references Montenegro's largest river, the

Günther-Treumann.
Die Lustige Witwe.
788

FIGURE 1.1. *Die lustige Witwe* actors Louis Treumann (Danilo) and Mizzi Günther (Hanna). Bildarchiv Austria, Österreichische National-bibliothek.

Zeta. The royal house of Montenegro was itself called Petrovic Njegos, the name of the embassy's attaché in Léon and Stein's libretto.[53] Politically, it was a somewhat provocative choice (considering the perennial instability in the region), while musically the choice of Eastern Europe invited a musical style that contrasted with the Parisian one.

The use of Montenegran costumes was apparently obvious, as seen in fig. 1.1.

Critics were not fooled by the kingdom's pseudonym either. The critic of the *Deutsches Volksblatt* described "a very transparent paraphrase of nationality, whose truth is fully revealed by the costumes."[54] Julius Stern sarcastically noted, "Pontevedro is the theater-official name of the country where all the people wear Montenegrin caps and dance the kolo."[55] In the *Arbeiter-Zeitung*, David Josef Bach wrote, " 'Montenegro,' or, as the daftness of our theater censor wants it, 'Pontevedro.' "[56] The etymologically improbable name of Pontevedro seems to be inspired by Pontevedra, a town on the coast of northwest Spain; in 1893 Lehár's entry in the Sonzogno opera competition had been bested by an opera by Josef Forster entitled *Die Rose von Pontevedra*.[57]

The libretto was given first to Richard Heuberger; presumably the many sexually charged party scenes of *Die lustige Witwe* reminded the librettists of Heuberger's sole great success, *Der Opernball*, which was similarly based on a French comedy.[58] After composing several songs—which appear not to have survived—he was fired by the librettists because, as leading actor Louis Treumann wrote, "despite all his talent and significant technical ability [he] lacked two elements that were essential for this composition: the exotic and the erotic."[59] Emil Steininger, the secretary of the Theater an der Wien, suggested Lehár as a replacement. The match was canny—both Léon and Lehár had shown their interest in and proficiency at a wide range of new and old operetta styles, and in *Die lustige Witwe* they would use this skill to its best advantage.

MUSICAL DUALITIES

With a precision unmatched by other operettas of its era, the score and libretto of *Die lustige Witwe* stage the plight of the fin de siècle resident of Vienna. The Pontevedrans are ethnic outsiders from the provinces now in the center of a dazzling metropolis, forced to balance the boredom of wage labor work and the pull of urban temptation against the weight their homeland traditions. Of course the ending is happy: traditional dance and racy nightclub can coexist, as can political expediency and romantic love. Like many operettas, *Die lustige Witwe* is wish fulfillment, displaying an opulently staged, romantic solution to problems found in its audience's everyday lives.

The music dramatizes the libretto's duality between Paris and Pontevedro. Carl Dahlhaus explored the idea of a musical duality in *Die lustige Witwe* in his 1985 article, "Zur musikalische Dramaturgie der *Lustigen Witwe*," in which he argued that Lehár's music operates according to a principal of *Stilmischung* or style mixture: a buffo Parisian style is used to stage the external plot—the political intrigues and farcical action—and a sentimental, romantic folk song–influenced style is used to portray the characters' internal psychological states.[60] Dahlhaus considers the distinction between Paris and Pontevedro to be primarily temporal (Paris represents modernity and the folkloric numbers are outside of time). But the split is geographical as well. *Witwe*'s external, presentational numbers might be understood to represent the public and political urban life in Paris in all its superficiality, while the numbers portraying the characters' inner feelings and love of country are sentimental, folkloric, rural, and nationalistic—that is to say, Pontevedran.[61]

Moritz Csáky interprets the Parisian setting, carried over from the play, as a straightforward code for the operetta's tale of affairs and lust: "Paris became a topos for erotic freedom, for the 'sweet tête-à-tête' in a '*chambre separée*' [quoting *Der Opernball*, which also takes place in Paris]. Paris became a metaphor for the only recently openly articulated longings of the new generation."[62] But the city's symbolic role in *Die lustige Witwe* is more specific, standing for a certain form of dramaturgy as well as a moral code. This is revealed in the element of operetta most frequently ignored by historian Csáky: the music, which represents the contrasting world of the Pontevedrans and the Parisians. It suggests that the operetta is less a break with nineteenth-century tradition than a synthesis of several competing strains that had been fighting for supremacy since the passing of the Golden Age, with the conflict among innumerable polemics thematized in the plot. *Die lustige Witwe* dramatizes the contrast between Pontevedro and Paris as, in short, the contrast between Parisian and Austro-Hungarian operetta styles. It is a synthesis of the Austrian/French dialectic, but one whose drama is generated by the friction between the two schools.

The table outlines the distribution of the opera between the Parisian and Offenbach-style numbers and the Pontevedran/*Volkston* ones. Several numbers do not fit clearly in either category or mix the two; these are included in the third column. As is immediately apparent, the first act is dominated by the Parisian numbers, the second by the Pontevedran ones (most importantly the extended Vilja-Lied), and the last again by Parisian (though it is quite short and serves more as a coda than anything else).

The texts of the Parisian numbers, such as Danilo's entrance song "O Vaterland, du machst bei Tag," the septet "Wie die Weiber," and the Grisetten-Lied "Ja, wir sind es, die Grisetten," speak of big city ambivalence, cynicism, and showmanship. The national and folkloric ones such as Hanna's "Vilja-Lied" and Danilo's "Es waren zwei Königskinder" articulate patriotism, sincerity, enthusiasm, and genuine emotion. For both Danilo and Hanna, the plot's challenge is to put the Offenbachiade of Paris in its proper, external place, to not permit the intrigues to compromise their relationship, and to allow for the triumph of the true self, the nation, and love, as exemplified by the operetta's finale. The operetta is not so moralizing as to assign an explicitly negative value to the frivolity of Paris—after all, it is a fun and enjoyable spectacle. But ultimately it is the sentimental *Volkston* that prevails. Hanna marries Danilo, and the homeland is saved; Valencienne and Camille are foiled. Lehár, Léon, and Stein found a way to revive

MUSICAL NUMBERS, *Die lustige Witwe*

Parisian/Buffo	Pontevedran	Mixed/Ambiguous
	Act 1	
		1. Introduktion
2. Duett, Valencienne and Camille, "So kommen sie"		
	3. Entreelied, Hanna, "Bitte, meine Herren" (some mixture)	
4. Auftrittslied, Danilo, "O Vaterland"		
5. Duett, Valencienne and Camille, "Ja was—ein trautes Zimmerlein"		
		6. Finale I "Damenwahl"
	Act 2	
	7. Introduktion, Tanz und "Vilja-Lied," Hanna	
		8. Duett, Hanna and Danilo, Lied vom dummen Reiter
9. Marsch-Septett, "Wie die Weiber man handelt"		
	10. Spielszene und Tanzduett, Hanna and Danilo	
		11. Duett und Romanze, Valencienne and Camille, "Wie eine Rosenknospe"
		12. Finale II
	Act 3	
13. Tanzszene		
14. Chanson, Grisetten-Lied, "Ja, wir sin des, die Grisetten"		
14a. Reminiszenz, Danilo, "Da geh' ich zu Maxim"		
		15. Duett, Hanna and Danilo, "Lippen schweigen"
16. Schlußgesang, "Ja, das Studium der Weiber!"		

Offenbach and yet inter him again, a way to have their satiric and sentimental cake and eat it too.

The operetta begins by setting the tone with Parisian music, but it is almost immediately juxtaposed with the Pontevedran. The short prelude (in lieu of an overture) is a galop marked presto (score No. 1) whose Offenbachian tone is obtained with near-unison use of the large orchestra, maniacally repeating figures, extremely fast tempo, and even the genre of the galop itself (related to the cancan). But when the curtain rises, the focus turns to the Pontevedran partygoers, and the tone of the music shifts as well. Pontevedran Baron Zeta notes that that party is being held to celebrate the birthday of the unnamed Pontevedran *Fürst*, "to whom we patriotically dedicate ourselves." No sooner does Zeta proclaim his patriotism and duty than he switches into a mazurka and recalls his status as a senior representative of rustic Pontevedro in urban Paris (ex. 1.2).

Though the oboe figure over "bin Landesvater *per procura*" recalls the repeated mordent motive of the prelude, the easygoing tempo and wind solos give the section a small-scale, rustic tone despite the official nature of his proclamation. (Pontevedro is evidently not a nation that can be taken very seriously.) Thus, while the celebrations of social Paris are marked with the explicitly Parisian music of French operetta, Zeta's responsibilities to home and country are depicted with the folkloric, generalized Eastern European music of the mazurka.

This association is strengthened when it is repeated in Hanna's entrance song (No. 3). She is greeted by Cascada and the other Parisians in a waltz, but then introduces herself by proudly proclaiming her Pontevedran soul and incomplete adjustment to Parisian life. On the line "Hab' in Paris mich noch nicht ganz so acclimatisiert" (I haven't yet completely acclimated to Paris), she falls, like Zeta, into a mazurka. When the male choir reenters, she shifts back to a waltz, noting with Parisian cynicism, "I have often heard, well, that we widows are coveted!" For the Pontevedrans, the mazurka is the music of their home identity while the waltz is identified with a new Parisian attitude.

Lehár made no attempt to achieve any ethnic unity in his folk music influences. The Croatian kolo in Act 2 is the most geographically appropriate dance to Pontevedro, but Lehár's vocabulary extends through the whole realm of the Austro-Hungarian Empire.[63] Dahlhaus describes this eclecticism as innate to music-theater in general, comparing it to the plurality found in ballet music. It, he claims, gives national music a symbolism that is coloristic rather than specifically referential and trades in familiar clichés in a way that had become ritualized.[64] The waltz that provides the apotheosis of Hanna and Danilo's relationship, "Lippen schweigen" (No. 15), is the principal example of Viennese color.

But the waltz was not the only dance music of 1900 Vienna. Indeed, by offering a wide selection of different ethnic musical styles, Lehár makes the most authentically Austro-Hungarian use of regional music possible. This mixture reflects not

EXAMPLE 1.2. Franz Lehár, *Die lustige Witwe*, No. 1, Introduktion, m. 98

only the diverse populations of Vienna but also the complexities of many of its citizens' own identities, including that of the composer himself. Lehár referred to himself as a *Tornisterkind* or "backpack child." While ethnically Slovakian (and identified as such by the Viennese press), he was resident in Hungary for much of his youth, as he moved from garrison to garrison with his family, and educated in Prague.[65] In the army, he had been stationed in Poland, Breslau, the Balkans, and many other locations. He was not atypical: while nationalism sought to sort people, practices, and symbols into clear-cut national categories, in practice few people or places would ever be so straightforward. Imaginary Pontevedro is a perfect representative for this mixture: it possesses no distinctive sound but rather mixes a variety of national musics from different regions. In this sonic world, the Pontevedrans stand in for all expatriates in Vienna who could hear one, or more than one, of the musics as their own. Throughout the score, the ethnic dances are associated entirely with the Pontevedran characters and never the Parisians. (Both Parisians and Pontevedrans can enjoy the waltz.)

The score's eventual tour of regional music—which includes multiple mazurkas, a polonaise, the kolo, and the use of a tamburitza band at the beginning of Act 2—recalls the "Fünf-Kreuzertanz" (Five-Penny Dance) chapter of Felix Salten's *Wurstelprater*, in which the narrator strolls through the titular amusement park and hears a medley of dance music from Austria, Bohemia, and Hungary. Salten writes: "Here no one revolted against the song of another....Whether the music was a waltz, a Ländler, a polka, or a csárdás, all the people here have one thing in common: that they are foreigners in this giant city that devours their toil."[66] The various musics exist in involuntary harmony, assuaging the homesickness of the alienated expatriates and diverting them from their difficult, poorly paid work. While nationalism separates them as members of different groups, here their homesickness unites them. The Pontevedran music speaks not to one specific group of immigrants but, like that of the Prater, to all groups.

While Hanna adopts Parisian language only when she is self-consciously voicing Parisian sentiments, her would-be paramour Danilo speaks it all too readily. Upon his entrance, the score makes an auspicious return to Parisian style (No. 4). His entrance song immediately follows hers and stands in stark contrast to it (ex. 1.3). In a jaunty tone without significant lyricism, he laments the woes of his bureaucratic job and celebrates the glories of the nightclub Maxim's. The form is a modified version of Offenbach's couplets (lacking the choral interjections). In the refrain, a descending scale insistently repeats, and the litany of his favorite showgirls' pet names (Lolo, Dodo, Joujou/Cloclo, Margot, Froufrou) sounds like the nonsense syllables of an Offenbach operetta.

The role of Danilo was tailored to the particular talents of Louis Treumann, the Theater an der Wien's new leading man and the self-proclaimed inventor of eccentric dance in Vienna. Previously known for portraying comic, non-aristocratic characters, Treumann engineered a change of *Fach* when he moved to the Theater an der Wien from the Carl-Theater in the fall of 1905. Treumann's initial role at his new theater was the aristocrat-turned-beggar in Leo Ascher's *Vergelt'sgott!* and it aptly marked the first step in his transformation from comic relief to leading man. The engineer of this shift was Victor Léon, who wrote a long letter of advice to him on September 20, 1905, before the *Vergelt'sgott!* premiere, telling him that he must no longer rely on comic dance duets with "die Günther" (co-star Mizzi Günther) but that he "must appear as a *completely different* person, a new and unexpected Treumann." He encouraged Treumann to develop the character with "*interiority*"

EXAMPLE 1.3. Lehár, *Die lustige Witwe*, No. 4, Auftrittslied (Danilo), refrain

and through "*temperament*" ("*Stimmung*") and repeatedly assured Treumann that following this advice would lead to "*artistic*" acclaim, rather than just popular success (all emphases original).[67] The association of interiority with artistic worth and merit, and comedy with mere popularity, is one that would be made by many advocates for Silver Age operetta, and one that its critics, longing for a return to Offenbach, would declare backward.

Treumann's star image is inseparable from the character of Danilo.[68] Danilo's speech is capped with a jagged ritornello that suggests an eccentric dance, and the pattering rhythm of his vocal line recalls the English style—all typifying the old Treumann, not the new one. (Complaining about work or penury had become Treumann's signature: after singing a song on this theme in *The Geisha*, his entrance songs in *Die Rastelbinder* and *Die lustige Witwe*, both written for him, were on similar subjects. Likewise, in *Vergelt'sgott!* he entered complaining that he was out of money and wanted to shoot himself.) The difference is significant, because Danilo is merely awaiting reformation. Soon enough his purported true self—a patriot who is desperately in love with Hanna—is revealed. Léon, in creating this role specifically for Treumann, thematizes the actor's own evolution from comic, distanced, eccentric dancer to soulful lover (conveniently allowing Treumann to display his dramatic range as an actor and dancer). The "real Danilo" is the new Treumann, a figure of identification for the audience and later a major operetta celebrity. He is also the new operetta.[69] Ironically, the old operetta is the one in the modern Parisian suit, while the new Treumann wears the Montenegran cap of folklore and displays Silver Age operetta sincerity.

The Parisian tone is epitomized most of all in second act ensemble number "Wie die Weiber" (No. 9) and the third act "Grisetten-Lied" (No. 14). Both are marches, and both include the percussive nonsense syllables familiar from Offenbach, which provide rhythm and motion, chatter without meaning—sequences of "zippel zippel zippel zapp" and "und so und so und so" that mean nothing in particular. The numbers are explicitly externalized and meant for a large ensemble; they deal with generalizations and types rather than individual characters—the over-the-top performing personae of showgirls and the men's view of the entire female gender, respectively. They are spectacular production numbers of the sort that would be found in the variety theater (known in the German-speaking world by the French-derived term *Varieté*), unnecessary to the plot and showing little relation to the inner states of the main characters but adding gloss and panache to the score. The perspective is essentially distanced, offering the audience a non-mimetic spectacle to admire and enjoy without emotional commitment.

The Pontevedran numbers, in contrast, are united not in ethnicity but in earnestness. They come in two forms: first, national dances and dance-like songs for fast numbers, and second, the folk song–like strophic forms. The most popular number of the entire score, the "Vilja-Lied" (No. 7), includes both. Framed in the libretto as part of Hanna's "true Pontevedran party" and performed in Pontevedran national costume (as seen in fig. 1.1), it is introduced by a polonaise including a tamburitza band of triangle, cymbals, and various other clamorous instruments. The chorus makes its entrance on a long melisma on "ah," then continues "Mi velimo da se veslimo" ("we like to celebrate")—it is revealed that "Pontevedran" is the same as Serbian (ex. 1.4).

In contrast to Dahlhaus's view that the score shows no technical innovation, a closer look at this number reveals some eccentricities that differentiate it from the

EXAMPLE 1.4. Lehár, *Die lustige Witwe*, No. 7, Introduktion, Tanz, und Vilja-Lied, choral entrance

extremely diatonic Parisian numbers. In the melisma, the harmonic movement from a G-minor chord to an A-major chord is surprising and non-functional, though the strange A major is resolved as a V/V to D major in the fourth bar. Hanna's subsequent strophic song is marked "declaimed like a folk song" and has a simple, flowing rhythm and harmony, but the hovering on the seventh degree of the scale gives the theme a haunting instability, as does Hanna's later cadence in the final chorus on a high B, the third degree of the scale.

The text is similarly unstable: it tells of a forest spirit, or *vila*, from Slavic myth (the plot also recalls the ballet *La Sylphide* and the willis of *Giselle*). Yet for a folk song, the story is oddly unresolved: in the first strophe the hunter sees the nymph and longs to be her lover; in the second strophe she beckons to him, and he enters

EXAMPLE 1.5. "Die Königskinder," folk song, reading from *Deutsche Weisen*, ed. August Linder (c. 1900), No. 222

her house, but after one kiss she disappears forever. That is all. The hunter is left lovesick, and the dance music returns. Even without the missing ending, the song is an obvious parable for Hanna and Danilo, with Hanna as the mysterious forest girl who disappeared years ago from Danilo's life. The folkloric aspects—not only the music but the national costume—are laid on thickly.

The conflict between the Parisian and Pontevedran styles comes to a head in the Act 2 finale (No. 12). After being caught in the gazebo with Camille (where she is actually covering for Valencienne), Hanna proclaims in a bright 6/8 march that she will marry Camille without any love or expectation of faithfulness, "in the Parisian style."[70] After this merry salute against romantic love, Danilo announces that he will tell a story. Like the "Vilja-Lied," it is a story of a failed romance, a prince and princess who love each other. The prince is unable to state his love openly, and the princess leaves him for another (ex. 1.5). The song is itself a quotation from a German folk song, a fact that has not been noted by previous scholars. "Es waren zwei Königskinder" is a well-known folk ballad of sixteenth-century Germanic origin that has been transmitted in several settings. Eckhard John describes it as "one of the best-known traditional songs in the German-speaking realm."[71] It appears in many major nineteenth-century German collections, including *Des Knaben Wunderhorn*; the musical setting dates from the nineteenth century. Its appearance in *Witwe* uses the melody found in Ludwig Erk's important collection *Deutscher Liederhort* and amounts to both a textual and musical quotation, albeit somewhat altered to fit into triple time (ex. 1.6).[72] Danilo begins with the folk ballad's text: the two royal children are in love but are separated by a lake:

Es waren zwei Königskinder,	There were two royal children,
Die hatten einander so lieb,	They loved each other,
Sie konnten beisammen nicht kommen	They could not be together

EXAMPLE 1.6. Lehár, *Die lustige Witwe*, No. 12, Finale 2, m. 293

In the full ballad a "treacherous little nun" betrays the royal love, and the prince drowns trying to reach the princess. But instead of recounting the whole story, Danilo notes the quotation, singing "as a poet once described." The parallels with Hanna and Danilo's own relationship are obvious (though their class difference has been eliminated), and at one point Danilo even slips into the first person and then corrects himself. The musical setting is of the utmost moderato folk song simplicity, with strings and harp (the harp gives it, perhaps, a folkloric quality, but the triple meter and rhythms are closer to the waltz than to Pontevedran music; the signifiers are intermingled). As Danilo becomes more and more agitated and unable to keep up the fiction that he is not in fact the prince himself, the ending collapses into a kind of *Sprechstimme* (marked "*schreiend,*" shouting) on the words "Then take him whom you desire!"

Then, Danilo ironically recapitulates the refrain of his entrance song, "Ich gehe zu Maxim." What was previously superficial fun has now been exposed through the "Königskinder" folk song as a defense mechanism. The line "they let me forget the dear Fatherland" has now become "they let me forget that which I find so frightening!" This reprise is a key element of what became known as the tragic second-act finale, in which what seems to be a happy ending is suddenly torn asunder in melodramatic fashion. In their 1947 history of operetta, Franz Had-

EXAMPLE 1.7. Lehár, *Die lustige Witwe*, No. 10, Spielszene und Tanzduett

amowsky and Heinz Otte gave such a finale prominent placement in their defini-tion of "Silver Age" operetta, writing that the leading couple's "obstacles become insurmountable in a grandiose Act 2 finale, which quakes with false sentimental-ity"; Adorno similarly identified the "tragic finale to the second act" as operetta's salvo at autonomous musical form.[73] *Die lustige Witwe* is, however, by no means the first example of a musically ambitious and dramatically pessimistic second act finale—that distinction is usually given to *Der Zigeunerbaron* (1885)—but *Die lustige Witwe*'s musical model, in which the meaning of a prominent number from earlier in the operetta is reversed, would indeed become de rigueur in the twenti-eth century.

In this case the tragedy of the second-act finale is immediately forestalled: Hanna's reaction to Danilo is an aside but jubilant: "Me alone! He loves me alone." Danilo has allowed his Pontevedran soul and true love for Hanna to escape. All that remains in the third act is for them to untangle their confusion. This is in part because their love had in fact already been articulated, albeit wordlessly. Before being split up by escapades in the gazebo, Hanna and Danilo had already declared their love in the "Tanzduett" (No. 10). The music is Pontevedran, a few dances followed by the Viennese waltz that will become the third act love duet "Lippen schweigen," first played by the orchestra and then hummed by Hanna and Danilo (ex. 1.7). This wordlessness is as important an element of the Pontevedran num-bers as the frequent nonsense syllables are to the Parisian ones. If the Parisian numbers are linguistically typified by the percussive nonsense of "trippel trippel" and "zippel zippel," the Pontevedran numbers are defined by the melismatic sighs of the "Tanzduett" and "Vilja-Lied." The Parisian noises are markedly mechanistic, articulation without melody, while the Pontevedran sounds are organic, melody without articulation. The Parisian yelps imply rhythm, motion, dance, and externality without deeper significance, while the Pontevedran sighs imply an emotion that is too internalized to apply the external medium of speech.[74]

The plot's challenge for Danilo and Hanna is to embrace this inner desire, to give it words beyond parable and humming without surrendering to the superficiality of the Parisian nonsense. At the very end of the operetta, they finally put words to their wordless waltz, but they are, ironically, words about the need to remain silent, for the music has already spoken. They reach this point—as they reach many of the other emotional high points of the score—through pure farcical plot mechanics: this time the transparent trick of Hanna's claim that should she remarry she will have to give up all her money. The Frenchmen are put off, and Danilo promptly proposes, now without appearing to do so solely in pursuit of her fortune. She accepts and says that her wealth will remain and will now pass into his hands. That was all it took. The *Neue Freie Presse* found this unconvincing: "She speaks to him so nicely with her eyes, in the wild tenderness of Slavic dances, that he finally kisses her, the house applauds encouragingly."[75] But the essential battle, the struggle to bring Danilo to do his Pontevedran duty, to sing in Pontevedran style, and to acknowledge the fraud of his Parisian Maxim song, had already been achieved in the second act.

PREMIERE AND SILVER LEGEND

Convention has long portrayed *Die lustige Witwe* as a victorious underdog, succeeding despite minimal support from the theater and an unsuccessful first night. Indeed, as already noted, *Die lustige Witwe* was rushed into production after the withdrawal of the flop that preceded it, *Der Rebell*. According to *Rebell* librettist Rudolf Bernauer's possibly fanciful recollection, Karczag begged for the revision of his work as soon as possible rather than put on another operetta by Lehár, whose most recent work was a "sentimental, boring business with an impossible title." The new Lehár, Bernauer wrote, was "openly a fiasco," and a few days after its premiere he received another telegram from the theater management: "Completion of *Rebell* allows no delay. New operetta catastrophic revenue as feared. Reminding you of your promise. Yours, Karczag Wallner."[76] But after more revisions, the telegrams stopped; the problematic new operetta had apparently "suddenly received a jolt and now brings only sold-out houses."[77]

Indeed, Karczag and Wallner evidently had little faith in the work and placed limited financial investment in it: because of the short rehearsal period, the first stage rehearsal took place at night after an evening revival performance of Sidney Jones's *The Geisha*. To address major problems with choreography, a dance rehearsal took place the next day behind the safety curtain while the orchestra rehearsed in front of it. The operetta received one more stage rehearsal, a dress rehearsal (with at least one critic in attendance), and then opened.[78] Yet Bernauer's account of the operetta's initial reception is at odds with the reviews and other descriptions of Die lustige Witwe's first night, which describe a strong reception with many numbers encored. Reviews were entirely positive; Ludwig Karpath's notice opened, "Finally, an operetta as it should be."[79] But by both Léon's and Wallner's accounts, Die lustige Witwe did only moderate business in its first week or two.[80] These early performances may have served as a final rehearsal period, allowing the cast to turn the operetta into a success before a live audience. Apparently it was word of mouth—aided by the dissemination of the score in sheet music form— that led the operetta to become such a success. It then became an international phenomenon, a major success in London, Paris, New York, and elsewhere.[81]

Die lustige Witwe's success doomed the pointed stylistic plurality that it celebrated. Most of the subsequent operettas of the twentieth century followed Witwe's model in one or more particulars. English operettas faded, no full-fledged Offenbach revival took place, and a mixture of waltzes, folk song, and non-parodic buffo writing became the most popular model for composition. Die lustige Witwe bestowed upon operetta a stylistic unity that it itself did not possess. Until the influx of American dance styles and the creation of revue-operetta in the late 1910s and early 1920s, Die lustige Witwe was the reigning model for Viennese works.

When this model became codified, and when operetta had become a product for syndicated international export, the genre had taken a step toward the autonomy retroactively bestowed upon Die lustige Witwe. Outside its home territory, of course, Die lustige Witwe itself became a phenomenon rather than a product of a particular time and place in operetta history. It became easier to speak of "operetta" rather than "operettas" and to consider works independent of their place and time of origin. For Theodor Adorno, Die lustige Witwe represented a kind of last bastion of true art in the operetta, after which all subsequent efforts were mere commercial copies. Witwe, he wrote in 1934, "stands on the border, one of the last operettas that still had something to do with art and one of the first that unthinkingly renounced it."[82] But previous operettas had been just as commercial and just as apt to copy previous hits. It was the scale of Die lustige Witwe's success that had the homogenizing effect.

While operetta's success led many members of the musical establishment to criticize it, it prompted others—prominently including Lehár himself—to claim for operetta a place in the high-art pantheon.[83] The ascent of the Silver Age meant, for supporters of operetta, an objective improvement in the genre's musical quality as measured in individuality of style, complexity, and craftsmanship. This improvement would, they claimed, cultivate the ears and improve the discernment of the masses. Many opponents found this aspiration misplaced. For Karl Kraus, Die *lustige Witwe* opened the floodgates for a succession of sentimental, materialist works that neglected the social satire he considered the essential function of true operetta.[84] Kraus's critique, filtered through Adorno's construction of aesthetic autonomy, became the conventional musicological approach to Silver Age operetta as a once-valuable genre that lost its independent voice and declined into mass production.[85] This narrative obscures the construction of *Witwe* as well as the social role of subsequent operettas, whose function may have shifted but which were nonetheless more than simple commodities.

But in 1905, all of this lay in the future. In January 1906 the authors of the failed *Der Rebell* were still rewriting their operetta for the Offenbach revival that would never occur, Karczag was still handing out free tickets, and the world of Silver Age operetta was only nascent. It was, arguably, crowned with Felix Salten's feuilleton essay "The New Operetta," published in December 1906, which declared *Die lustige Witwe* the music of the era, with a new rhythm befitting the spirit of an age that was no longer that of Johann Strauss II. "It is," Salten wrote, "hard to say what defines the sound of an age. It is ten thousand tiny truths, a country's air, a language's accent, the steps and gesticulations of a people."[86] For Salten, *Die lustige Witwe* now represented not multiple worlds but a single one, yet operetta's ability to contain the diversity of its ecosystem within the sphere of a single work would be one of the defining traits of the twentieth century.

2

Sentimentality, Satire, and Labor

In 1906 composer Oscar Straus sought a new operetta libretto. He whiled away his evenings at a café in the Prater, Vienna's largest park and pleasure garden.[1] In honor of Straus's presence, the café's resident *Damenkapelle*—a salon orchestra of women—would occasionally play his compositions. Straus recalled such an occasion at the café, Zum Eisvogel, to his biographer Franz Mailer:

> One evening the pretty woman conductor came to my table with a request for an autograph and asked me, wholly naively: [in Viennese dialect] "Say, why don't you compose us a real Viennese waltz some time?" Just to please her, I sketched on a napkin a few bars of a waltz, which were later to become the principal waltz in my operetta. So the idea came to me totally spontaneously: such a Viennese Damenkapelle with a young woman conductor would actually be a very charming premise for a Viennese operetta. Viennese melodies were already swirling through my head, and the thought began to take shape.[2]

Another evening at Zum Eisvogel, he was purportedly approached by a young author, Hans Müller (1882–1950), who gave him a newly published book of his short stories, *Buch der Abenteuer*. Straus was apparently taken with "Nur, der Prinzgemahl," a story featuring a Damenkapelle of the same sort.[3] Librettists Felix Dörmann and Leopold Jacobson adapted the story into an operetta.

To find inspiration for an operetta in a café may be regarded as good fortune; to find inspiration twice at the same café (and not at the Café Sacher or the Café Museum, at that) looks like embroidery. The resulting operetta, *Ein Walzertraum*, was the biggest success of the decade excepting *Die lustige Witwe* itself, and its success similarly birthed contradictory creation myths. But while *Die lustige Witwe* has been memorialized as the unlikely triumph of a team of scrappy underdogs, *Ein*

Walzertraum is remembered as a fairy tale conceived under the Viennese sun of the Prater in a series of strokes of inspiration and coincidence. This is particularly remarkable because *Ein Walzertraum* is not set in Vienna at all but rather in the fictional Germanic state of Flausenthurn. Like Pontevedro in *Die lustige Witwe*, Vienna's mythic presence becomes more potent through its absence: it is repeatedly described, imagined, and performed by its homesick principal characters.

The placement of *Ein Walzertraum* in the Prater, the epicenter of Viennese leisure and pleasure, home of the iconic Ferris wheel (of *The Third Man* fame), serves to mark it as a work of *gemütlich* (cozy) relaxation, a label both typical and ominous for Viennese operetta. For many critics, the operetta was a repudiation by Straus of his earlier, critically prestigious satiric style in favor of the more remunerative territory of nostalgia and escapism. In operetta historiography, this shift—one that has been mapped over the genre as a whole from Offenbach to late Lehár—has often been assessed as a decline, such as in the monumental history of Volker Klotz.[4] The perceived centrality of sentimentality and pleasure was key both to Silver Age operetta's appeal and to its critical and historiographical marginalization. Critics from Karl Kraus to, much later, Siegfried Kracauer and, later still, Carl Dahlhaus positioned such operettas against an earlier, prelapsarian satirical Offenbach.[5]

But the sentimentality of operetta was not haphazard. Operetta's shift to sentimentality and romanticism was concomitant with changing audiences and theatrical systems; the hostile reception toward this transformation can be attributed to an elite musical establishment reacting with surprise to something that was fundamentally no longer for them. Kracauer claimed that "it was, in fact, to this class that the mixture of satire and ecstasy of Offenbach's operettas principally appealed. These people lived a life apart from the dominant society of their time"; they were so-called Bohemians who were "distinct from the great mass of the bourgeoisie."[6] But unlike Kracauer's idealized Offenbach, in the twentieth century operettas in Vienna aspired to—and eventually achieved—the status of mass culture. And yet the Parisian bacchanal of *Die lustige Witwe*, if ultimately subdued by the end of that operetta and never particularly subversive, continued to be an important stylistic and thematic element of many operetta scores. As always, operetta was a hybrid.

This chapter discusses this dialectic of satire and sentimentality in operetta through the lens of operetta's engagement with labor and leisure. Addressing these issues means confronting operetta's paradoxical place as an art of both the insider and the outsider, its roots in cabaret, and its status as a silently Jewish art—a discourse that originates in operetta's very early reception and continues to today. It requires unpacking the blunt notion of "escapism," asking what these audiences were escaping from and where they were escaping to. Despite its idyllic setting, *Ein Walzertraum* is not a fairy tale; it presents its own escapism in morally ambiguous terms and denies its audience a happy ending. I will first consider the emerging generation of new operetta composers, their work in cabaret theaters, and their reception in the specialist music press. I then consider these issues in light of two works—*Ein Walzertraum* and a fascinating flop: Franz Lehár's *Eva* (1911), a Cinderella-like story set in a factory that attempts to reckon with the moral value of escapism and economic disparity, something rarely seen on the operetta stage. Its provocative subject prompted an unusual discussion of strikes and riots, suggesting that "escapist" operetta was never distant from its audiences' daily lives.

OSCAR STRAUS AND THE NEW WORLD OF UNTERHALTUNGSMUSIK

Most of the principal composers of the Silver Age first emerged from the chaos of the 1900–1905 period. The four considered in this study are among the most consistently popular of the twentieth century: Franz Lehár, Leo Fall, Oscar Straus, and Emmerich Kálmán. Lehár was the first to graduate from promising to established, as already seen. Kálmán's career began somewhat later; in 1906 he was still writing music criticism in Budapest (see chapter 3). Leo Fall had already made his debut in Vienna in 1905 with the ill-fated *Der Rebell*. Despite its aborted run, Fall's music caught the eye of Victor Léon, who provided the librettos for his next two operettas. These works, *Der fidele Bauer* and *Die Dollarpinzessin* (1906 and 1907) would put him at the side of Lehár as one of the most popular operetta composers. Richard Heuberger (now best known for his work as a critic for the *Neue Freie Presse*), Edmund Eysler, and Heinrich Reinhardt, all hailed as potential revolutionaries in the early days of their careers, enjoyed steady but less meteoric careers.

Oscar Straus (1870–1954) remains the least-studied of this quartet, and only a few of his works remain in the modern repertory. A native of Vienna, he began to study with Max Bruch in Berlin in 1891. He then held conducting and musical assistant positions in theaters in Brno, Teplitz, and finally Mainz. His opera *Der Weise von Cordoba* premiered in Pressburg [Bratislava] in 1894, but at some point during this period his focus shifted to lighter genres. In 1898 he decamped for Berlin, where he, like Leo Fall, began his career in the world of Berlin's cabarets, a fast-moving, ragtag scene of artists, impresarios, and controversy into which Lehár never ventured. Straus served as music director for the influential if short-lived Überbrettl, the first major Berlin cabaret, and Fall for Die bösen Buben (The Naughty Boys), which began soon afterward.[7]

Much like the creators of operetta, early cabaret artists were torn between an ideal of irrationality and a desire for respectability. The most energetic advocate for cabaret in Germany was novelist and poet Otto Julius Bierbaum (1865–1910), who never opened a theater himself. Instead, his cabaret impresario is the fictional protagonist of his 1897 novel *Stilpe*, who voices cabaret's mission in rapturous terms, a description that equally recalls Nietzsche and Offenbach:

We want to throw a golden net over all people, over all of life. Those who come to us, in the Tingeltangel (cabaret), will be those who flee the museums in fright, and those who flee the church as well. Those of us who are seeking only a little colorful entertainment will find what they're looking for: a cheerful spirit to brighten life, the art of the dance in words, colors, lines, movements, a naked desire for the beautiful, the humor that takes the world by the ear... —ah, toss me a pair of fig leaves full of words, pump me full of associations, let me babble incoherently, let me blow out colored torrents of words as huge as the water sprays from the nose of an enraptured whale![8]

Never mind that this rapture leads to disaster and ends with Stilpe taking his own life onstage. What counted was the delirious vision.

Ernst von Wolzogen founded the Überbrettl in 1901 with similar ambition, his Nietzschean tendencies indicated in the enterprise's name. But he also prioritized a performance space that was clean and tidy (as he wrote in his memoirs, "no stink of beer and wine and tobacco fumes, rather a proper theater") and maintained a conventional and hierarchal division between performers and spectators ("a stage and a real space for the orchestra between me and the audience").[9] The very first program included a song by Straus; its pointed lack of delirium suggests more the cheerful spirit to brighten life than the enraptured whale.[10] Set to a text from Bierbaum's *Deutsche Chansons*, a collection of poems intended to spur German-language cabaret culture, "Der lustige Ehemann" is a duet about a happy husband and his wife (ex. 2.1). Despite the cabaret's purported aspiration to lofty culture and art, the song seems to be light escapism, proclaiming that "die Welt, die ist da draussen wo,/Sie interessiert uns gar nicht sehr" (The world is out there somewhere/It doesn't interest us very much).

Stylistically, Straus's setting has much in common with both Offenbach and the English operettas that had proved so popular on the continent only a few years earlier: short, repetitive phrases made up of stepwise motion and arpeggios, little rhythmic variety (resulting in a mechanical quality), simple diatonic harmony, nonsense syllables ("la, la, la") and strophic forms. The music was most notable for its propulsive energy and catchy themes. While certain words could be underlined, the composer never aspired to more than setting the words, rather than expressing them. (Performance style obviously played an important role in determining this song's meaning, but unfortunately critics did not remark upon it beyond generalities.[11]) But even though "Der lustige Ehemann" rejected romantic excess and its music could be plausibly read as modern, its evocation of Biedermeier comfort did not register as satiric to its contented audiences. According to Peter Jelavich, "Far from being an expression of modern times, the number represented a nostalgic looking-back to a supposedly idyllic, cozy, premetropolitan age. It did so in a distinctly apolitical manner."[12] The Überbrettl as a whole similarly failed to live up to the hyperbole of its own name and shuttered quickly.[13]

Straus's first operetta was, in fact, far more successfully satiric than "Der lustige

EXAMPLE 2.1. Oscar Straus, "Die lustige Ehemann," opening

Ehemann." Written in 1902 to a libretto by the Überbrettl lyricist "Rideamus" (né Fritz Oliven, a lawyer), it is entitled *Die lustigen Nibelungen* (the title preceded and perhaps even inspired *Die lustige Witwe* and was itself drawn from "Der lustige Ehemann").[14] Straus and Oliven were seemingly unable to find a theater willing to produce the work in Berlin. The reasons for this difficulty are unclear, but the unusually sharp content of the work may have been at fault.[15] When Straus eventually returned to Vienna, he found a city eager for new operetta talent, and one of the most important theaters in the city, the Carl-Theater (also known as the Carltheater), programmed *Die lustigen Nibelungen*, which finally premiered in November 1904.

Die lustigen Nibelungen is closer to an Offenbach imitation than anything else in the era. But in the place of Offenbach's mythic subjects are figures of Germanic myth, drawn from the *Nibelungenlied*. The operetta echoes Offenbach when it places these timeless figures in an unmistakably contemporary context, making fun of inflation, stuffy mores, and other sins of Wilhelminian Germany. While the plot roughly follows that of the *Nibelungenlied*, Straus takes the inflated self-importance of the Wagnerian *Gesamtkunstwerk* down a peg through parody in detached, satiric operetta style.[16] The operetta became something of a darling of Offenbach advocates, but it did not lead to a lasting Offenbach revival, and further satiric endeavors, such as Lehár's 1907 self-parody *Mitislaw der Moderne*, were relegated largely to smaller spaces or special occasions.

After *Die lustigen Nibelungen*, Straus remained in Vienna. But his style then, infamously, swerved. *Nibelungen* was the high-water mark of twentieth-century operetta satire; while other composers dabbled in the occasional satiric musical number, few would attempt such an explicitly satiric work. Satire came to be a peculiarly double-edged sword: a marker of its creators' outsider status but at the same time operetta's most intellectually significant, "insider" attribute, linked to the supposed irrationality that marked it, for some critics, as an irrational resistance to bourgeois conformity.

JUDAISM, OPERETTA, AND MARGINALIZATION

The discourse surrounding satire and detachment versus romanticism and immersion also had ethnic dimensions. In his fervently nationalist and frequently anti-Semitic memoir, Wolzogen notes that his cabaret musicians were almost all Jewish. Germans, he wrote, have taste in music that "is deeply anchored in the racial, through which it proudly stamps its uniqueness on the powers of feeling.... The Jewish musician, on the other hand, is already used to being so far removed from the background of his race by virtue of thousands of years of wandering that he is able to produce even Jewish music rather as a clever imitator."[17] From Wolzogen's perspective, such imitation was ideally suited to the mission of the Überbrettl at the time. Satiric operetta was often assigned a kind of outsider status that was associated with Jewish artists. As operetta moved into more romantic realms, condemnations also focused on Judaism, but replaced the outsider artist's detachment with the degeneracy of anti-Semitic eugenics. Scholarship has tended to cast such marginalization and forced outsider status in a more positive light, such as Jefferson Chase's study of "*Judenwitz*" (Jewish humor): Jewish artists possess the potential to "develop authorial voices reflecting both their outsider background and sense of mainstream community membership...a source of resistance against discrimination."[18]

Straus's satire was an outlier, but Silver Age operetta was frequently identified as a Jewish art.[19] Operetta appeared to offer Jewish artists a haven and community that the government-subsidized theater and opera did not. Unlike those in serious music, few converted.[20] In the world of operetta, this relative comfort and acceptance represented a considerable shift from the nineteenth century, when the theater politics of the 1870s and 1880s had defined Jews in opposition to traditional Viennese life (see chapter 1). By the Silver Age, Jews were a larger and more visible element of the city's populace as a whole.[21]

With a few exceptions, Jewishness was present onstage only as subtext, as Marion Linhardt has demonstrated.[22] This was part of the premium placed on assimilation by many Viennese Jews. (For many histories of Jewishness in German-language music and theater, operetta is not considered Jewish enough for inclusion, despite the demographics of its creators.[23]) There are only a few explicitly Jewish characters in operetta, such as in *Der Rastelbinder*, *Frühling am Rhein*, and *Die Herzogin von Chicago*, and their reception was often negative. Most notoriously, the Jewish *Neue Freie Presse* critic Ludwig Hirschfeld criticized the depiction of Jewish peddler Pfefferkorn (played by Louis Treumann in his days as a comic supporting player) in *Der Rastelbinder*, writing that the songs were not only sung but also "*gejödelt*" (yodeled) as would befit a Yiddish theater in the Taborstrasse, to which Lehár should repair should he wish to continue in this vein.[24] (Lehár was, of course, the most visible non-Jewish operetta composer, though Léon and Treumann were Jewish.)

Yet Jewish identity can nonetheless be located in operetta beyond anti-Semitic stereotypes: it can be seen in the very assimilative ideal of Viennese Jewish culture. The relative scarcity of characters specifically identified as Jewish meant that Jewish actors often occupied social roles onstage that were inaccessible to them in real life. But their Jewish identities did not necessarily go unnoticed. Indeed, Felix Salten suggests that Judaism could even be attractive. He wrote of Louis Treumann's Danilo, "Like this operetta he is un-Viennese...delicate and slim and limber and a bit feminine."[25] These terms, as Marion Linhardt points out, are a conglomeration of anti-Semitic descriptions of Jews of the late nineteenth century.[26] The Jewish Salten describes the Jewish Treumann as a racial and gender Other, but triumphantly so, for, as Salten says, "he is so elegant, all the girls will fall in love with him."[27] And, more than in this particular instance, the stories of operetta frequently embraced eventual assimilation under Austro-Hungarian colors, a three-act transformation of (usually tacitly) Jewish subjects into Austro-Hungarian ones (who remain tacitly Jewish).[28] This preference for a message of assimilation may explain why operetta has so infrequently been identified as "Jewish" music, but it certainly did not protect it from anti-Semitic attacks. In 1914 Walter Dahms would sound the alarm in the *Neue Preußische Zeitung*, in the interest of protecting the character of Prussia's youth: "It cannot be repeated often enough: protect the German folk song against the (mostly Jewish) pop song!"[29]

CRITICAL PERSPECTIVES

These issues of satire, entertainment, and cultural value have dominated operetta historiography, but they were also the preoccupation of music journals from the start. The most thorough public airing of these grievances began in November 1910, when *Die Zeit* published a fusillade by "young writer" Erich Eckertz, originally given as a lecture at the Universität Wien. Eckertz launches a scathing yet vague attack against all current operetta.[30] While most pre-*Witwe* polemics looked back to the good old days of (Jewish) Offenbach, Eckertz's ideal models are Lucian, Aretino, Mozart, and Goethian *Singspiele*. Johann Strauss is also a "refined" composer, but Offenbach's efforts are "a miscarriage." It is obvious why operetta and its creators are so abhorrent to Eckertz: the essay is full of terms redolent of fin de siècle racial theory. Operetta, whose artists were at the time almost all Jewish, is condemned because it is associated with disease, bodily impurity, and bastardization: "degeneracy" (*Entartung*, as later adopted by the Nazis), "as ineradicable as the plague," a "cultural malady," a "poisoned embryo," a "filthy monstrosity," and a "garbage pile."

Die Zeit later published a remarkable roundup of responses to Eckertz's condemnation, mostly from the high-art music and theater world, few so obviously anti-Semitic but most sympathetic on some counts. Most of the respondents addressed *Die Zeit*'s general question regarding operetta's worth rather than Eckertz's arguments in particular. Max Reger stated the high-art perspective in the starkest, most direct terms: "The colossal success of this genre can be ascribed to the bad taste of the great masses." Ferruccio Busoni seemed offended by the mere question, writing a single sentence: "For me, from an artistic standpoint, modern operetta is not worthy of discussion." But others attempted to put themselves in the ears of the operetta audience and characterized its relatively simple and predictable music and plots as meeting the needs of that audience. Heinrich Mann's response to Eckertz was that "the people [*das Volk*] also require a theater for the petit bourgeois of the intellect, for whom theater of quality is inaccessible, posing impossible demands."[31]

This is a theme that extended well beyond Eckertz's condemnation: operetta, though not to the writer's taste, served a necessary purpose. A review by the musicologist Hans Joachim Moser, published in 1913 in the magazine *Der Greif,* provides another example. In a passage that recalls Georg Simmel's "The Metropolis and Mental Life," Moser writes that "the economic struggle of the present with its monstrous demands on the power and will of the individual, the feverish growth and striving of the large city and its millions have already made every day a Dionysian work symphony."[32]

Moser argues that at the end of a long day, the worker needs a counterbalance. An operetta performance continues the overwhelming sensory stimulation to which the masses have become accustomed but now exploits the harmony of a tidy *Gesamtkunstwerk* to negate the city's chaos. After a day of work, laborers seek what Moser calls an Apollonian, ordered world. Operetta can "unite all the means on offer—scenic pictures, language, and music—toward this purpose, and can fully and completely thrill the wearied receptivity of the modern listener and viewer." Moser's essay then turns to the material predicted in his title, "The Operetta Epidemic." He condemns the decadence and obscenity of modern operetta and, in language similar to Eckertz, urges a return to "the *Hausmusik* of our German masters."[33]

Unsurprisingly, operetta composers themselves were more forward looking. In *Die Wage* in 1903, as quoted in chapter 1, Franz Lehár wrote that since most contemporary operas tax the understanding of the vast majority of the populace, operetta has a new task. Not all citizens have the privilege and leisure to appreciate complex music, but operetta could provide "recuperation after the day's trouble and toil."[34] Notably Lehár seems to think this recuperation is an essential function of music as a whole, but one that for many people operetta was best equipped. In 1910 Franz Gräflinger took the more conventional approach of defining operetta as easy entertainment for those who simply do not want more serious fare: "Among the great masses there are thousands and thousands who say: I want to go to the theater to be entertained; for me the daily routine is serious enough, at least in the evening I want to laugh away my sorrows and stress."[35] For him, operetta was not an antidote to a social ill but rather a simple diversion.

These writers might be seen in contrast to an important later work on these issues, namely Theodor Adorno and Max Horkheimer's *The Dialectic of Enlightenment.* In the chapter "The Culture Industry," Adorno writes, "Serious art has denied itself to those for whom the hardship and oppression of life make a mockery of seriousness and who must be glad to use the time not spent at the production line in being simply carried along." But, and here is where Adorno diverges from earlier writers, modern entertainment has become not the remedy for too much work but simply the continuation of labor for those unable to do anything else. Adorno identifies both the production of mass entertainment and the resulting product as an "automated sequence of standardized tasks." The culture industry,

Adorno writes, "endlessly cheats its consumers out of what it endlessly promises."[36] In other words, audience members do not get fun but an advertisement for fun, something that only echoes and reinforces the capitalist system in which its viewers are trapped. Silver Age operetta failed to actually provide the irrationality that would allow release.

Applying Adorno's post–World War II writings (which above all concern film) to pre–World War I operetta is rather anachronistic. But in the case of operetta, criticism became historiography: the assumption that operetta existed as a generic body of standardized repertoire existing well beneath the level of high art underlies much of its subsequent musicological dismissal. This is a judgment that can cross ideological and methodological lines. For Carl Dahlhaus, operetta is an interesting manifestation of cultural history, but unimportant for "compositional history."[37] This distinction implies that it is a repertoire that has failed to transcend its social contingencies. In other words, it reflects rather than comments on the conditions of its own production and thus, it is implied, is of a lesser order.

But, like many operettas, *Ein Walzertraum* suggests something more self-aware than an assembly line. By the twentieth century, operetta had developed an elaborate system of signifying conventions that were often deployed meta-theatrically.[38] Indeed, the unease that Adorno had with the culture industry is written into the texts of many operettas themselves. Reflexivity is a fundamental feature of Silver Age operetta. (It is also one that Dahlhaus outlined in his sole article on operetta, on Lehár's *Die lustige Witwe*, as discussed in chapter 1, but he explicitly declined to suggest this as a general trait of the genre, rather considering it as an aspect of what he saw as *Witwe*'s special status.) Two examples support this argument: first, Oscar Straus's operetta *Ein Walzertraum*, which is aware of the ephemerality of its own escapism and presents that escape in a way that encapsulates the specific leisure experience of Vienna, and second, Franz Lehár's *Eva*, which attempts to depict life under industrialization itself.

LADIES' ORCHESTRAS

Ein Walzertraum seems to locate itself deliberately far from these conversations, preferring instead a fairy-tale castle and the sensual refuge of the Damenkapelle, as discussed in the opening to this chapter. The operetta takes place in the imaginary principality of Flausenthurm, and the setting is, crucially, the present.[39] The state's aging princess must marry and have children to maintain the royal line, and Viennese officer Lieutenant Niki is recruited for the job. As the operetta begins, the couple has just returned from their wedding. Niki happens to hear a Viennese Damenkapelle playing in the castle park and falls in love with Franzi, the Viennese woman who conducts the visiting Damenkapelle. Complications ensue. The ending of *Walzertraum* is bittersweet: Prince Niki ultimately leaves his true love to do his duty for Flausenthurm. But Niki is still afforded some comfort: Franzi, the Viennese conductor, has secretly taught Princess Helene how to play Viennese music on her piano.

Damenkapellen (usually translated as "ladies' orchestras") were all-woman salon and concert orchestras that began to appear throughout Europe around 1850 and reached the height of their popularity around 1900. At turn of the century, approximately two hundred Damenkapellen were playing across Europe, in theaters and most commonly in cafés and restaurants.[40] Many toured for engagements of at least a month (such as the orchestra in *Ein Walzertraum*), but some stayed put. Their repertory consisted of dance music, arrangements of larger works, and other light classics, the same repertory a male orchestra would have played in these contexts. (They were eventually followed by all-girl dance bands such as the one depicted in *Some Like It Hot*.[41]) Many of the surviving accounts of Damenkapellen concern Viennese groups, which seemed to have enjoyed the widest renown.[42]

The women of Damenkapellen proclaimed themselves "Künstler," artists performing real music; the skill level of their musicians seems to have varied. The musical material, however, was only a small part of the Damenkapelle experience. Male observer's descriptions of their performances inevitably comment on how the performance's visual pleasure matched the auditory one. Spectators urge the reader or listener to imagine how the women looked, placing the reader directly in the place of a male gaze watching the orchestra play. Observing Damenkapellen seems to be an inherently subjective event, and many portray the event as a liminal experience. George Bernard Shaw saw an unusually large Damenkapelle on tour in England:

> Fancy...the apparition in full sunlight of a charming person of the other sex in a crimson silk military tunic and white skirt. Fancy at her heels a string of nearly sixty instrumentalists, all more or less charming, and all in crimson tunics and white skirts. Fancy a conductor distinguished by a black silk shirt, and sleeves made somewhat shorter and wider than the others, so as to give free play to a plump wrist and arm.... This is no vision of an autumnal journalist at a loss for copy; it is to be seen daily at the Albert Palace.... [The women] spread themselves like a vast bouquet over the orchestra.... The effect of the "lady orchestra" as a whole is novel and very pleasant.[43]

For Shaw, the orchestra's femininity, as well as serving a decorative purpose, serves to enhance the actual playing, as their feminine qualities lend grace and moderation to their musical expression.

Perhaps the most vivid description of a Damenkapelle was written by Joseph Roth in 1931—by which time they were very much a nostalgia trip. Roth identifies their vogue as being a few years before World War I—that is, the age of *Ein Walzertraum*. Their vision, he writes, provoked something like a paroxysm of ecstasy in the viewer as the women "pour all the vitality of their radiant bodies into the violin and cello." What's more, in his view they were representations of the emancipation of women. Unlike their "charmless sisters" in London who "cover mailboxes with

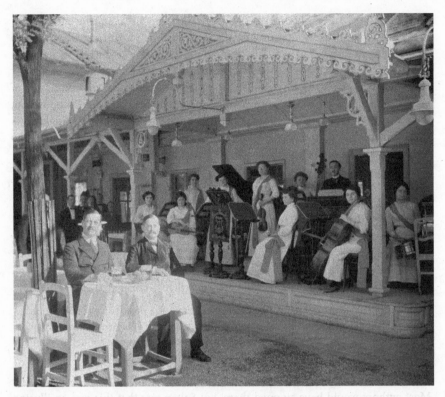

FIGURE 2.1. Damenkapelle E. Hornischer at Zum Eisvogel, 1912. Albertina.

gasoline and burn them...the good maidens of whom we sing here reigned over the estrade, podium, and garden pavilion, and their shawms stirred our hearts in more than one way. They were a superb combination of nymphs and Amazons." Their virtues are projected through their white dresses as well as their service to the muses, and Roth specifies that the men were not allowed to proposition them. Yet for Roth they are still "always naked."[44]

Ein Walzertraum links its Damenkapelle to the same location where the operetta itself supposedly originated: the Prater, a large public park in the second district and the site of the Wurstelprater amusement park memorialized by Felix Salten. Its green space, cafés, summer theaters, and other pastimes catered to all classes of Viennese citizens. A photograph taken at Zum Eisvogel, the Prater café that features in *Ein Walzertraum*'s founding myth, shows a Damenkapelle that meets all of Roth and Shaw's specifications. (fig. 2.1) The photograph is, highly unusually, in color (a technology in which photographer Arthur von Hübl was an early pioneer). The orchestra members sit on a stage framed by a gingerbread proscenium; the ensemble consists of nine women and one man (the latter standing behind what is likely a harmonium), and the women wear long white dresses with bright red sashes. But even this photograph that purportedly—as its title proclaims—is a representation of a Damenkapelle, the foreground is occupied not by the women but by a café table where two mustached men sit with glasses of beer. Even for von Hübl, the male photographer who arranged the composition, the presence of men at leisure mediates the Damenkapelle experience, making its social function clear and provide a visual analogue to the written accounts. The ostensible subject of the photograph is in its background.[45]

As transporting as it could be for the viewer, there existed in the Damenkappelle a tension between the women on display and the women who aspired to be valued and paid for their skill in a traditionally male art. The Damenkapelle was in some respects not dissimilar to operetta itself, offering the modern pleasures and titillation of the Parisian cabaret but—with few exceptions—never threatening traditional morality or bourgeois family values. Felix Salten noted contradictions when describing the Damenkapelle in his tour of the Viennese Prater in *Wurstelprater*. He begins with the same vision of beauty that so enchanted Shaw and Roth:

> The maidens' white dresses spread such an illusion, the purity of a confirmation, poetic happiness. Ladies' orchestra. When a ladies' orchestra plays in an inn's garden, there's a special atmosphere. It's something of a joke, when young women in white dresses sit on the stage and play music as one "desserts," [sic] somehow at the same time it's touching.[46]

Most authors would have stopped there, but Salten saw that this was an illusion and a slightly incomplete and precarious one:

> The struggle for life in white confirmation dresses. Many of these maidens are long withered, many look dissatisfied and sorrowful, many tired and bored. Earnestness and sobriety show in their faces. They work. But their work is the Tralalala! And when their little band makes its jubilant music, then we ask less, whether the maidens have this jubilation in their hearts or only on their sheet music.[47]

For most, though, the Damenkapellen bestowed an over-the-top beautiful visual onto music that already was entrusted with the power to conjure otherworldly beauty. The Damenkapelle, even more intensely than light music alone, represented for male writers escape, fantasy, and the comforting embrace of sentiment without specificity.[48]

WALTZ DREAMS

Ein Walzertraum's Flausenthurm is, like all operetta principalities (*Der Rebell*'s Balkanien, *Die lustige Witwe*'s Pontevedro), tiny and endearingly inept. But if Pontevedro represents a shambolic exoticism, Flausenthurm takes on the tidier boredom of a small Germanic state akin to *Wiener Blut*'s Reuss-Schleiz-Greiz (1898). (Politically, Flausenthurn is a post-unification anachronism; *Wiener Blut* is at least set during the Congress of Vienna.) But while *Wiener Blut* is the story of the Germanic Count Zedlau's happy assimilation into the carefree dissipation of Viennese life, *Ein Walzertraum* is its inversion: Viennese Niki must reconcile with the bourgeois boredom of Flausenthurn, a transformation that is never portrayed as anything other than a compromise.

In Act 1 the homesick Niki hears the unmistakable sound of a Viennese waltz wafting through the air; his comrade, Lieutenant Montschi, says it must be the Damenkapelle. Niki describes the feelings elicited by this music by singing a waltz whose refrain would become the operetta's greatest hit tune, "Leise, ganz leise." This is the waltz Straus supposedly formulated for the ladies at Zum Eisvogel (ex. 2.2). The audience does not witness Niki hearing the waltz for the first time; they have only his own account of hearing it. Yet the music he sings presumably replicates the tune of the music he heard in the distance, an impression reinforced by its reflexive status as a waltz and by the solo violin that joins his vocal line, suggesting that Franzi herself is playing. The experience of hearing the music is rendered in the terms of that music itself. Like the literary accounts of men hearing these orchestras, Niki's own voice and subjectivity take the central role. As Montschi listens, he is able to imagine the experience and sing the waltz himself, joining Niki in simple harmony.

The harmony makes a smoothly prolonged journey to the tonic to the refrain to introduce the song Niki heard in the distance. But once the refrain begins, Straus declines to make a particularly strong cadential statement. The men sing high in their ranges, first just Niki and then both in thirds, producing a sound that is disembodied and lacks the rhythmic drive and corresponding physical propulsion of a faster waltz. Such elegant understatement is typical of twentieth-century Viennese operetta—it recalls *Die lustige Witwe*'s "Lippen schweigen"—but here emphasizes the orchestra's ephemerality. In this context, it suggests that the love that Niki seeks will remain out of reach. Where the first strong cadence was found in the first phrase, here any cadence is avoided (appropriately on the words "Hoffen und Bangen, Liebe, bist du!" [Love, you are hope and yearning!]).

The Damenkapelle is finally revealed in the opening of Act 2. No photographs of this sight survive. A photograph of Mizzi Zwerenz as Franzi (fig. 2.2), however, shows her wearing a long white dress with a sash, of the sort described by Salten and Shaw and as seen in the image of the real Damenkapelle. The clearest description of the staging is found in the manuscript full score, which indicates that the premiere production included an actual Damenkapelle onstage in addition to the pit orchestra. It is unclear whether this group played themselves or mimed to a group of backstage musicians (perhaps the male ensemble that was seen onstage in Act 1, which may have been drawn from the usual pit orchestra), and none of

EXAMPLE 2.2. Straus, *Ein Walzertraum*, No. 7, Walzerduett, end of verse and refrain

EXAMPLE 2.2. (continued)

the reviews offer definitive clarification. But the score is clearly written for two separate ensembles, one onstage and one in the pit.[49]

The onstage orchestra is first introduced much in the same way as it had been in "Leise, ganz leise": as a tantalizingly invisible sound. While the curtain is still closed, the opening of the second act, a march, is played by the pit orchestra. Then the same music is uncannily transferred to the stage, continued by the concealed stage orchestra. The curtain finally rises to reveal the sight of the Damenkapelle, which proceeds to accompany the chorus in the successive number. At the very end they are joined by the pit orchestra, and the two ensembles play together.

FIGURE 2.2. Souvenir Postcard, *Ein Walzertraum*. Bildarchiv Austria, Österreichische Nationalbibliothek.

While the Damenkapelle appears as a diegetic ensemble, this number is not clearly marked as diegetic. But in keeping with the instrumental format of a traditional Damenkapelle, Franzi does not sing, and indeed conducts and plays the violin onstage. (This was presumably mimed; in the manuscript score the violin solos are assigned to the concertmaster of the pit orchestra.) Franzi had, of course, already been introduced to us in the violin solo of "Leise, ganz leise." When the Damenkapelle reappears at the end of the act, the effects are similar.

The stylistic dualism between lyricism and Offenbachian comedy closely recalls *Die lustige Witwe* and is characteristic of Silver Age operetta as a whole, but its application by Straus is not as consistent or clearly thematic as that of Lehár. Volker Klotz claims that a "stylistic rupture" goes through the center of *Ein Walzertraum* between a "wild Offenbachiade" and the sincere numbers such as "Leise, ganz leise." For Klotz, this leads inevitably to a negative value judgment. The Offenbachian elements are valued for their "rash impetuosity" and satirical zest while the waltzes are downright "vulgar" in their sentiment.[50] But while the two categories diverge in musical style, Klotz never clarifies what about the cabaret-style music is satirical, anarchic, or otherwise subversive. Straus's cabaret numbers seem less akin to Offenbachian sophistication or anarchy than Oskar Panizza's founding call for the art of cabaret as "something wholly naive, set forth in full poetic freshness...folk poetry."[51]

What Klotz identifies as the "wild Offenbachiade" should also give pause: the duet "Piccolo, piccolo," a close descendent of "Der lustige Ehemann." It is an interesting counterpart to "Leise, ganz leise": the texts of both songs are explicitly odes to music, but if the waltz evokes something unreachable, the buffo number is comically direct. Lothar, an old man trying to seduce the uninterested and age-inappropriate Franzi, plays a duet with her violin on a piccolo; the disparity between them as partners is echoed in the disparity of their instruments (ex. 2.3). The violin is praised for its ability to sigh, and "the piccolo does exactly the same." The refrain proclaims that the piccolo's piping is the sound of wisdom. (Klotz points out that the number poses a failure—the inability of the violin and piccolo to play together and produce the described effects—but one which is transformed, in performance, into success.[52]) While "Leise, ganz leise" practices harmonic evasion and chromaticism, the duet features compact and repetitive melodic cells, almost exactly the style of "Der lustige Ehemann" and not something meant to evoke mystery or romance, despite the obvious sexual subtext. Like most old man characters, Lothar is a comic rather than a threatening figure; again operetta is disinclined to give its characters nefarious intentions.

While Viennese operetta frequently traded on dramatic juxtaposition, Klotz's binary of good satire and bad sentimentality offers limited insight into the world of *Ein Walzertraum*. The cabaret and the Damenkapelle were differentiated in their aesthetic stance, musical character, and critical prestige. But for their audiences, they had many similarities: to start, both incorporated a mixture of the naive and sentimental. This innocence is in fact the key to the work's effect. The operetta provides for its audience the escapism that it thematizes for its leading character. Despite its indulgences, bourgeois morality wins in the end. Niki stays with Helene, who does her best to transform their marriage into a love match. The Viennese waltzes she plays on the piano are an echo of the idyllic vision of the Damenkapelle at one more degree of remove from Vienna; but like the operetta as

EXAMPLE 2.3. traus, *Ein Walzertraum*, No. 14, Buffo-Duett, refrain

a whole they promise consolation, not escape. For Niki, just as for the audience, the pleasure with Franzi and her music is only fleeting—and this pleasure was inevitably told from a male perspective. For Franzi and Helene, the very concept of an escape from duty is never an option.

Other more recent writers have cast *Ein Walzertraum* as preemptively nostalgic for a bygone imperial era. Richard Traubner writes that "the charm of the piece lies in its romantic yearning for Old Vienna, a Vienna that was already fading into the romantic mists at the twilight of the Austro-Hungarian empire."[53] There is evidence that this view became common soon after 1918: Siegfried Kracauer memorably dubbed Ludwig Berger's 1925 film *Ein Walzertraum* a "retrospective utopia," describing it as the origin of an "enchanted Vienna which was to haunt the screen from then on...the persistent image of this retrospective utopia overshadowed the misery of twentieth century Vienna."[54] However, the operetta was written in 1907, when the operetta genre was newly reborn and the empire lived on. Critics described the operetta sentimental and emotional, but none found that it alluded to a bygone or soon-to-vanish world.

Ein Walzertraum's melancholy indeed suggests that its audiences were in search of catharsis or release from sorrow. But the vagueness of this ennui is its defining feature. Like the ambiguous and invisible waltz, the pathos of its yearning was contingent on the viewpoint of the audience member watching it. In this, its formulation as a "dream" is entirely apt, and its fairy-tale quality adapted itself to the dreams that were present, allowing audiences to project their own personal problems onto Niki's homesickness and submission to duty. The ending is not entirely sad: Franzi teaches Helene to play Viennese music and Niki contents himself with ersatz waltzes in his provincial realm. Full escape is impossible, but he learns to make peace with his situation. For something that proclaims itself a fantasy, the ending is surprisingly realistic. You cannot live in a dream, even if you're a character in *Ein Walzertraum*.

Ein Walzertraum's bittersweet ending was unusual for its time; several critics, seeking a reference point, compared it not to another operetta but to the somewhat similar ending of Wilhelm Meyer-Förster's popular 1901 play *Alt-Heidelberg* (Old Heidelberg), in which a prince must leave his barmaid girlfriend in order to take the throne.[55] (The play was later adapted by Sigmund Romberg and Dorothy Donnelly as the operetta *The Student Prince*.) Thanks in part to its success, sad finales became more common in the 1910s and later—most prominently in the later works of Franz Lehár, particularly his collaborations with Richard Tauber. Like *Ein Walzertraum*, Lehár's "tragic" operettas had a vague escapism at their heart, an escapism that could take the shape of the viewer's own longing. The signature of these works was the "Tauber-Lied," an effusive love song delivered by Tauber, nominally to the operetta's soprano but in practice directly to the audience (discussed in more detail in chapter 5). While the Tauber-Lied ostensibly dramatizes a specific situation in the operetta, it is sung to a text so general that it could address any love story at all. Likewise, Franzi's position as a symbol of Vienna, music, and all that cannot be reached invites a broad range of emotional antecedents, enveloping its whole audience, despite their own diversity of experience.

What Niki is longing for, in addition to a love match, is the pleasure of friends, leisure time, and home denied by his job, problems that have less to do with national politics than the ordinary concerns of the imperial working class. The pleasure and beauty represented by the Damenkapelle summons the geographically specific site of the Prater, where the operetta was conceived and where most of the audience would have spent its spare hours and social lives. Like *Die lustige Witwe*, it speaks to an audience that works too much and perhaps lives far from their home and family. For the Vienna of the relatively newly minted wage laborer, these particular concerns were personal.

Ein Walzertraum was an immediate hit. Writing in the *Neues Wiener Journal*, composer Heinrich Reinhardt praised the libretto for quickly setting the scene and described Straus's score as "exceptionally ingratiating, fine and also often very catchy." Straus was credited as a composer of "well-credentialed Überbrettl songs" and distinguished for his "rhythmic liveliness and melodious piquancy." The choruses were "sonorous" (*klangvoll*), not parodic. Only sometimes, though, did his music find the "specifically Viennese tone" that some scenes demanded. Perhaps Reinhardt, a composer of decidedly provincial Viennese works, was jealous.[56] In contrast, in the *Fremden-Blatt*, Julius Stern began by identifying the operetta specifically as a turn toward a specifically Viennese operetta, "where it lives and smiles and lives a warm life." Straus's Viennese credentials satisfied, the operetta provided waltzes "sung by Viennese men and women."[57]

Not all agreed on the libretto. In the *Arbeiter-Zeitung*, David Josef Bach called it "crass." With typical acerbity, he said the librettist Dörmann, "who with his *Ledigen Leuten* undoubtedly displayed talent, now evinces only the wit and spirit that, every night in the cabaret, makes a bed or sofa collapse under the force of the eroticism present. It doesn't go this far in *Walzertraum* because, because—only because it's just not possible. God, how witty the literate Herr Dörmann is!" In this Bach identifies what will be a key characteristic of Silver Age operetta: the application of proclaimed high literary and artistic ambition with material that is decidedly common. He deems the music masterfully banal and clichéd, not "helpless dilettantism" as much as highly developed calculation.[58]

This calculation was enough to make *Ein Walzertraum* the biggest success since *Die lustige Witwe*. Straus followed it with *Der tapfere Soldat*, whose source material suggests a satiric spirit that would be welcome to many: George Bernard Shaw's *Arms and the Man*. But for the most part the spirit of romantic comedy prevails. Shaw allowed his play to be used on the condition that his name appeared nowhere near it, and he gave up all royalties. This latter decision he surely regretted: *Der tapfere Soldat* did only modest business in Vienna, but in London and New York, given the more appetizing title of *The Chocolate Soldier*, it was an enormous success.

EVA, A SOCIALIST OPERETTA?

As its title proclaimed, *Ein Walzertraum* never claimed to represent social reality. Yet for all the charges of escapism, its ending was faithful to its audience's experiences. This prompts the question: what would happen if operetta did attempt to depict something more closely resembling its audience's lives throughout? Such a subject risked dullness. Since operetta cannily positioned itself as the very op-posite of the toil of daily wage labor (as discussed in Danilo's entrance song, ex-amined in chapter 1), why would audiences want to see onstage that which they were trying to escape? Nevertheless, there was an attempt to give a more accurate portrayal of social reality in operetta: *Eva*, composed by Franz Lehár and first per-formed in 1911. Since *Die lustige Witwe*, Lehár had been the foremost composer of Viennese operetta. But while many other composers sought to duplicate *Witwe*, the experimentalist Lehár took it as a point of pride that each successive operetta would offer something immediately recognizable as new for him.

This experimentalism quickly took him further along the path of the senti-mental and grand. While he often exploited the *Heiterkeit* (merriment) of Offen-bachian musical style, Lehár had made only a few early attempts at satire, none of which approached the success of his major works.[59] In 1910 *Ziegeunerliebe* (Gypsy Love) moved in the direction of national opera, with the *style hongrois* (Hungarian style) permeating the score (much in the manner of Johann Strauss II's *Zigeuner-baron*), a sad ending, and an opening storm scene that is positively Wagnerian in its sonic scope, as discussed in the next chapter.

Eva followed. Other than the ever-present waltzes, it is not marked as Viennese. Freely adapted from Ernst von Wildenbruch's play *Die Haubenlerche* (The Crested Lark), the plot concerns an orphaned girl brought up by factory workers in Bel-gium who catches the eye of new factory owner Octave Flaubert, a *Lebemann* (playboy) from Paris. Flaubert is played, of course, by Louis Treumann, the first Danilo in *Die lustige Witwe*.[60] While they love each other, the usual complications of social rank ensue.[61] When the factory workers learn of the relationship, they re-volt, accusing Octave of having no intention of marrying Eva. He leaves in despair. Eva then moves to Paris and transforms herself into a demimondaine, supported by an ostensibly platonic relationship with an elderly duke. ("Are there really such selfless dukes?" cracked Julius Stern of the *Fremden-Blatt*, who further noted that the platonic nature of their relationship was spelled out in the program.[62]) Shocked at Eva's ability to convincingly move in his own circles, Octave reunites with her and marries her, rescuing her from two different forms of working-class toil.

The first two acts are set in Octave's glass factory, and the final act is in Paris. The combination of factory worker characters and Parisians would presumably allow for the usual stylistic juxtapositions, but this is only partially realized. The virtu-ous factory workers—particularly Eva herself—receive music of cloying sweetness. It is not, however, the simple and sincere tunefulness of the *Volkstück*-influenced Zeller or Millöcker, but rather a rich orchestral carpet that prefigures Erich Wolf-gang Korngold. In Eva's first song, there is, as in *Ein Walzertraum*, the sense that the music can summon a distant paradise—in this case, the figure of Eva's dead mother. Using melodrama, Eva imagines what her mother, whom she never met, might have looked like (ex. 2.4a). Eva's vision is essentially that of an operetta itself, a beautiful mirage.

EXAMPLE 2.4A. Lehár, *Eva*, No. 2, Melodram und Lied. START OF VERSE

EXAMPLE 2.4B. Lehár, *Eva*, No. 2, Melodram und Lied. WALTZ REFRAIN

Valse moderato

EVA

Wär' es auch nichts als ein Au - gen - blick,   wär' es auch nichts als ein Traum vom Glück;

müßt' gleich dem Früh - ling es wie - der ent flieh'n,   wär's nur so lang wie die Ro - sen uns blühn!

Lehár expresses this dream with a sicilienne-like vocal line and undulating, delicate accompaniment. It is lyrical and, while never dissonant, harmonically restless to a degree that is rather unusual in operetta. Eva's music modulates every phrase or two, particularly after a few lines of text. This long, meandering verse is followed by a waltz refrain, making it a simple binary take on a conventional song form (the verse does not return) (ex. 2.4b). The waltz is comparatively diatonic and harmonically stable, but its text, in which Eva wishes she could for just a moment meet her mother, is strikingly similar to that of "Leise, ganz leise." For all of Lehár's aspirations, Eva seems to live in the same world as the characters of *Ein Walzertraum*, where music can offer a utopic and ephemeral vision of a better world. But the romantic lightness of the music again suggests that this dream is to remain forever out of reach.

While the comic numbers do not stray as far harmonically, the number of sections and tempo changes and the rich contrapuntal orchestration defy the formulaic construction of most operetta numbers as well as the traditional signification and dramatic role of music in such a light style. In fact, the use of cabaret style is present primarily in a diegetic context, associated with the Parisian characters. The first number in which the Parisians appear is a musical scene for Octave and the factory man Prunelles. It begins a with a short dialogue section of irregular

EXAMPLE 2.5A. Lehár, *Eva*, No. 3, Szene und Duett. ALLEGRO VIVACE

short phrases sung over a light theme in the flute and oboe, giving the words an inconsequential tone.[63] When Octave begins to think of Paris, the music seems to anticipate his question to Prunelles, "Sie war'n schon in Paris?" (You've been to Paris?) (ex. 2.5a) The tempo quickens and the orchestra's flute figure is transformed into a more aggressive, march-like theme under the vocal line. This theme grows into assertive syncopated figure that evokes the tumult of the city.

When the glass factory reminds Octave of a popular *chanson* he heard in the Parisian cabaret, the orchestra again anticipates him by obligingly striking up the chanson's theme (ex. 2.5b) so Octave can sing it for Prunelles and the audience.

EXAMPLE 2.5B. Lehár, *Eva*, No. 3, Szene und Duett. ALLEGRETTO MODERATO

The chanson is unmistakably of the cabaret style, with simple, repetitive rhythm and melody and the onomatopoetic "klinge linge linge ling" of tinkling glass (accompanied by a glockenspiel). The text proclaims that happiness and love are, like glass, easily broken. Elsewhere, Lehár would have set such a sentiment to appropriately gloomy music, but the disjuncture between text and words sets this number apart as a cabaret product, one that is cynical and detached compared with Eva's earnestness.

The external world of Paris and cabaret exist here only as quasi-diegetic material. The rest of the number is much more character-specific and dramatic, with the music serving a narrative function rather than a presentational one. This is true of most of the score: it advances the plot, and the music serves to deepen and expand upon the expressive meaning of the words. It elaborates upon that which cannot be seen, such as Paris, Eva's mother, and Eva's desires. In its tendency to anticipate the character's words, it suggests that it is revealing their thoughts and feelings, possibly before they themselves are aware of them. Such a relationship, while typical of post-Wagnerian opera, is antithetical to satire and Offenbachian operetta.

The glass chanson reappears as one of the reprised numbers in the Act 2 finale, which in conventional fashion inverts the signification of music that has already been heard. Here, Lehár exploits the juxtaposition of the words and music to great effect. While originally meant lightheartedly, now the moral that happiness and love are easily broken carries catastrophic consequences for Eva, and the gaiety of the march turns sinister. It is only because of the strength of the original signification that the reversal has such a strong effect: these are the loose morals of the cabaret put into action in Eva's life. Eva then reprises her dream music, referring no longer to her mother but now to her own seemingly impossible aspirations.

Eva's dreams in part put her out of time. Like many Cinderellas of the twentieth century, she is a working girl who longs for domesticity, a model that Maya Cantu found slightly later on Broadway and identifies with "the decades of American history in which women first started to enter the white-collar labor force in significant numbers."[64] Eva, however, is not a secretary but a factory girl (as the work's subtitle, *Das Fabrikmädel*, recalls), and for her the most accessible alternative to factory labor is not only life as a housewife but a thinly veiled representation of sex work. Her improbable transformation in the operetta's third act, a rapid and unlikely journey from laborer to semi-prostitute to future respectable wife, is the operetta's most unusual feature.

The plot seems to present a morally conventional setup: Eva is a virtuous poor girl destined to reform the dissolute, wealthy Parisians. The classic Silver Age plot model is ready to deploy Eva to tame Treumann into a married, bourgeois gentleman. (Octave is conscious of his advantages from the start, remarking, "Well then, look at me, I've never done anything.") And indeed, this is the ultimate happy ending of *Eva*, but it takes a strange path to get there. Albert Gier posits that this difficulty is due to the libretto's joining of Wildenbruch's cautionary tale—the story of the seduction of a proletarian girl by an aristocratic man—with the fairy tale of Cinderella, in which the protagonist's enduring innocence is paramount.[65] At the start of the operetta, only Eva is dissatisfied with her life in the factory; the other factory workers are hard working, upstanding, and peaceful. The Parisian world is portrayed as titillating but lazy and morally depraved, with little true love or faithfulness. Yet it is this world Eva longs to join, as represented in her song to her mother and alluded to by her very name's signification of temptation and lost virtue. And join it she does, in a *lieto fine* that is portrayed as thoroughly positive. She has, it seems, pinned Octave down into marriage, but only through becoming a Parisian society lady, a world in which she will remain. Women previously shown through the supporting character Pepi to possess limited virtue now somehow become acceptable when Eva joins their numbers. The third act, brief as it is, offers no resolution to these tensions.

Eva's good-hearted factory workers and superficial demimonde also invite an allegorical reading. The character Eva's sympathetic depth of feeling and sincerity embody Lehár's attempt to "elevate" operetta to serious art. But when the libretto makes her into something like the figure she is imagining in her effusive, sincere opening song, it essentially transplants her into the world of Offenbach operetta, the cabaret realm of Octave's glass song. This is the very world it had explicitly distanced itself from in the previous two acts. It is tempting to read *Eva* as an attempt at rapprochement between Lehár's image of operetta and its heritage, but the perfunctory nature of operetta third acts does not afford the time or space to enact such a reconciliation. Eva's dreams get far more music and stage time than the dramatization of their improbable fulfillment. The result is, in fact, the inverse of *Ein Walzertraum*: in *Ein Walzertraum*, a fantasy-like story comes to a surprisingly pessimistic, realistic conclusion. In *Eva*, what begins as an unusually naturalistic story has a not-at-all-realistic Cinderella-like happily ever after.

Some critics praised Lehár's ambitions. His diligence was lauded by the *Neue Freie Presse*: "It's clear to see that this operetta wasn't written in the haste of a few weeks but rather with great artistic care."[66] The *Neue Wiener Journal,* with some more trepidation noted, "One could just as easily call this a *Volksstück* opera."[67] But ultimately the reception of *Eva* would coalesce around another issue. Though Lehár denied that the operetta contained any social message, critics disagreed. The scene in contention is in Act 2 in which the factory workers, thinking that Octave Flaubert is about to "ruin" Eva by seducing her without marrying her, briefly rebel against him. The operetta's premiere took place only a few months after the *Teuerungsrevolte,* or price hike revolt, a demonstration that began in the outer Viennese district of Ottakring. Organized by the Social Democrats, the workers' protests resulted in a tense confrontation between workers and police and ultimately looting.[68] For bourgeois critics of *Eva*, this unrest was still fresh. The liberal middle-class *Neue Freie Presse* was the most alarmed:

> The thing that disturbs most in this book is the social affectation. Social consciousness is thoroughly superfluous in operetta. Blue shirts [i.e., of factory workers] and silent fists are out of place, and social politics, ethics, and labor issues are intolerable in sung texts. For the purposes of operetta these things are too serious...and when the hordes of workers appear in the dramatic climax of the second finale and begin to grumble, so the practiced operetta audience in the stalls begins to grumble inwardly as well.[69]

Tellingly, the critic does not notice what is going on up in the cheap seats. Later, the director of the Theater an der Wien, Wilhelm Karczag, disingenuously claimed that the scene had nothing to do with politics. With the insouciance of an impresario who was turning a profit, he wrote that *Eva* merely endeavored to portray human characters:

> Again and again I read that in *Eva* Franz Lehár wants to solve social problems. For God's sake, where in this operetta is there a single word about social problems? Because the workers revolt, it's socialism?... The workers want to protect Eva from the young factory boss who wants to seduce her. That's just a simple human matter and has nothing to do with socialism. Only a superficial, thoughtless judge could, when hearing the complaints of the worker, opine that this is a socialist demonstration.[70]

On the other side, David Josef Bach, critic for the *Arbeiter-Zeitung*, the Social Democrats' official newspaper, also had concerns. Surprisingly, Bach liked the score and found it a convincing mix of lyricism and hits. Referring to the popular libretto team of Willner and Bodanzky, however, he notes that "the libretto market's most renowned firm now seems to favor social politics as a commodity."[71] For Lehár, musical complexity was also a commodity, its exchange value to be cashed in for respect and acclaim.

For many critics, operetta's place in the world of commercial theater and mass audiences doomed it aesthetically from the start. Its willingness, even eagerness, to speak of the hopes and fears not of its creators but of its audience was the key both to its success and to the critical controversy it engendered. Operetta promised a brief respite—as Eva sings in Act 1, "even if it's no more than a moment, even if it's no more than a dream of happiness, just as spring must pass." The same awareness of ephemerality, of a special but limited place in its audience members' lives, haunts *Ein Walzertraum*. More recently, operetta has often been described as a glimpse into the glory of the past. But for those past audiences, it offered not a mirror of reality but only a fleeting vision.

Hungary, Vienna, and the "Gypsy Operetta"

According to the 1903 guidebook *Budapest: The City of the Magyars,* any visitor to the city must seek out a "Gypsy" violinist. The visitor should bypass the common tourist stops and find "one of the smallest and most unpretentious coffee-houses," for "it was in one of these that I heard Rácz Laczi play."

> There is savagery in his music, in his devilish snap virility and fire. There is the forest wind hidden within his black violin, the cry of pain, the crash of thunder; again he will draw from his magic sobbing strings notes that bring tears and a lump in the throat....Sometimes the day has gone wrong and he comes to the café in a bad humor; then his fiddle growls, venting his feelings. Again his mood changes and he suddenly stops short, crouches low and with a shout like a lion-tamer training a refractory beast to leap he swings his band with him again into a wild czardas.[1]

The Roma musician is an authentic, unmediated vessel for volatile, extreme emotions. When imported into Germanic art music, his music would be called the *style hongrois,* associated not only with the Roma but with Hungary as a whole.

The Viennese image of Hungary, connoting romantic individualism, interiority, chivalry, and passion, was ideally suited to twentieth-century operetta. In operetta, Hungarian music—particularly in the figure of a "Gypsy violinist" or music alluding to one—was a Dionysian counterpart for the more refined, Apollonian Austrian waltz. The twentieth-century revival and deconstruction of the Hungarian "Gypsy" figure (a literary device far removed from the realities of Roma people) was the first defining achievement of Hungarian Emmerich Kálmán (1882–1953), who would become one of the most important operetta composers of twentieth-century Vienna. In his 1912 operetta *Der Zigeunerprimas* (The Gypsy Bandleader[2]), Kálmán reinvented operetta dualism for the Dual Empire, juxtaposing Viennese style and style hongrois, setting both sides of the empire to music.

Der Zigeunerprimas follows in the footsteps of Johann Strauss II's 1885 "Gypsy operetta" *Der Zigeunerbaron* (The Gypsy Baron). But unlike Strauss, Kálmán could claim to portray Hungary to the Viennese from a Hungarian point of view, a persona cultivated by the composer himself. The intense interiority of his stage Hungarians was linked to his own construction of a national authenticity, one that has persisted to this day in the frequent characterization of Kálmán as "the melancholic of operetta."[3] In a radio broadcast of *Der Zigeunerprimas* made around 1950, shortly before his death, the composer explained:

> Hungarian music lies very near to my heart. As a young apprentice in Budapest, I was in regular contact with the best Gypsy orchestras. I had also a short period before received from the Hungarian Gypsy orchestra leader Pali Rácz a photo with a dedication. I made a small tribute to the family Rácz in the character of Pali Rácz, title role of my operetta *Der Zigeunerprimas*.[4]

Such claims must be taken with skepticism: Pali Rácz died in 1885, when Kálmán was three years old (he perhaps saw the great Rácz's eldest son of the same name). That the recording is in German, not Hungarian, is significant: Kálmán's myth was calibrated for a Viennese audience. While his career began in Budapest, as an operetta composer he came of age in Vienna, and *Der Zigeunerprimas* was calibrated to please not Hungarian but Viennese tastes. Kálmán gave the Viennese the "Gypsy fire" they expected of him, something that had been largely absent from the operettas he had written in Budapest.

The operetta Gypsy had little relationship with actual Roma people. Following in the footsteps of many other scholars, throughout this chapter I use the term "Gypsy" to refer solely to this fiction (corresponding to the German *Zigeuner*), in acknowledgment of the term's historical usage, its distance from real experience, and the lack of other options.[5] For the Viennese, the style hongrois offered a space for the romantic, raw subjectivity that was increasingly central to operetta in the twentieth century. It occupied an expressive space that contrasted with the more extroverted waltz and, perhaps more important, with the parodic, alienated, sometimes mechanical world of Offenbach-derived operetta. Gypsy music was thus not only exotic but also—sometimes even primarily—music of interiority and sincerity. It was thus ideally suited for twentieth-century operetta. As the *Neue Freie Presse* eventually wrote of Kálmán's *Zigeunerprimas*, "The real world of Gypsies is almost like it was composed of elements from an operetta: a little bit of sentimental romanticism, a little bit of frivolity and pride, and a great deal of love—seemingly everything that belongs to an operetta."[6]

Yet Kálmán often put his own claims to authenticity into self-conscious quotation marks. The music can be simultaneously expressively sincere and presented as only an imitation of Gypsy music. It might be performed by a despairing non-Gypsy character, found in a dream sequence, or even shown as a conscious career choice for a musically inclined family. Kálmán thus presented a style hongrois that was passionate and dark without being heavy or threatening, and occasionally even took on utopian tones. His Gypsy figures are domesticated and aware of their own artificiality. Thus Kálmán traded on his supposed access to an authentic voice while wearing it lightly, delivering it with a wink. (Critics did not point out that Kálmán had access to a theatrical world and an authorial platform that actual Roma did not.) Later, the implications of Kálmán's work would take on a more pointedly political tone: Kálmán had created an emotional and musical logic for the Dual Empire just before it disappeared.

This chapter traces the place of Hungary in Viennese operetta from several perspectives. Kálmán's early career provides an example of the exchange between the Budapest and Vienna operetta industries and shows his evolving persona as a Hungarian composer. His early operetta *Ein Herbstmanöver* also illustrates the role of the Austro-Hungarian military in operetta culture. Ultimately though, Hungary, style hongrois, and "Gypsy music" would come to have a specific symbolism in Viennese operetta, seen in works from *Die Fledermaus* to *Der Zigeunerbaron* to Franz Lehár's *Zigeunerliebe*. This style proved to be the key to Kálmán's career in Vienna, as his breakthrough *Der Zigeunerprimas* demonstrates. Kálmán created a unique mixture of operetta elements, incorporating both the genre's most forward-looking, international ingredients and the romantic Hungarian voice that he would claim as his own. He would explore it further in some of the most popular operettas of the 1910s and 1920s including *Die Csárdásfürstin* (1915; see chapter 4), *Die Bajadere* (1922, see chapter 5), *Gräfin Mariza* (1925), and *Die Herzogin von Chicago* (1928; see chapter 6). Operetta's imperial image was not complete without what Viennese critics often referred to as "dash of paprika."

VIENNA'S BUDAPEST, KÁLMÁN'S BUDAPEST

Austrian culture's portrayal of Hungary and Hungarians was based on national stereotypes, many of which overlapped with those ascribed to Gypsies. A description by Maurus Jókai in the Austro-Hungarian monarchy's official ethnography, *Die österreichische-ungarische Monarchie in Wort und Bild* (its editorship credited to Crown Prince Rudolf himself and issued in a series of volumes beginning in 1886), is a case in point:

> The Magyar's temperament is an idiosyncratic mix of sanguine, phlegmatic, and melancholic. . . . In the past (and also recently), the Magyar nobleman was the proudest man in the world; only in Hungary does the farmer consider himself an aristocrat, and he still is today, not only among other races but also in Hungary itself, and it is hard to believe that there exist anywhere else as many levels of rank in forms of address as there are among the Magyars.[7]

Like its language, seen as impenetrable by German speakers, Hungarian culture is portrayed as old-fashioned, proud, and mysterious. Austrians also frequently saw Hungary as culturally and technologically backward.

At times, Austrians seemed jealous of what they perceived as Hungarians' comparative unity and homogeneity. Both Austrians and Hungarians were expected to be Austrians or Hungarians while simultaneously also being Austro-Hungarians. Robert Musil described Austria-Hungary's predicament ("Kakania" is derived from k.u.k. or *kaiserlich und königlich*, "imperial and royal," used to describe the Austro-Hungarian government; "imperial" refers to the Empire of Austria, "royal" to the Kingdom of Hungary).

> Their [the state's] understandable motto in the face of such times was "united we stand" (from *viribus unitis*, "with forces joined"). But the Austrians needed to take a far stronger stand than the Hungarians, because the Hungarians were, first and last, simply Hungarians and were regarded only incidentally, by foreigners who did not know their language, as Austro-Hungarians too; the Austrians, however, were, to begin with and primarily, nothing at all, and yet they were supposed by their leaders to feel Austro-Hungarian and be Austro-Hungarians—they didn't even have a proper word for it.... So this was the way Kakanians related to each other, with the panic of limbs so united as they stood that they hindered each other from being anything at all.[8]

From an Austrian perspective, then, the identity of the Hungarian people was comparatively straightforward. Operetta, at least before World War I, similarly represented Hungarians as homogenously nationalistic and rarely represented "Austrians" as such at all, preferring the metropolitan identity of the Viennese or the specific regional accents and quirks of nearby provinces. Other imperial cities such as Prague rarely figure in Viennese works.

Budapest was not a frequent setting for Viennese works either, though the actual city's rapid development and the popularity of the genre in its theaters meant that the city nonetheless became a relevant concern in Vienna's operetta business.[9] Many of the operettas performed in Budapest originated in Vienna, while Hungarian operettas—shaped by the *népszínmü*, a form of folk theater similar to the *Volksstück*—were only rarely performed in Vienna.[10] (Before Kálmán, Theater an der Wien impresario Wilhelm Karczag was probably the city's most important operetta export to Vienna.) In Vienna, Hungarian operettas were most often performed by touring companies; until Kálmán they rarely had widespread influence on Viennese composers or were particularly fashionable.

To the Viennese, Hungarian operetta was old-fashioned and rustic, far from the urbane Offenbachian operetta. The Viennese also found that genuine Hungarian operetta lacked the stereotypical Gypsy music that the Viennese considered the Hungarian stock in trade. Describing two operettas by Jenő Huszka (1875–1960), latter-day historian Richard Traubner shows some of the Viennese bias: "*Bob* [*Bob herceg*, 1902] and *Lili* [*Lili bárónő*, 1919] have a certain grace about them...but they lack the fiery Hungarian csárdás strains which foreigners, if not the Budapesters themselves, admire in Hungarian operetta." Traubner identifies Viktor Jacobi (1883–1921), composer of *Leányvásár* and *Szibill*, as a more exportable talent, but his extra-Hungarian success came primarily in London and New York, not Vienna.[11]

It was Kálmán who, by beginning his career in Budapest but moving to Vienna and assimilating Viennese tastes, synthesized the Hungarian spirit that the Viennese wanted. He followed a path to operetta composition that, while beginning in Budapest, was otherwise similar to those of Lehár, Fall, and Straus. Born Imre Koppstein in 1882 in the small town of Siófok on the edge of Lake Balaton, he came from a comfortably middle-class Jewish family of merchants and showed early musical talent as well as an interest in his town's small theater. He began his education at a Jewish school in Siófok, but when he left for a Christian *Gymnasium* in Budapest at the age of ten, he changed his name to the non-Jewish and explicitly Hungarian Kálmán Imre (such changes were common among Hungarian Jews as a sign of "magyarization"). He subsequently studied composition at the Academy of Music in Budapest. Upon his move to Vienna, he changed his first name as well, to the German equivalent, Emmerich (like most operetta artists, he remained a secular Jew).[12]

His primary teacher at conservatory, as for his contemporaries Béla Bartók, Zoltán Kodály, Ernst von Dohnányi, Albert Szirmai, and Viktor Jacobi, was Hans Koessler. Koessler trained his students in the Germanic tradition of Bach, Brahms, and Beethoven and had little interest in Hungarian nationalism.[13] It was in Koessler's vein that Kálmán's first works were written, including an early tone poem, *Saturnalia*, which earned him his first good reviews in 1904. (It was overshadowed by the premiere of his classmate Bartók's *Scherzo*.[14]) But after the success of this single work, he seems to have hit a dead end and could not find a publisher for his subsequent compositions. He spent some time studying law, to no clear end, and from 1904 to 1908 wrote music criticism for *Pesti napló*, a daily newspaper. As with Oscar Straus, it is not entirely clear what made him turn from serious to light music, but he began by writing a few successful cabaret songs and then turned to operetta. The move from prestigious albeit unemployed composer of art music to a composer in the remunerative field of operetta was something he described with some self-deprecation:

> I came to my colleagues with a tragic look on my face. "If things keep going this badly, I'm going to do something terrible," I said to them with a dark look. "Well, what then, what is it?" said my appalled friends. And I answered with a flat voice: "I...WILL...WRITE...AN...OPERETTA!!!" The reaction was deep distress and obvious consternation.[15]

The account is like a melodramatic tableau from one of Kálmán's own operettas. While it captures the disrepute of operetta, the decision was not unexpected considering that it occurred after Kálmán's successful foray into the cabaret world. At a moment when more and more formally trained composers were entering the operetta world (including several of Kálmán's conservatory classmates), his decision was not as shocking as it would have been a generation earlier. It was, however, a fateful one.

MILITARY OPERETTA AND *TATÁRJÁRÁS*

Kálmán's first operetta, *Tatárjárás,* was written to a libretto by Károly (Karl von) Bakonyi and premiered in Budapest on February 22, 1908. By contemporary Viennese standards it was a modestly scaled work, with short finales and only few incongruously grand moments. But it was a hit, and Kálmán had a stroke of luck: in March, Wilhelm Karczag happened to be visiting Budapest, saw the operetta, and decided to immediately bring it to his Theater an der Wien.[16] The plot of an aristocratic lady and a battalion of hussars was appealingly old-fashioned and had some similarities to Oscar Straus's *Der tapfere Soldat,* which had opened at the Theater an der Wien in November 1908 to considerable success. (*Der tapere Soldat*'s attitude toward the military is somewhat more skeptical, thanks to its roots in George Bernard Shaw's *Arms and the Man.*) Karczag had the libretto translated and somewhat rewritten by Viennese regular Robert Bodanzky, the title was changed to *Ein Herbstmanöver* (Autumn Maneuver), and it premiered on January 22, 1909.

The operetta was amenable to translation primarily because of its central plot feature: the Austro-Hungarian army, an institution long credited as a unifying force in the empire. Lawrence Cole has gone so far as to characterize Austria-Hungary as a "military monarchy," meaning that the military had special status and power, the parliament was limited in its control over the military, and the army had social precedence.[17] Military music had a prominence in operetta that rivaled that rivaled the status of the waltz. Many operetta composers, including Lehár, Leo Fall, and earlier Carl Michael Ziehrer, had served as military bandmasters, and compositions written expressly for military bands formed a major part of their early output. Band concerts included military music, dance music, and excerpts or potpourris from operas and operettas.[18]

Marches had featured in Viennese operetta since its early days, some in diegetic context but many with no soldiers in sight. The bright energy, forward momentum, and strong rhythmic emphasis of a march made it perfectly suited for operetta and an ideal replacement for the markedly French galop. Franz von Suppé ended many acts of his operettas with marches, a habit picked up by other composers. In 1885 Karl Millöcker wrote, "Suppé's influence, which composers have devoutly treasured ever since, is still recognizable today in his potent act finales, into which he usually slips in at the end of the piece a melodious march, which remains in the ears of the audience long after the performance."[19] This practice persisted in the twentieth century, when marches frequently appear absent any military context (such as "Wie die Weiber" in *Die lustige Witwe*). In a 1910 condemnation of operetta in the *Neue Musik-Zeitung*, Walter Kellerbauer wrote that operetta dramaturgy consisted of "pointless dances or senseless marching around"; in 1910 Alfred Wolf wrote that operetta scores were based on "one march and two waltzes."[20]

The perceived symbiotic relationship between the military and operetta provided additional ammunition to critics who charged operetta with being overly complacent and beholden to state powers. For critics there existed a clear counterexample in Offenbach, who satirized the army—for example in General Boum's *couplet* in *La Grande-Duchesse de Gérolstein* (as well as Offenbach's followers Gilbert and Sullivan, who satirized the armed forces in works such as *The Pirates of Penzance* and *H.M.S. Pinafore*). The Offenbachian legacy of operettas concerning tiny, inept principalities (such as Pontevedro and Balkonien) did lend an occasional anti-militaristic strain to Viennese operetta. But when an operetta played in Vienna and when the army involved was the k.u.k., strict reverence was the only option (as in *Ein Walzertraum*). This attitude was not only patriotic but required by the censor.

Yet the march nonetheless served a regulatory function. While Gypsy music conventionally illustrated a volatile interior subjectivity—a vital element of twentieth-century operetta—marches remained the music of an exterior, social sphere. Gypsy music and slow waltzes like those of Kálmán, Lehár, and Straus indulged in rubato, romanticism, and drawn-out sentiment while marches retained their rhythmic regularity and, usually, major-key pep. Even Gypsy characters march in some of Kálmán's operettas (notably in the Act 2 quartet of *Der Zigeunerprimas*), and the music's military association seems to have faded.

For Kálmán, military music served to successfully translate *Tatárjáras* into *Ein Herbstmanöver*, from Budapest to Vienna. Both the military-centric plot and the marches of the score seemed to require little translation to play to the Viennese. The trousers role of Marosi made soubrette Louise Kartousch, who sang two different march songs (No. 2 and No. 4), a star in Vienna. But other elements of Kálmán's score registered as out of step with fashion. As the *Neue Freie Presse* critic wrote, "Kálmán's music is nothing but Hungarian, meaning that he treasures every yearning, dragging melody or every agitated rhythm. They would enchant his countrymen for hours on end, but become monotonous to the Viennese ear and boring after five minutes."[21] *Die Zeit* questioned whether Hungarian sounds were appropriate for Vienna: "Whether one can, in Vienna, muster up full enthusiasm for the operetta's essential 'joi' [an enthusiastic exclamation] disposition remains to be seen."[22]

Ein Herbstmanöver is remembered mostly for launching the careers of two important actors: Kartousch and tenor Max Pallenberg. The composer was not, initially, so lucky. Kálmán wrote that, as an unknown, he was paid poorly and treated badly by the theater. Nor was he besieged by librettists offering new works.[23] Unlike Lehár, whose rapid ascendance was abetted by exceptional timing and good relationships with the Viennese operetta community built through his career as a conductor, Kálmán would have a difficult time becoming established. Only a few years after the start of the Silver Age, operetta had a small group of brand-name A-list composers, and the ranks were not as immediately accessible as they had been for Lehár, Fall, and Straus. Kálmán lacked Lehár's network, and his music had not garnered the rave reviews of Lehár's or even Leo Fall's debuts. Kálmán would not return to the Theater an der Wien until 1912 (with the flop *Der kleine König*). Though he remained in Vienna, his next premiere was in Budapest, on March 16, 1910. The subject was again military. *Az Obistos* (The Soldier on Leave) was later adapted by Victor Léon for Vienna into *Der gute Kamerad* (The Good Comrade) and premiered at the Bürgertheater in October 1911. The Bürgertheater (not to be confused with the Burgtheater) was a small theater that was considerably less prestigious than the Theater an der Wien, and the work was not particularly successful. World War I gave it a new lease on life as the propaganda operetta *Gold gab ich für Eisen*, as will be seen in chapter 4.

STYLE HONGROIS AND OPERETTA

While the military subject matter of *Ein Herbstmanöver* appealed to imperial sentiment, Kálmán soon discovered a more potent tool to attract the Viennese. The Viennese demanded a heightened romanticism from Hungarian music, which meant, for operetta, something on a grand scale. This was quite unlike the modest, conservative works of actual Hungarian operetta composers. Viennese exposure to Hungarian music was largely limited to the stereotypes of the style hongrois, as practiced by visiting *Zigeunerkapelle* (Gypsy bands, whose musicians may or may not have been Roma) and the art music based on their style (such as Brahms's *Hungarian Dances* and *Zigeuenerlieder* as well as Liszt's *Hungarian Rhapsodies*). The Viennese operetta industry subscribed to Franz Liszt's equation of "Gypsy music" and Hungarian folk music, though in other quarters debates about the ownership and heritage of "Gypsy music" were contentious and sustained.[24] (The actual hardships of Roma life had no relation to operetta reception.)

Gypsy characters and music in operetta are stereotyped as potently expressive, what Lynn Hooker has termed an "oriental fantasy."[25] Like those found in opera, operetta Gypsies are commonly fortune-telling, colorfully dressed, loose-living women or larcenous, violin-playing men.[26] Most often, they appear only in minor supporting roles (such as Manja in *Gräfin Mariza*), but their musical style is often adopted by non-Gypsy characters such as Sylva Varescu in *Die Csárdásfürstin* (see chapter 4). Musically, the premier operetta style hongrois number is a *csárdás*, a vocal number related to the *verbunkos* tradition, which had long been used to transmit Hungarian color. Both verbunkos and the csárdás are in duple meter and in two parts—first a free, rhapsodic section with melodic ornamentation and dotted rhythms (the *lassu*), followed by a fast section often featuring *moto perpetuo* sixteenth notes in repetitive patterns and syncopated quarter notes (the *friss* or *friska*).[27] (The term "verbunkos" is often used interchangeably with "csárdás," though a few scholars have argued for a geographical distinction.[28] Twentieth-century operetta uses "csárdás" exclusively.) In operetta, this dance music form became a song form, usually a showpiece solo song to express an extreme emotional state, either the deepest abjection or the most frenzied jubilation (as is traditionally associated with style hongrois music). Some of the more elaborate csárdáses include a stage band in the style of a *Zigeunerkapelle*, including a solo violin, usually a clarinet, a cimbalom, and metallic percussion instruments such as cymbals or a tambourine.[29]

Two well-known examples from Johann Strauss illustrate this function. In *Die Fledermaus* (1874), the non-Hungarian Rosalinde disguises herself as a Hungarian countess and sings a virtuosic csárdás number, "Klänge der Heimat" (ex. 3.1). Unlike most subsequent csárdáses, the text does not specifically mention Gypsies. The first few phrases show a veritable encyclopedia of style hongrois markers: the clarinet melisma in the first measure, the oscillating thirds in the second, the vocal line's *alla zoppa* syncopation and leap of a sixth on "Heimat," ornamentation on "weckt mir das Sehnen," the *Kuruc* fourth on "Auge mir," and the rubato on "Wenn ich euch höre." Later, the fast section's scalar passages, sudden leaps, and final wordless cry are also typical of style hongrois operetta music.[30] Yet the number serves little purpose in the plot; the *style hongois* topic is invoked for its virtuosity and novelty.

In contrast, Strauss's later *Der Zigeunerbaron* (1885) includes many Roma characters and uses style hongrois in a more extensive, non-incidental, and even political way. The score contains another prominent csárdás (Sáffi's entrance song, No. 6, "So elend und so true... O habet acht"), but the style hongrois is not limited to this single number; rather, it inflects all the Gypsy characters' music.[31] The idea of a "Gypsy spirit," familiar from Liszt, is also pivotal to the plot, in which the titular non-Gypsy character's joie de vivre leads to his appointment as *Zigeunerbaron*, baron of the Gypsies. The Gypsy identity has already been distilled into character traits—carefree passion and freedom from convention—that can belong to anyone, Roma or not. The equation of Gypsy music with expressivity and a state of mind rather than an ethnic or racial identity persists in twentieth-century Gypsy depictions, which were never creations of Roma people nor particularly interested in authentic reproduction of their musical styles. In most cases, this inauthenticity is signposted in the plot, as it is in *Zigeunerbaron* and *Fledermaus*.

EXAMPLE 3.1. Emmerich Kálmán, *Ein Herbstmanöver*, No. 13, Lied und Tanz, opening

Despite *Der Zigeunerbaron*'s success, Gypsies vanished from the Viennese stage for some time. In 1910 Franz Lehár used a Gypsy-themed subject in his first major attempt to write a score of operatic breadth and complexity. *Zigeunerliebe* (Gypsy Love) features complex orchestration, demanding vocal writing, and elaborate musical "scenes" that are more complex and longer than the usual songs. The style hongrois intensifies the libretto's romantic tone and rural setting and gives Lehár an expanded palette for his musical ambitions, one far from the triviality of Offenbach-inspired scores. The plot, however, couches its own unreality in a bourgeois frame. On the eve of her wedding to a dull man, the non-Gypsy heroine, Zorika, encounters a Gypsy named Józsi, and in an act-long fantasy dreams of living in a caravan telling fortunes and stealing watches. The Gypsies represent less real people than a reverie for Zorika, a dream of freedom before she must confront an inevitably bourgeois marriage. The brief sight of a Gypsy in Act 1 sets off the entire Gypsy dream inside Zorika's head. But when she awakes in Act 3 she realizes that it was all a fantasy.[32]

The plot presents the romance of Gypsy life purely as an impossible hypothetical, the creation of a non-Roma girl's unconscious. To Zorika, Gypsies and their music mean freedom from the narrow confines of her middle-class life. For Lehár, the Gypsy music's unusual color and perceived emotional depth helped him create a score of greater ambition and scale than was conventional for operetta. This has led to a divisive reception: at the time, critics found Lehár's work far too serious and insufficiently comic, while for later scholars it is still too much operetta. Jonathan Bellman writes scornfully of one Act 1 dance in *Zigeunerliebe*:

> Characteristic rhythms...are mixed and matched in a wholly improbable fashion that results, uncharacteristically, in even four-bar phrasing....Similarly, the plot reduces the complexities of the Gypsy stereotype to pap....Allusions that in an earlier time might have been oblique are now baldly stated, and a character that might have inspired both dread and desire is a long way from either.[33]

Such is often the curse of operetta, caught between its ambition and its own conventions. For its Viennese audiences, operetta's version of Gypsies replaced anthropological authenticity with personal authenticity. It did not matter how accurate the representations of Roma or Roma music were, because the music itself carried the promise of representing deep interiority. Bellman mildly qualifies his condemnation with the concession that Lehár's operetta was written for a "commercial market." This is ironic: Lehár saw Gypsy music as a vehicle to carry him further from the lightness and triviality of mainstream commercial operetta. The perceived freedom and virtuosity of Gypsy music (and the libretto's stereotypical evocation of Roma culture) are presented as an antidote to both operetta triviality and the routine of Zorika's life. That chaos is a force that the operetta ultimately exploits for musical and dramatic energy, albeit within the confines of its genre.

Lehár's construction of authenticity was built on tropes that existed within the world of operetta, not in relation to any actual Roma music or musicians. What Bellman identifies as the distinctive elements of Gypsy music—irregular phrasing, complexity in general—had become, by the twentieth century, closely aligned with high-culture sensibilities, and the language of *Zigeunerliebe* follows the more foursquare conventions of popular music with a few colorful borrowings from the Gypsy tradition and a larger orchestra.[34] (Bellman acknowledges this complexity as a stereotype; he sees Lehár's work as an aesthetic failure, not an ethical one.) But operetta's lack of engagement with Roma traditions, in fact, is an explicit subject of Kálmán's later *Zigeunerprimas*.

EXAMPLE 3.2. Johann Strauss II, *Die Fledermaus*, No. 10, Csárdás, opening

Lehár's grandiosity fit the Viennese conception of the power of Hungarian music. Kálmán's slightly earlier *Ein Herbstmanöver*, in comparison, did not (and for the Viennese it was largely unsuccessful in summoning "dread and desire"). *Ein Herbstmanöver* does contain the obligatory czardas. Dramatically, it is unusually low-key; it is sung by male lead Oberleutnant Lörenthy in a mood more elegiac than lamenting and plays no significant role in the plot. Musically, its form is much closer to its Hungarian inspiration than most other operetta versions (ex. 3.2). It features a "Gypsy band" onstage, which takes command in the opening *lassú* and the *friss* dance at the end. The band's introduction is dense with Hungarian tropes: oscillating thirds, the Hungarian anapest rhythm, and the raised fourth of the "Gypsy scale" in the first and seventh measures. Yet most of this disappears when voice enters. In Kálmán's Hungarian operetta, the csárdás retains its generic status as a dance and the style hongrois is not deployed for the emotional affect expected in Viennese operetta style. Once he relocated to Vienna, however, Kálmán would become the foremost practitioner of the Viennese idea of Hungarian style.

DER ZIGEUNERPRIMAS: IRONIC INTERIORITY

While Lehár's heritage was occasionally pointed out by the press, Kálmán's Hungarian nationality was the central attribute of his public persona.[35] This characteristic was rarely expressed in musically specific terms but rather described in the expressive language typical of discourses of national identity. Genuineness of feeling and rawness of expression were Gypsy music's most important attributes, and Kálmán's nationality and claim to close proximity to the sources of Gypsy music allegedly allowed him to channel their expressive language more directly. Independent of whether Kálmán actually wrote more authentic Gypsy music than non-Hungarian composers, the Viennese critics believed he did, as it was understood to be intrinsic to his nationality. The Hungarian Gypsy musician, in the Viennese view, served as an amanuensis for this surplus of emotion, and it made for a powerful display onstage.

Kálmán found his personal formula for Viennese success in 1912. Unlike his first Viennese operetta, the experimental flop *Der kleine König, Der Zigeunerprimas* adopted most of the conventions of Silver Age Vienna. Written for the Johann-Strauß-Theater to a libretto by Julius Wilhelm and Fritz Grünbaum, the operetta gives the style hongrois a leading role in the plot and infuses it throughout the score.[36] Moreover, Gypsy music is not used as exotic, interpolated color but as a structural element of the operetta on a level with the waltz.

The libretto of *Der Zigeunerprimas* may have been inspired by the success of *Zigeunerliebe* in Vienna, or perhaps merely by Kálmán's Hungarian heritage. Either way, it offers a new perspective on "Gypsy life." Rather than cloaking the Gypsy experience as fantasy, it is concerned with the phenomenon of Gypsy music—and thus also Hungarian music—as an expressive vehicle. The stereotype of the Gypsy in the modern world is not only distanced but played for laughs. And unlike most Gypsy operettas, almost all the major characters are Gypsies. Moreover, they are Gypsies who are themselves engaged in selling their Gypsy identities in the music business.

The protagonist and title character of *Der Zigeunerprimas* is the aging Gypsy violinist and bandleader Pali Rácz, who is engaged in a rivalry with his son Laczi. Conservatory-trained Laczi plays in a new style that the traditionalist Pali considers nonsense. True to operetta's penchant for love triangles, both father and son want to marry the same woman, Julishka. Although gout and old age hamper old Rácz's playing, he is not eager to cede his role as *Zigeunerprimas*, Gypsy bandleader, to his newfangled son, nor does he want to give up Julishka. The audiences of Paris, however, prefer the modern dance music of Laczi to Rácz's amet-

ric scrapings, and eventually Rácz senior is persuaded to put down his treasured
Stradivarius and acknowledge he is too old to marry Julishka, ceding both violin
and girlfriend to his son.

Despite the characters named after the famous Rácz clan of musicians, the plot
has only tenuous basis in fact, as already noted.[37] In the operetta the title character,
Pali Rácz, has sixteen children; historically, he reputedly had at least thirty-four. At
the time of the operetta's premiere, the real Laczi, who was probably around fifty
years old, was still going strong as a bandleader. Several recordings made around
1907, however, reveal a musician playing predominantly in a traditional Roma
style rather than modern dance music or classical repertoire.[38]

The operetta's raison d'être was a triumphant return to the stage by Alexander
Girardi, the living symbol of Golden Age operetta, who had retired on the eve of
the Silver Age after Franz Lehár's failed *Die Juxheirat* (1904). In *Der Zigeunerprimas*, he played old Rácz (in the operetta, the surname alone refers to the father).
As the senior bandleader reluctantly agrees to resign his position to his modern
son, the allegory of passage from the Golden to Silver Age of operetta could hardly
be more obvious.[39] The *Neue Freie Presse* considered Pali "more than simply a
thankful role for Girardi" but "sublimated reality."[40] The generational gap between
father and son mirrors the biographical differences between Golden and Silver
Age operetta composers: the former, like Johann Strauss II, are largely self-taught
and grounded in popular and folk music; the latter, like Kálmán and Lehár, are
conservatory-trained and began careers in art music before switching to popular
entertainment. The plot similarities to Wagner's *Die Meistersinger von Nürnberg*
are equally obvious (Rácz is Hans Sachs, Julishka is Eva, and Laczi is Walther),
though, as Stefan Frey points out, the generations have been reversed for modernity: it is now the elderly Rácz whose style originates in Romantic inspiration
while the son Laczi produces academically polished, mass-produced music for an
industrialized age—music the rural Rácz decries as fit only for the soulless urban
market.[41]

But, as so often in operetta, this allegory is defused even as it is presented. The
Gypsies of *Der Zigeunerprimas* are ordinary people running a family music business, not an exotic or mysterious Other. While Rácz first appears, he is in tattered
Gypsy garb, orally instructing a classroom of his children and grandchildren in the
art of Gypsy music. But he is doing so inside his own luxurious house and refers
to his students as an implicitly industrial "Gypsy factory." The romantic image of
the inspired Gypsy has been put in brackets.[42] In Act 2 he performs not dressed as
a Gypsy but rather in a dapper tuxedo (as the real Rácz Laczi does in the pages of
the guidebook *The City of Magyars*, described at the start of this chapter).

Musically, Kálmán—a conservatory-educated composer like Laczi, but one
who claimed access to Rácz's outsized Hungarian soul—exploits his ability to write
both Viennese waltzes and style hongrois music. But he is not a fundamental-

EXAMPLE 3.3. Kálmán, *Der Zigeunerprimas*, No. 6, Finale I, first vocal entrance

ist about their placement. Kálmán offers a distillation of the differences between the father and son's styles in a short dialogue in the Act 1 Finale (No. 6) (ex. 3.3). Laczi protests that he wants to find his own style of music, not merely imitate his father, singing in in flowing compound meter (orchestrated with oboe and bassoon, the passage recalls and arguably parodies the music of Walther von Stolzing in *Die Meistersinger*). His father responds that he is a good son but a bad musi-

EXAMPLE 3.4. Kálmán, *Der Zigeunerprimas*, No. 3a, Melodram, opening

cian, singing in duple divisions, his vocal line immediately jumping up a fifth and then descending (the melodic type of Gypsy music throughout the score) in steady eighth notes. Rácz's is doubled in the accompaniment with a variety of melodic ornamentations—grace notes, mordents, and turns—all of which exemplify the style hongrois.

In the battle between these two styles, Laczi seems to have the upper hand. Some of the diegetic music played by Laczi is later transformed into non-diegetic song, suggesting that it has greater expressive power than Rácz claims—or, at least, reinforcing that it is the mainstream style of modern commercial operetta like *Der Zigeunerprimas*. In No. 3a, Laczi is heard playing offstage (ex. 3.4). The number begins *in media res* with a single phrase in 4, then moves to a slow waltz. All this material will be repurposed in ways that suggest that both Laczi and Julishka remember the moment and that potentially even positions Laczi as a surrogate

EXAMPLE 3.5. Kálmán, *Der Zigeunerprimas*, No. 10, Duett, refrain

for Kálmán himself. First, the 4/4 phrase is reprised in the very next number, "Laut dringt der frommen Chor," where Laczi uses it to declare his love—of music (Julishka complains that he is not listening to her). The waltz resurfaces in Act 2, where it provides the refrain to Laczi and Julishka's duet No. 10, "Bist plötzlich durchgegangen" (ex. 3.5). Julishka recalls Laczi's violin music as she laments their impossible love (she is still engaged to his father). For the Gypsy, the music is inspired by one's inner spirit, but here Julischka's emotions are given shape by preexisting music.

Rácz's violin playing is written in a virtuosic Gypsy violin idiom, and appropriately none of it is transformed into non-diegetic music. When Rácz sings, however, he often defies the style hongrois and falls into slow Viennese waltzes suitable for the elderly Viennese eminence Girardi. Such numbers were expected, and national identity never seems an important matter in *Der Zigeunerprimas*. (Appropriately, Rácz's songs are written for a narrow, low range, and the melodic line is invariably doubled in the orchestra, suggesting that Girardi's singing voice may have shown signs of aging as well.[43]) While this sudden departure from a Hungarian musical identity may seem jarring, for the Viennese, at least in operetta, the style hongrois could be heard as primarily aesthetic rather than as a signifier of personal or national identity.

The operetta shows respect for Rácz's skill and tradition (particularly in his sentimental slow waltz song addressed to his violin, "Mein alter Stradivari"), but age has dulled his skills and fashions have changed. The operetta's affectionate and forgiving attitude toward its characters allows for a certain amount of slippage between the plot's literal level of the aging Rácz's declining skills and its allegorical depiction of changing musical fashion: it can acknowledge that Rácz and Alexander Girardi's days, like their music, have passed while still giving them their due. (If *Der Zigeunerprimas* is indeed the *Meistersinger* of operetta, it is one without a Beckmesser.) This foreshadows the nostalgia that would grow in later decades. That Hungarian Gypsy music here represents the past is ironic given that in the world of operetta its sound was ascendant.

Kálmán could also mix Hungarian style with modern dance music, which would become one of his stylistic signatures, even more than the romanticism represented by Laczi's violin music.[44] This hybrid can be seen already in full form in *Der Zigeunerprimas*'s so-called "Hazazaa" number. This was a late addition to the score, and it is not entirely clear when it was composed (though it was certainly performed in the Budapest premiere, which was on January 24, 1913).[45] It is sung by Sári (one of Rácz's daughters) and her French beau, Gaston. The introduction presents a memorable melodic "hook" whose syncopation could belong equally to Gypsy music or a cakewalk. The text, like many dance songs, deals with dance and, in particular, the excellence of this particular dance, the Hazazaa. (The title word does not seem to mean anything at all, but it sounds exciting.)

The opening is marked "stark im Bauerton" (strongly rustic), established by the clarinet's grace notes doubling the voice and the folk-inspired figurations echoing the voice, as well as the traditionally Gypsy instruments of drum, triangle, and clarinet (ex. 3.6). The Hungarian anapest rhythm appears in slightly altered form on "und da gibt's kein Halt." In the refrain, the Lombard rhythm on "das tanzt ihr" and "alte." The text reinforces the music's mixture. The number's style represents a rapprochement between Racz and Laczi, between old world and new, but one that is never instrumentalized within the operetta's plot. Sári explains the movement of the Hazazaa in terms of Gypsy music: "da lernt man lachen und weinen/mit beiden Beinen,/das ist der Hazazaa!" (so you learn to laugh and cry with both your

EXAMPLE 3.6. Kálmán, *Der Zigeunerprimas*, No. 5 replacement number, Hazazaa, vocal entrance

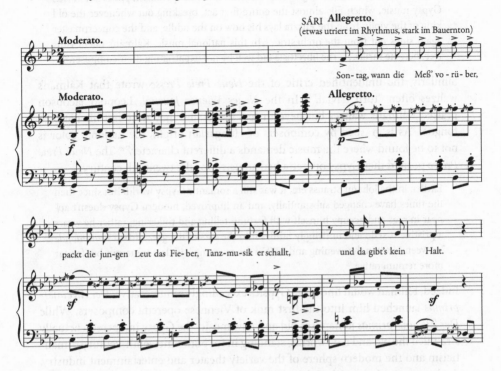

legs, that's the Hazazaa!). The second strophe, however, adds references to modern technology when Gaston comments that to do the dance one would need sixty horsepower, "and a few horsepower for the big toe." (Excessive physical demands were a frequent complaint against ultramodern dances.)

The number gleefully mixes the old and the new. In a way, Kálmán played the role of Sári, introducing something that was old and traditional as a sexy new fashion. His Hungarian style, critics agreed, was something new and exciting. Critics seemed to find Kálmán's perceived ability to transmit genuine Gypsy feeling his strongest suit—and showed little concern about anthropological authenticity. While Kálmán's short radio broadcast makes the sensible argument that his knowledge came from actual experience gleaned in Budapest, critics tended to define his talent in the familiar terms of fin de siècle belief, ascribing the superior quality and perceived authenticity of Kálmán's Hungarian music to his ethnic identity. (Ironically, this contravenes the message of the operetta itself. Performing and composing are not, it seems, the same thing.) Additionally, many were skeptical about his ability to adopt the Viennese language of the waltz. In the *Fremden-Blatt*, Julius Stern wrote:

Waltzes aren't Kálmán's strongest suit. The heat of his temperament pours out in rich Gypsy music, which fills almost the entire first act, breaking out whenever the old king of the violin from the Puszta lays his bow on the fiddle, and the concertmaster again sings out from the orchestra.... In this national music, Kálmán's talent runs free, here he thrills.... The librettists did well by not expatriating their composer.[46]

Similarly, the unidentified critic of the *Neue Freie Presse* wrote that Kálmán's waltzes often "turn trivial."[47] In the *Neues Wiener Journal*, Leopold Jacobson praised Kálmán's waltzes but nevertheless noted that they were not his national tongue: "As is grasped by composers of Hungarian origin, the national color is not to be found where the music demands a different character."[48] The *Neue Freie Presse* posited that Gypsy operetta had adjusted for the twentieth century:

> Earlier, in the Johann Strauss era, it was still a romantic Gypsy world. But since then the times have changed substantially, and an improved, modern Gypsy doesn't appear in rags and occupy himself with fortune-telling and tinkering; rather he wears a pristine tuxedo and untiringly fiddles into the ears of the great urban *beau monde* between 11:00 in the evening and 5:00 in the morning—it's less romantic, but far, far more remunerative.[49]

Indeed, Kálmán would find stage Gypsies exceedingly remunerative. *Der Zigeunerprimas* launched him into the first rank of Viennese operetta composers. While *Der Zigeunerprimas* juxtaposes old and new music, the Gypsy in operetta actually straddled the old and new worlds, standing in for both nineteenth-century romanticism and the modern sphere of the variety theater and entertainment industry. And it was, perhaps, Kálmán's unique background that inspired him to combine the cabaret and the Gypsy in operetta music.

But while Kálmán's style seems to capture the empire just before its demise, its role in the revival of operettic exoticism may have been its most influential contribution. To some extent, this was merely a continuation of the Slavic music of *Die lustige Witwe* and Lehár's *Zigeunerliebe*. But Kálmán's immense success at establishing exotic music as the sound of an emotional, interior space (a role different from that of the Slavic music in *Die lustige Witwe*) would set the tone for a large number of exotic operettas in the 1920s, to be considered in chapter 5. It was another means for operetta to retreat from the depiction of an exterior reality into that of a subjective fantasy, and one where the exotic was not so much a mysterious or threatening Other as a reflection of the deepest mysteries of the self.

4

Operetta and the Great War

In Peter Konwitschny's production of Emmerich Kálmán's operetta *Die Csárdás-fürstin,* first performed at the Semperoper in Dresden on New Year's Eve 1999, the operetta's subtext was brought to the foreground. *Die Csárdásfürstin*, which dates from 1915, concerns Edwin Ronald Carl Maria von und zu Lippert-Weylersheim, a Viennese aristocrat who has the misfortune to fall in love with a Budapest cabaret singer, one Sylva Varescu. His parents think he should marry the more appropriate Countess Stasi. But in the Dresden production, this conventional plot was eventually invaded by soldiers, nurses, and unexpected explosions. By Act 2, the action was taking place in a trench. As in the second act of most operettas, the standard pair of couples threaded their way through a plot of reversals and revelations, but this time with breaks to duck and cover.[1]

The production was greeted with outrage, and the fact that seemingly unnecessary bombs had been dropped in, of all places, Dresden aroused particular consternation and even legal action.[2] Konwitschny's production played on the incongruity between *Die Csárdásfürstin*'s apparently trivial plot and the dire circumstances of the world in which it premiered, bringing the world outside the premiere's theater to the stage of the Semperoper. (He also provided some novel, locally relevant puns on Countess Stasi's name.[3]) In the director's words, "A world gone mad can't be shut out of such a story; it always sneaks in again through the back door."[4] Yet how did the 1915 audiences of *Die Csádásfürstin* see it? Richard Traubner refers to *Die Csárdásfürstin* as possessing "genial high spirits," implying that the operetta was simply an antidote to the war, not a reflection of it.[5] Other accounts of wartime operetta find a more sinister silence. During the war itself, cultural gadfly Karl Kraus (1874–1936) claimed that operetta like *Die Csárdásfürstin* was a synecdoche for the very blindness that had led to this tragedy in the first place, as his quasi–alter ego The Grumbler puts it in his epic war play *Die letzten Tage der Menschheit* (The Last Days of Mankind): "And did you not notice how the tragedy [of the war] became a farce, became an operetta, thanks to the simultaneous appearance of the latest malice and fossilized forms, one of those disgusting modern operettas with an insulting libretto and music that is a torture?"[6] For Kraus, the war was the culmination of operetta's march-crazed dreams of frivolous destruction and operetta was a symptom of the inhuman culture that allowed the war in the first place. Operetta's purportedly oblivious survival was just another symptom of the impending apocalypse—Vienna may have risen to the strains of Mozart, but it would fall to those of Lehár.

This chapter considers Kraus's military-operetta complex. What would become known as World War I inflicted tragedy on the Austro-Hungarian Empire on both a personal and national scale. Ultimately, the state itself would be dissolved. But Kraus was not wrong about operetta's wartime ubiquity. Even amid the war's carnage and the empire's precarity, one thing that kept going with hardly a pause was operetta. As Marion Linhardt writes, "It is one of the commonplaces of Austrian, and especially Viennese, theatre history that the First World War...was a time when operetta, already the dominant form of popular theatrical entertainment, drew larger and more enthusiastic audiences than ever before."[7] This chapter will examine two of these popular works in detail, both by Kálmán—first his propaganda operetta *Gold gab ich für Eisen* (1914), then *Die Csárdásfürstin*—as well as discuss the representation of and symbolic power ascribed to operetta by Kraus during this time. These works will be considered in light of theater scholar Martin Baumeister's model of "mobilization," which considers the relationship between the state and operetta creators as part of World War I's total war.[8] Wartime operetta gave voice to a wider variety of voices than Kraus's critique allows for, particularly in light of wartime discourses of nationality, class, and religion, sometimes turning those very "fossilized forms" against their own pasts.

OPERETTA AND PROPAGANDA:
GOLD GAB ICH FÜR EISEN

When the war broke out in 1914, Emmerich Kálmán had just begun work with Leo Stein and Béla Jenbach on a new operetta entitled *Es lebe die Liebe!* (Long Live Love!) under contract with the Johann-Strauß-Theater. After the declaration of war on July 28, it was delayed indefinitely. The future of theater was uncertain. At the Theater an der Wien, Wilhelm Karczag dissolved his company, putting the actors, orchestra, and stage technicians on leave, and in early August he wrote to actor Hubert Marischka, "I am not currently in a position to determine when and to what extent I will be able to resume business."[9]

Other theaters reopened swiftly with patriotic programming. On August 17, the Deutsches Volkstheater was the first, presenting Friedrich Schiller's *Wallensteins Lager* (Wallenstein's Camp), a military drama that despite a rather ambivalent message nonetheless celebrates the power of war to bring together disparate populations from Central Europe. Through September and early October, various theaters produced revues and "patriotic scenes" such as the play *In dieser großer Zeit* (In These Great Times, Colosseum) and Edmund Eysler and Franz Lehár's "musical scenes" *Komm', deutscher Bruder!* (Come, German Brothers!, Raimundtheater).[10] As documented in letters in the censor's archive, impresarios actively sought the patronage and support of government officials to give their commercial performances the appearance of government-sanctioned propaganda. Prior to the opening of *Komm', deutscher Bruder!*, for instance, the management of the Raimundtheater invited Count Richard Freiherr von Bienerth—a former prime minster of Austria and then governor of the province of Lower Austria—to attend the gala premiere, as his reputation would enhance the event.[11]

As for the Theater an der Wien and operetta, less than a week after Karczag wrote to Marischka, another rumor spread. "The opera and the Burgtheater are, at present, closed until September 1, and perhaps will be for longer," music theorist Josef Polnauer wrote to Alban Berg on August 18. But, he added, "On that account, the Theater an der Wien wants to feature a 'patriotic' operetta, by a certain Kalmán [sic], who slapped together the operetta *Ein Herbstmanöver*."[12] The rumor was correct. The theater reopened on October 18, 1914, with a new patriotic war operetta, *Gold gab ich für Eisen* with music by Kálmán.[13]

The operetta, masterminded by librettist Victor Léon, was in fact a reworking of Kálmán's second operetta, *Az Obsitos* (The Soldier on Leave), which had first been performed on March 16, 1910, in Budapest in Hungarian, with a libretto by *Tatárjárás* author Karl von Bakonyi. Léon and Bakonyi had adapted it into the German-language *Der gute Kamerad* (The Good Comrade), which had premiered in 1911 at the Bürgertheater in Vienna with the unusual genre designation of "Theaterstück" (theater piece) with music in two acts. Both *Tatárjáras* and *Der gute Kamerad* take place in 1859, during the Second Italian War of Independence. In 1914 Léon adapted the work again, moving the setting up to the present and calling it *Gold gab ich für Eisen* (I Gave Gold for Iron), a "Singspiel in 1 Prelude and 2 Acts, freely after an idea by Karl von Bakonyi." The plot concerns cavalry officer Franz, who had been fighting in the army for fifteen years and had while dying told his best friend and fellow officer, Alwin, to return to Franz's village to speak with his mother, Karoline, and give his sister, Marlene, the requisite blessing to marry, as well as return to them an iron ring that had belonged to Karoline's grandmother. When the regiment is marching through the area of the village, Gubendorf, a few weeks later, Alwin goes to return the ring and is unintentionally mistaken for the long-gone Franz himself. Afraid to tell Karoline that her son is dead, he plays along until he falls in love with Marlene. The bittersweet truth is eventually revealed. Franz is lost, but Alwin gets married.

Notably, none of the three versions are designated as "operetta"; all are described in alternative ways that suggest rustic simplicity—and, in wartime, add distance from operetta's French roots, both linguistic and dramaturgical. The score does not include Kálmán's signature post-*Zigeunerprimas* style hongrois musical mode, nor does the libretto feature many of the genre conventions that had, by 1910, become obligatory for large-scale operetta in Vienna.[14] The most radical changes from the conventional ideal are, however, the sad ending and the modest and unglamorous country village setting. In its Viennese premiere in 1911, it enjoyed a modest 53 performances; critics found its, melancholy tone dreary and dull, and it was eclipsed by Kálmán's far more successful *Der Zigeunerprimas* the following year.[15]

But the war gave it another lease on life. By 1914 Kálmán's star had risen considerably, and the show was staged at the larger Theater an der Wien. Kálmán and Léon transformed the historical *Der gute Kamerad* into the timely *Gold gab ich für Eisen*. The operetta was rushed into production; an incomplete libretto was submitted to the censor on September 2, barely a month after the war broke out.[16] Several critics thought it was a surprisingly apt work considering its prewar origins. The *Neues Wiener Journal* went so far as to say that in peacetime the work was too "pathetic" and excessively sentimental but in wartime had far greater resonance.[17] Echoing the language of Felix Salten's "The New Operetta," the *Fremden-Blatt* critic Julius Stern said that the work was a "friendly evening, full of soul and comfortable amusement, in which the day, the hour in which we are living now, with its frights and its hopes, is reflected back to us... and the most notable thing is that this piece was not originally conceived for this day or this hour."[18]

The camaraderie and emotional resonance described by these critics are key to the operetta's propaganda effect. In Jason Stanley's definition, propaganda "closes off debate by bypassing the rational will. It makes the state move as one, stirred by emotions that far surpass the evidence for their intensity."[19] The operetta's gentle approach was suited to the early days of the war, when its true horror was yet to reach the majority of the Viennese audience. Through its mix of cheery and poignant moments, as well as some more unusual contrivances, *Gold gab ich für Eisen* presented the war as justified, winnable, and an opportunity to prove one's manly and, crucially, womanly steadfastness. Not only was the setting was moved up to the present day (wartime 1914), but, most important, a happy ending was appended in which it is revealed that Franz did not die after all—he makes a propitious reappearance in a new finale.[20] The musical changes primarily reinforce the patriotic character of the work through the addition of marches in the overture and several patriotic anthems and traditional operetta marches celebrating the might of Austria-Hungary and Germany (with titles like "Österreich wird die Frauen preisen," [Austria will praise women] and "Mein Vaterland, du bist in Not"

[My fatherland, you are in neeed]). Now the work's old-fashioned, provincial character was a strength. Its score was, according to the *Neue Freie Presse*, "in a manner of speaking, Austro-Hungarian music" with an "almost rustic rural character,"
representing a move away from the more urbane, cosmopolitan character that operetta had by 1914 conventionally cultivated.[21]

In October 1914 the war was still, in the words of Stefan Zweig, "a rapid excur-
sion into the romantic, a wild, manly adventure."[22] This upbeat spirit is represented
by the trouser role of Xaverl, performed by star soubrette Louise Kartousch (who
had also sung a trousers role in *Ein Herbstmanöver*). Xaverl's No. 7 was intended
to be a pointed salvo against Austria's most immediate nemesis in which Xaverl
boasts about how he has "eine Masse Serb'n g'fress'n" (gobbled up a ton of Serbi-
ans) and names several Serbian sites where he saw action (Schabatz [*Šabac*] and
Voljewo [Voljevo], both sites of fighting at the time). The specific locations were
struck by the censor, and the number became a generic celebration of the joy of
fighting.[23] By making this a trouser role, the creators further avoided reality. The
sight of a woman singing and dancing as a soldier was titillating and prevented
any accusations that an able-bodied actor would be better off actually fighting than
singing about it. The role of Xaverl is in fact entirely comic—the script makes a
number of puns on Kartousch's name that break the theater's fourth wall and assure the audience that this is all in good fun.[24]

But *Gold gab ich für Eisen* does not present a uniformly jingoistic picture; its
dominant tone is, as critic Stern noted, one of gentle pathos. After the prologue,
the perspective provided is largely a female one: the setting for the remainder of
the operetta is the home front, and the plot concerns the family's affairs rather than
the military. The audience, privy to the prologue, spends the entire operetta in an-
ticipation of the moment of revelation when Karoline and Marlene's hopes will be
dashed and they discover that Alwin is not really Franz. The pain seen in *Gold gab
ich fur Eisen* is mostly the psychological toll of uncertainty and insecurity on the
home front—that is to say, the situation in which the audience found themselves.

The operetta's focus on the lives of women and on the home front distinguishes
Gold gab ich für Eisen from many wartime theater pieces, but women were a key
audience for wartime propaganda campaigns in general. In Vienna, the Frauen-
Hilfsaktion Wien actively promoted the maternal instincts of Austrian women
as a crucial resource in the war effort, one based on, as Maureen Healey writes,
"supposedly universal feminine traits of maternalism, love, and selflessness."[25] The
operetta similarly focuses on the power of women's feelings, even tacitly endorsing
their power to sympathize away Death himself. In the new ending, the threat of
loss has been eliminated, and the material sacrifice to which the title alludes is, in
the plot, purely symbolic. The operetta made perfect propaganda: it acknowledged
and expressed sympathy for the audience's situation and depicted it as the worst
part of the war, to be followed not by death but rather by their family members'

triumphant return home.[26] Several critics praised its moderation. The *Neue Wiener Journal* claimed that the cast "tried to make the pathos real and gripping but also cautious and noble."[27]

The home front focus of *Gold gab ich für Eisen* suits a period of "total war." As Martin Baumeister observes in his study of wartime theater in Germany, "To be successful, propaganda must be more than simple indoctrination and manipulation.... The totalizing logic of the war...puts pressure on the systematic exhaustion of all available material and immaterial resources."[28] This means, Baumeister argues, that while unofficial propaganda may advance many of the same messages as official works, it may also manifest many other values and traditions. *Gold gab ich für Eisen* is not state-endorsed propaganda, and its creators did not actively seek to present it as such. Furthermore, as a preexisting work it exists within established theatrical traditions. But despite its distance from official dicta, it nonetheless transmits many of the same messages as officially sanctioned material.

Gold gab ich für Eisen's most characteristic propaganda feature, in fact, is its unusual effort to explain and make emotional sense of the war. The centenary of the Battle of Leipzig in 1913 had brought recent attention to the Napoleonic era.[29] By referencing established discourses of war and memorial associated with this period, Kálmán and Léon construct a historical legacy for the alliance of Austria-Hungary and Germany against France in both dramatic and musical terms. The operetta references these campaigns repeatedly, sometimes in elements held over from its earlier incarnations set in 1859. But this history had much greater import in wartime than in peace. The relationship between the present and past campaigns is established through the plot point of an iron ring referenced in the title and repeated invocations of the folk song "Ich hatt' einen Kameraden" (which lent the first German version its title). Even though the two conflicts are separated by a century and are fundamentally separate, by invoking a historical precedent the operetta imposes a historical narrative on the present-day war, a fight whose causes were, for many Viennese citizens, obscure. As Jay Winter writes, "The search for the 'meaning' of the Great War began as soon as the war itself."[30]

Franz's ring, which Alwin must return to Karoline, is engraved with the words "Gold gab ich für Eisen" (I gave gold for iron). These rings were popular relics from both the Napoleonic and, eventually, World War I years. On March 23, 1813, Marianne Prinzessin Wilhelm of Prussia had issued a call for women living in Prussian territories to cast aside vanity and donate their gold jewelry for the sake of the war effort, and in exchange they received in exchange just such a ring.[31] The ring donation effort had been revived in Austria in the very early days of World War I and was in full force by the operetta's premiere in October. (A poster advertising a ring collection effort in St. Veit an der Glan on September 28, 1914, prematurely states that the proceeds will go toward "cripples, widows, orphans, and those returning home."[32]) In the first act of the operetta, the revived gold drive

EXAMPLE 4.1. "Der gute Kamerad," folk song, reading from Friedrich Silcher, ed., *Volkslieder gesammelt und für vier Männerstimmen* (1902), 5–6

is seen onstage, and Marlene and the women's chorus sing an ode to the donation drive (No. 4, "Österreich wird die Frauen preisen").

Aryan Theater founder Adam Müller-Guttenbrunn (see chapter 1) resurfaced in the pages of the *Tägliche Rundschau* of August 4 to critique the donation effort as "a parody of 1813 for the sake of feminine vanity."[33] Feminine vanity or not, the creation of war-linked art objects recalls the "trench art" relics examined by anthropologist Nicholas Saunders. Saunders argues that these artworks made of the literal detritus of war form a "memory bridge," serving "as solid and multisensorial remembrances of wartime experiences or as…the embodied absence of a loved one."[34] While the iron in the iron ring is not literally made from a bullet, it similarly refashions the metal of war. This function is also taken by the operetta itself: using the tools of a nineteenth-century work rather than a Silver Age one, *Gold gab ich für Eisen* explains the industrialized war of present in the context of a more humane, preindustrial past.

The operetta further invokes 1813 in its quotation of the popular poem and folk

song "Der gute Kamerad," sometimes known by its first line "Ich hatt' einen Ka-
maraden" (ex. 4.1). Originating in the Napoleonic period, the song is a chimera of
several nineteenth-century textual and musical sources.[35] The main body of the
text, "Der gute Kamerad," is an 1809 poem by Ludwig Uhland memorializing the
loyalty and honor of the soldier-narrator's fallen comrade, shown here in a vintage
translation. (A soldier song version dating from later in the nineteenth century
adds a refrain promising "in the homeland, we shall meet again!" at the end of each
strophe; the operetta uses the earlier version.)[36]

"DER GUTE KAMERAD," TEXT

Ich hatt' einen Kameraden,	I had a faithful comrade,
Einen bessern find'st du nicht.	None better you could find.
Die Trommel schlug zum Streite,	The battle drum beat gaily,
Er ging an meiner Seite	He marched beside me daily,
In gleichem Schritt und Tritt.	And never fell behind.
Eine Kugel kam geflogen,	A cannon ball came flying—
Gilt sie mir oder gilt sie dir?	Is't for me or is't for thee?
Ihn hat es weggerissen,	It threw him down, and dying
Er liegt zu meinen Füßen,	Before my feet he's lying,
Als wär's ein Stück von mir.	Just like a part of me.
Will mir die Hand noch reichen,	His hand he wants to give me,
Derweil ich eben lad.	While I must load anew;
Kann dir die Hand nicht geben,	My hand cannot be given—
Bleib du im ew'gen Leben	Now fare thou well in heaven,
Mein guter Kamerad!	My comrade good and true![37]

The song was conventionally performed by soldiers marching off to war. The act of
singing such songs together created a united front, purpose, and community in a
time of deep sadness and confusion. This was, similarly, the function of the operetta. The iconic status of the song, as well as its connotations of Germanic nationalism, made it an apt choice for inclusion.[38] It instantly evoked an experience that
existed outside the theater. Its text also deals with a longed-for reunion between a
soldier and his comrade, a parallel for Franz and Alwin.

The song is first heard in the prologue, which was a late addition to the operetta, not present in the script submitted to the censor. It largely recycles material
that was already part of later portions of the score but performs the crucial function of introducing Franz before his supposed death (and his relationship with
Alwin). Alwin pledges to Franz that in the case of Franz's death he will return the
ring to Franz's mother, and the prologue ends with the two rushing off to fight.
We do not see the actual battle. The score takes an overtly bellicose tone from the

start, beginning with a march for brass, drums, and woodwinds (No. 1, Vorspiel und Melodram). The march is interrupted at one point by a bugle call from the stage (no stage action is indicated in the score or staging manual and the curtain remains closed). The curtain then opens on an empty battlefield, and an unseen male chorus sings from backstage a short "Heil," paraphrasing the text though not the music of the Austro-Hungarian "Kaiserhymne," the version of "Gott erhalte Franz den Kaiser" that served as the personal anthem of Emperor Franz Joseph I.[39] But the soldiers are unseen, forcing the audience to imagine a visual analogue from their own experiences.

The prologue establishes music as a reciprocal link between home and war: military music heard at home recalls the front just as music heard at the front can recall home. As Franz expresses his desire to return home, he sings a gentle, lullaby-like theme (Adagio, already heard in the prelude played by the oboe, one of the least military of wind instruments; the reprise is seen on the second page of ex. 4.2). The quiet, gentle character of this theme makes it stand out among the noisier military music so far. As the enemy approaches, Franz again sings of his family, now in a broader and more richly voiced waltz (Tempo di valse lento, beginning of ex. 4.2), but again refers to the power of this simpler music to transport him, reaching a high A as he proclaims its power to transport him ("It sounds to me in struggle and strife like a dear greeting, in battle it was my safe-conduct"). Kálmán customarily used the slow waltz to imagine things from a distance, such as hypothetical futures or bygone pasts. But within the operetta's diegetic space, it is the naive song of Franz's childhood, whose reprise follows, that has this power, the power of familial love over the more cosmopolitan sophistication of the waltz. Indeed, this "Franzl" song will return several times over the course of the evening, and Franz's family invests it with the same power he does.

The prologue reaches its climax when, prompted by Alwin's words "we'll remain comrades," the two men break into "Ich hatt' einen Kamerad," (moderato, "im Volkston") and march off toward the enemy. The song's entrance is accompanied by a sudden modulation from D major to B-flat major. It is the first time the two have sung together and emerges as a strongly marked musical moment, even if the audience were not to recognize the extremely popular song. The modulation and the song's preexisting character also imply diegetic status, which is logical considering the song's traditional association with these very circumstances.

The action of the operetta consists of a series of close calls in which Alwin is nearly exposed, Alwin's dithering and falling in love with his "sister," and various characters' breaking into patriotic songs (including a novelty polka in dialect dedicated to Zeppelin, his airships, and the salute "this little bomb was a greeting from Berlin and Vienna!"). At the end of the operetta, when Marlene realizes that Alwin is not her son, Franz conveniently appears, singing the Franzerl song yet again. Upon the reunion, an invisible backstage chorus intones, "Ich hatt' einen Kam-

EXAMPLE 4.2. Kálmán, *Gold gab ich für Eisen*, No. 3, Finaletto, first vocal entrance

EXAMPLE 4.2. (continued)

EXAMPLE 4.2. (continued)

eraden, einen bessern findst du nit [*sic*, dialect]!" The song appears unprompted, like a film soundtrack, providing an appropriate musical articulation of the moment's affect. It is belatedly made diegetic: after the singing finishes and the same harp makes the same flourish it did in the prologue, the stage directions indicate "lauter Jubel, Bauers, Soldaten drängen hinein" (loud celebrations, farmers, soldiers push in), meaning that the invisible chorus was actually a group of farmers and soldiers observing the proceedings just out of view. Onstage, they begin singing in celebration to the theme of the Franzerl song, whose promise is now fulfilled. The impression is that of a collective unconscious, a reflexive utterance of patriotic songs as the occasion demands.

Yet *Gold gab ich für Eisen* had a strange post-Vienna life. It was a hit in Berlin, but its greatest success would come in enemy territory. It was rewritten yet again by librettist Rida Johnson Young and premiered on December 6, 1916, in New York as *Her Soldier Boy*, where it ran for a stellar 204 performances and was "the first [Broadway] show to address the war in such an overt manner."[40] In this version, the story was set among the Allies in Belgium, and, in a clever twist, Karoline was made blind, making her false recognition of Franz far more plausible. More important, most of the culturally specific material was reconfigured or removed to suit an Anglophone audience. Only a few of Kálmán's songs remained in the score; Sigmund Romberg and perhaps a few other uncredited composers wrote several new numbers.[41] Kálmán and the Karczag-Verlag were paid for these performances only with great difficulty.[42] Meanwhile, in Vienna, the mood seemed to have shifted: after *Gold gab ich für Eisen* and the Lehár-Eysler collaboration *Komm', deutscher Brüder!*, there were few subsequent propaganda operettas. The theatrical public seemed to prefer a kind of euphoric celebration, often with socially adventurous elements (such as the African American character in Leo Ascher's *Bruder Leichtsinn* and the Jewish ones in Edmund Eysler's *Frühling am Rhein*).[43] But one of operetta's most prominent critics had other ideas.

KARL KRAUS'S OPERETTA WAR

Gold gab ich für Eisen would also live on in the words of one of the war's fiercest critics, satirist Karl Kraus (1874–1936). For Kraus, military-themed wartime operettas were brainwashing practiced by the powerful to hypnotize the masses into compliance with a senseless war. Operettas reverberate through his wartime writings and plays. But Kraus had long been on a noisy crusade condemning operetta as part of the hypocrisy, pretension, superficiality, and moral laxity he saw everywhere in Viennese culture. Since 1899 he had done this in the pages of his magazine *Die Fackel* (The Torch), for which he served as editor and primary author and whose early covers depicted the titular torch dispelling clouds of illusion hovering over Vienna's skyline.[44] Kraus's writing flows in a stream-of-consciousness style that prefigures Robert Musil, constructing a dense network of allusion and metaphor.

Kraus's views on operetta have come to exert enormous influence on its reception, and his work is rarely discussed in English-language musicology, which makes him worth considering at some length here. Kraus was an important early advocate for a revival of Offenbach, whose work he believed served a *Fackel*-like function. Beginning in 1926, he even performed many Offenbach operettas as one-man shows.[45] But in twentieth-century operetta—most particularly that of Lehár—Kraus found everything that was wrong with Viennese culture, a conclusion he built into a metonym. His first extended essay on this theme was "Grimassen über Kultur und Bühne" (Grimaces regarding culture and the stage, 1908), and it was followed by "Ernst ist das Leben, heiter war die Operette" (Life is serious, operetta was cheerful, 1910) and many others.[46] This critique also occupies a central place in his most ambitious work, the epic and unperformable wartime documentary drama *Die letzten Tagen der Menschheit* (The Last Days of Mankind), begun during the final years of World War I and extensively revised and published in multiple versions over the course of the following decade.[47]

For Kraus, operetta was a manifestation of the bankruptcy of Austro-Hungarian civil society. In operetta and its fans Kraus saw in microcosm a world that found obedience and conformity easier than rational, original thought. In the fame and high pay of operetta actors, Kraus saw a society whose artistic values were out of joint. In contemporary operetta's perceived capitulation to sentimentality, he saw a genre that had sold out its noble satiric tradition in favor of selling more champagne.[48] Operetta served the same evil purpose as Kraus's greatest nemesis, the mass-distribution newspaper. Both closed the floor to debate by inducing public panic and encouraging submission to authority. As Edward Timms puts it, for Kraus "an operetta culture glosses over logical contradictions, encouraging a willingness to dance to the music of the time regardless of who is calling the tune." When the world comes to an end, Kraus observed in January 1908, "orchestras in all European cultural centers will still be playing the song 'Dummer, dummer Reitersmann' from *Die lustige Witwe*."[49]

The perceived failings of operetta were, to Kraus, such an effective metonym for the failings of the empire as a whole that he condemned the decadence of 1912 Vienna as an "Operettenkultur":

> Here all is surface; we let it all stoop and inform ourselves through feuilletons, beer money, and operettas... for ten [*sic*, actually six] years we have rhapsodized over the world of Danilo and Njegus [of *Die lustige Witwe*]....A society that devotes 75,000 Kronen a year to Herr [Louis] Treumann [the first Danilo] cannot complain about the billions that are sacrificed for military use. If society goes to pieces, it's only because it earlier was going so well. No sympathy for a society in which the thieves of culture do best! The performance statistics of a modern operetta are bloodstained

numbers, which in history books will represent a lost battle. At times, an operetta culture marches out with thirst for war. Its soldiers are writers. Wholly irresponsible subjects, who launch a premiere today and a war tomorrow.[50]

Kraus's invocation of Treumann and a sizable sum of money is telling and recurs many times in his writing—as does as his close association of operetta and the liberal press, two industries in which Jews played prominent roles.[51] To Kraus, operetta was the interface between the "culture thieves" and ordinary people. It was the exact opposite of true art (as epitomized in his pun on a typo between König Lear and König Lehár in *Die letzten Tage*[52]). The war represented the triumph of these culture thieves, and thus the entanglement of operetta with war was inevitable. The Grumbler in *Die letzten Tage der Menschheit*, quoted at the beginning of this chapter, echoing Marx, claims that "tragedy became a farce...an operetta, one of those disgusting modern operettas."[53] Kraus's conception of operetta always existed in opposition to his true monuments of culture, such as his beloved Offenbach as well as more central German figures like Goethe and Schopenhauer.

Operetta served a rhetorical purpose for Kraus, and his tendency to map it onto Viennese society as a whole means that, despite its ubiquity in his work, it usually appears in fragmentary form. In *Die letzten Tage*, operetta titles, songs, and actors are mentioned numerous times, and operetta music is heard in the streets and in a nightclub. But we never visit an operetta theater. When Kraus mentions a specific operetta, he quotes only fragments (usually single songs or the names of performers), their dramatic context excised or replaced. The street scenes, as well as *Die letzten Tage*'s Act 5 nightclub scene, present the audience with a panorama of voices, from unidentified citizens to soldiers (interested in heroism and operetta), journalists (ditto), newspaper readers (the least informed of all), and many others.

In *Die letzten Tage*, operetta is as ubiquitous as Kraus claimed it was in real life. But the experience of the play's characters never coheres into anything more than a snippet, a rush of excitement, a manic tune, or a disorienting pun. Kraus had little interest in operettas as coherent pieces of theater—indeed, he probably would have dismissed any assertion that a work by Lehár or Kálmán could be called such. Kraus does not endow specific pieces with specific qualities or meanings, favoring instead a generalized morass of "operetta." His *Zitättechnik* (citation technique or collage) depends on the audience to identify the musical references not as particular pieces with individual histories but rather as part of a culture, prefiguring Theodor Adorno's conception of popular music as a repertoire of standardized, interchangeable commodities.[54] Kraus mixes operettas from before the war with wartime ones, mentioning some by title and referencing some with only a few lyrics (some of which are anachronistic).

Kraus was familiar with *Gold gab ich für Eisen* and mentions it several times. At first, it is present only as a title. Near the end of *Die letzten Tage*'s Act 1, Scene 1 (which comes after a lengthy prologue), the following exchange occurs, in Patrick Healey's translation:

> *Two sales reps enter.*
>
> *The first agent:* You know what, for the first time, I gave gold for iron. [*Gold gab ich für Eisen*].
>
> *The second:* What? You gave it away? I don't believe it! You, giving? Grown up in—
>
> *The first:* Who said that I did it myself? Don't you understand German? Over there I see a poster for our première. *I Gave Gold for Iron.* I want to go.
>
> *The second:* Okay, I will go as well. Now it is really fascinating. Yesterday Gerda Walde was reading out from a special edition of the newspaper during the *Csárdásfürstin* about the 40,000 Russians on the barbed-wire entanglements—you should have heard the cheering, if you said it went on ten times you would still be way out.
>
> *The first:* Any wounded yet?
>
> *The second:* Already. But now it's most fascinating. Fairly recently one of them was sitting near me. Let me remember, ah, yes! — *I Used to Have a Comrade.*
>
> *The first:* You?
>
> *The second:* Who said, I did? It's from Victor Léon!
>
> *The first:* Okay?
>
> *The second:* Dynamite!
>
> *A newspaper caller:* Belgrade bombarded—![55]

The slangy wordplay of the passage is difficult to translate but depends on literal readings of the titles *Gold gab ich für Eisen* and "I Had a Comrade" as sentences. The latter, of course, is the song that also appears in *Gold gab ich für Eisen* when Franz and Alwin are preparing themselves for battle. The second agent comically misattributes the folk song to Victor Léon, the author of the earlier version of the operetta by that title. (This suggests that Kraus knew something about the operetta, though perhaps nothing more than could be gleaned from reading a review.[56]) The folk song in fact serves as a leitmotif in *Die letzten Tage*, both quoted and sung onstage. In most cases, it is sung by soldiers leaving for the war: at first a group simply marked "soldiers" (81), then later "reserve troops of somewhat older age" (325), then "older men" (427), then finally simply "old men" (553). At one point in between, the song is played by a café-style Gypsy band (417), recalling the parody of Mendelssohn's Wedding March in *Die Csárdásfürstin*.

The second agent also describes an actress reading a war bulletin from the stage in a performance of *Die Csárdásfürstin*. Kraus had already depicted a similar event in the wartime lecture "In dieser großer Zeit" (In these great times, published as a text in *Die Fackel* in December 1914), this time placing the event onstage during *Gold gab ich für Eisen*: "And gold for iron fell from the altar into the operetta, bombing was a *couplet*, and fifteen thousand prisoners were put in a special edition of the newspaper that a soubrette read aloud so that a librettist might take a curtain call."[57]

This is factually accurate, as detailed in Julius Stern's *Fremden-Blatt* review of *Gold gab ich für Eisen*, where the announcement is described in the upbeat tones Kraus so deplored: "Indeed, even the representative of our chief of staff, Generalmajor von Höfer, also collaborated on this [second-act] finale. That is to say, Miss Kartousch brought our army's most recent victory report from the northern battleground to read out loud. Celebration on all sides and the end...[ellipses in original]."[58]

Kraus's version adds the newspaper as a participant: he sees operetta as an instrument of mass deception on the same scale as the mass media. Barbara Denscher points out that the bulletin was also read on the same day by Carl-Theater intendant Siegmund Eibenschütz at a performance of *Zwei Mann von Heß* and by tenor Alfred Piccaver at a concert at the Musikverein.[59] But Kraus, typically, chose the event whose title suited his writing and with which he could indict a soubrette.

Steven Beller argues that Kraus's portrayal fails to recognize the subtlety of *Gold gab ich*'s portrayal of war. Alwin's refusal to reveal his true identity, Beller reasons, means he is a bad soldier who avoids doing his duty, yet the operetta praises him for this.[60] Kraus would have countered that the work's sentimentality was itself a trap, and the theater as mobilization model holds that nuance does not preclude a propaganda role. Yet it is possible to see *Gold gab ich*'s intentions more sympathetically than Kraus without denying its propagandistic effects. Kraus lumps operetta into a larger capitalist military-industrial-media-operetta complex, adopting it for a particular symbolic function in his constellation of Viennese malaise, and he restricts its meaning to a top-down hypnosis of the masses. Yet operetta creators were not generals, nor were they even located particularly close to the city or empire's most powerful.[61] Kraus's condemnations of the war frequently generalized between operetta and print media as complicit in the war effort—both industries whose practitioners were often identified as predominately Jewish.

But, particularly in the case of the war, the Judaism of Léon and Kálmán as well as many of their colleagues is salient. This may be one other reason that Kraus, who often used anti-Semitism as a rhetorical strategy, saw operetta as standing apart and exerting control on society rather than operating as an integral part of it.[62] This perspective casts the work of Kálmán and Léon in a different light. Marsha Rozenblit has argued that Jews were particularly loyal to the imperial state and Habsburg family during the war: "They...wanted to dispel anti-Semitic myths about Jewish cowardice and prove the loyalty of Jews to the state. The war provided these Jews with the perfect opportunity to affirm their loyalty to Austria."[63] Jewish organizations such as the Israelitische Kultusgemeinde issued declarations of support, going so far as to consider a fight against Russia a "holy war," one without moral conflict or ambiguity.[64]

Like most products of the Viennese operetta industry, *Gold gab ich für Eisen* contains no characters who are identified as Jewish. But it can be read as an act of patriotism by its authors, who are driven by their own marginalization. *Gold gab ich für Eisen*'s incorporation of traditional Germanic song, its avoidance of Frenchified operetta conventions in favor of *Singspiel*, its positioning within the discourse of the Napoleonic wars, and its emphasis on fighting in Serbia and Galicia (possibly a reflection of the time of its composition) all present it as a native Austro-Germanic product. Moreover, Kálmán and Léon successfully effaced the work's Budapest origins, which were not mentioned in any of the reviews. When translated into English, the show achieved an ironic success, but most of the Germanic elements were deemed to be too closely identified with the enemy for a British or American audience and were removed.

DIE CSÁRDÁSFÜRSTIN: "DO YOU KNOW HOW MUCH LONGER THE WORLD WILL TURN?"

The greatest operetta hit of the war period, Kálmán's *Die Csárdásfürstin*, would seem to be a test case for Kraus's critique: it is usually described as a popular, seemingly irrelevant pleasure. While *Gold gab ich für Eisen* offered comfort and patriotism that, until the wish fulfillment of the finale, was never completely divorced from reality, *Die Csárdásfürstin* presented its audience with an aggressively escapist vision. But in the midst of the plot's nightclub scenes and balls, the operetta contains a critique of Austrian morals as cutting as Kraus's, and its revelry is frequently tinged with apocalyptic hysteria. *Die Csádásfürstin* presupposes a world of enormous precarity. The vehicle for this Dionysian celebration should come as no surprise: "Gypsy" music, whose wild emotionalism is contrasted with the proper social rituals of the Viennese waltz. And, by the end of the operetta, it is not the Viennese but the Hungarians who have triumphed. Yet *Die Csárdásfürstin* remains an operetta: out of death and uncertainty it salvaged an exhortation to live in the present and a promise that the forced casting aside of social customs could mean that the Apollonian waltz and Dionysian, Hungarian cabaret were not irreconcilable.

The librettists were Leo Stein and Béla Jenbach—the former, one of the authors of *Die lustige Witwe*, and the latter, an actor of Hungarian background who was just embarking on a career as a writer.[65] The subject was seemingly original. The first act of the operetta's spoken dialogue was completed before the war; the second dates from the summer of 1915. All the song texts were written afterward by Stein—that is, in the midst of wartime. The premiere of the operetta, then titled *Es lebe die*

Liebe! [Long Live Love!], was repeatedly delayed; it finally opened at the Johann-Strauss-Theater on November 13, 1915, as *Die Csárdásfürstin* (the name change was due to the success of Oscar Straus's similar-sounding *Rund um die Liebe* [All About Love]).[66] The new title adopts the juxtaposition common to operetta since *Der Zigeunerbaron* and cues the audience that Kálmán's signature musical style will be prominent. But the choice of a Hungarian musical style and an aristocratic title alludes to Strauss's operetta in particular—aptly, since *Die Csárdásfürstin* also juxtaposes Austria and Hungary, albeit under radically different circumstances.[67]

Es lebe die Liebe! would also have been an appropriate title: the operetta offers a catalogue of late imperial courtship rituals and relationships, from romantic monogamy to arranged marriage to promiscuity. And the work's second and final title, *Die Csárdásfürstin*, expediently chosen as it may have been, is also appropriate: by featuring a Budapest nightclub singer as its heroine and an heir to a *Fürst* as its hero, the operetta also portrays a breakdown in hierarchies, the kind of misalliance endemic to operetta titles from merry widows to dollar princesses. The central conflict of a couple separated by social class is familiar, and including a nightclub singer as one of the characters is hardly unique. What gives *Die Csárdásfürstin* its particular character is its canny self-reflexivity and irony.

The work is structured in two juxtaposed sections. In the first act, we are presented with a bevy of colorfully named denizens of a Budapest cabaret, including the singer Sylva Varescu; her admirer, Viennese aristocrat Edwin von und zu Lippert-Weylersheim; and hangers-on Count Boni (Bonifacius) Kancsiánu and Féri von Kerekes. As much as Boni and Féri flirt, it is Edwin and Sylva who are seemingly committed to one another. Edwin is called for military duty (it is implied that this is not wartime but merely routine), and Sylva prepares to depart on a tour of America; however in a typical plot device Edwin first signs a pledge that he will marry her within ten weeks. What Boni knows—and ultimately reveals to Sylva—is that Edwin's parents in Vienna have already arranged for him to marry his cousin, the Countess Stasi.

The action then moves to Vienna (first coyly identified in the *Regiebuch* as "a large metropolis" but specifically named in the score and stage directions). Act 2 opens at the aristocratic Viennese party where Stasi and Edwin's engagement is to be announced. Sylva, accompanied by Boni, turns up incognito as "Countess Kancsiánu," claiming that she and Boni have been married. Stasi, introduced as a naïve but spunky girl, promptly falls in love with Boni. When Stasi finds out that Edwin loves another, she is sympathetic, but Sylva believes she will never be accepted by Edwin's family and has better things to do (cue tragic second act finale). As usual, the third act, set in a Viennese hotel, serves as a somewhat perfunctory attempt to bridge the musical and dramatic gap between the two social spheres, but the librettists added a socially provocative, almost prophetic twist: class distinctions are erased with a recognition scene. The elderly Féri von Kerekes realizes

FIGURE 4.1. *Die Csárdásfürstin* production, September 17, 1915. Bildarchiv Austria, Österreichische Nationalbibliothek.

that Edwin's mother is herself a former nightclub singer, a fact she has concealed for decades, thus dissolving objections to Sylva and Edwin's marriage and allowing for a happy ending.[68]

Die Csárdásfürstin's opening presents its audience with a mirror of themselves: spectators watching a performance. The *Regiebuch* specifies, "the first act takes place in Budapest in an Orpheum...the time is the present." "Orpheum" generally connotes a variety theater playing revues or cabaret acts, a few steps lower on the theatrical food chain than a top-ranked operetta theater like the Johann-Strauss-Theater or the Theater an der Wien.[69] The operetta's set featured a segment of the Budapest theater, including boxes, tables (in the *Parkett* seating area, that is, the "orchestra" or "stalls"), and a small stage, which can be seen from the side. Remarkably, there exists a photograph of this set with the entire cast casually posed in costume onstage (fig. 4.1). Leading actress Mizzi Günther is seated at a table covered in bouquets, leaning back into none other than Kálmán himself. The ornate onstage theater appears to be white with delicate Jugendstil figuration, presumably gold, reproducing the decor of the Johann-Strauss-Theater itself.[70] The costumes suggest that the photo was taken after the end of Act 1.[71]

The operetta opens unusually, not with the usual expository, informative "Introduktion" but rather with a spectacular exotic production number—a song and dance for Sylva entitled, "Heia, heia in den Bergen." Performed in the distanced space of a theater-within-a-theater, the text is not to be taken seriously as plot exposition. But Sylva is established as the queen of the theater space and Kálmán's high csárdás style as its sound. Sylva's song reproduces most of the tropes of Hungarian musical style (ex. 4.3) in a precisely notated fashion. The entire number is in the minor mode, beginning with a rhapsodic, slow section with melismas and an emphasis on the raised sixth degree of the scale (D natural in the third bar of the example); the movement from straight eighth notes to triplets in the vocal part on the words "in den Bergen ist mein Heimatland" creates a rubato effect. The orchestration includes a solo violin in unison with the vocal line, arpeggios in the harp in lieu of a cimbalom, and brass call-and-response style echoes of the vocal line, followed by a fast section also typical of a csárdás.[72]

But "Heia, heia" is a free interpretation of a folk style, not a bid for authenticity. What is typically operetta—and often overlooked—is that it is conscious of its own status as a bit of a cliché, as indicated by its free orchestration and a theatrical frame that places it not in its purported native habitat but rather as a novelty number in a commercial urban theater (and a theater whose parallels with that of the operetta's own space have already been made obvious, at that). Sylva proclaims she is from the mountains and wears a costume from Transylvania (known as Siebenbürg in German, but the Latin "Transilvania" is hinted at in Sylva's name), and she later says she is from Kis-Küküllö, an area populated by both Hungarians and Romanian speakers that was at the time part of Hungary.

At the end of the number, the onstage audience (the chorus and supporting characters) join in to sing a few phrases with Sylva, then clap along as Sylva dances, finally ending with a series of all-purpose "la la las" and three cries of "bravo." This unusual ending both collapses the number's multiple layers of performance and draws the real audience in further. It establishes Sylva's purportedly diegetic performance as part of a communal activity, establishing the fictional Orpheum as a close-knit society (which, we will see, it is). The final bravos are notated for both the chorus alone and prompt the real audience in the Johann-Strauss-Theater to applaud. (Performances of this number as an excerpt inevitably struggle with this ending, often cutting the bravos and coming to an abrupt stop.[73]) Die Csárdásfürstin's audience sees the way Sylva's onstage audience is participating—clapping, singing along, and even finishing the number—and absorbs some of their enjoyment and forgetfulness. It is no accident that this world is the one of Hungarian music, which is not only Kálmán's signature but also a style that connotes inwardness, distance from worldly concerns, and timelessness (as discussed in chapter 3). It is far from the historical frames of Gold gab ich für Eisen.

The song's falseness and collapsing of diegetic and non-diegetic performance

EXAMPLE 4.3. Kálmán, *Die Csárdásfürstin*, No. 1, Lied Sylva mit Chor, vocal entrance

EXAMPLE 4.3. (continued)

dort   wo   schen   blüht das   E - del - weiß,

dort   wo   rings - um glit - zern Schnee und Eis.

molto rit.

are an important element of its message: it presents spectacle, excitement, and pleasure through music and dance divorced from any real-world context. For some modern critics of *Die Csárdásfürstin*, this would seem to be the operetta's entire message in a nutshell, but it is only its opening move. At the same time, however, the song articulates an important feature of the Budapest theater: Sylva introduces herself as a symbol of romantic, eternal love, preaching a near-bourgeois fidelity not normally associated with the fleeting pleasures of the theatrical space she occupies (suggesting right from the start that she will make an appropriate partner for the earnest Edwin). "If you're mine, you must stay, must devote yourself, I must be your heaven and hell," she sings. (Notably, the relationship between style hongrois Jószi and bourgeois Zorika in *Zigeunerliebe*, discussed in the previous chapter, fell apart precisely when Zorika demanded similar monogamy and commitment.) This is further emphasized in No. 5, a number for Sylva, Edwin, and Boni that echoes the structure and style of "Heia, heia" in a non-diegetic context. Sylva advises, "Look in your own heart, not in the tumult of the world."

The Orpheum is presented as a world of escape; several subsequent numbers in Act 1 further elide the lines between diegetic and non-diegetic performance. The act contains two similar songs for Boni and ensemble, written in a bouncy cabaret style, both similar to *Die lustige Witwe*'s "Wie die Weiber": The first, No. 2, "Alle sind wir Sünder" (We are all sinners) expresses love for the ladies of the Orpheum, who do not take love and sex too seriously. In the second, No. 4, "Ganz ohne Weiber geht die Chose nicht" (Without women, nothing works), Boni says that he probably will never be able to give up women entirely. Musically, their brisk marches and syncopation mark them as the cousins of *Der Zigeunerprimas*'s "Hazazaa" and "Tief in unserem Vaterland" (Deep in our fatherland). They are also exactly the sorts of numbers one would hear onstage in a variety theater such as the one in which the act is set. Their message might seem opposed to Sylva's doctrine of fidelity, but this is not presented as a conflict. The key features of the Orpheum, ultimately articulated in Act 3's trio No. 14, "Nimm, Zigeuner, deine Geige," are the pursuit of love and the expression of self.

The true alternative is in fact Vienna's world of aristocratic courtship, the setting of Act 2. The gap between the two worlds is spatial—between the two halves of the Austro-Hungarian Empire—but it is also temporal and again self-reflexive. Act 1's Budapest was the world of pleasure and love—even true love—set to up-to-date, popular musical styles, the hallmarks of a Silver Age operetta. Vienna, however, is presented as a world governed by social strictures and manners that paper over hypocrisy and unhappiness. This is communicated through a musical setting that is distinctly that of the nineteenth-century Golden Age: it features satirical, Offenbach-like text settings as well as old-fashioned Strauss-like waltzes. As in *Die lustige Witwe*, musical style is deployed self-reflexively.

Like the first act, the action focuses on courtship and performance, the Budapest chorus girls supplanted by a Viennese ball. The setting is described in the *Regiebuch* as "a large hall in the villa of the Fürst Lippert-Weylersheim. Adjoining ballroom, from where music can be heard at the beginning of the act. We see young couples dancing."[74] In place of the exotic dance number that opens most Silver Age second acts, the music is an old-fashioned Johann Strauss II instrumental waltz, making Vienna itself serve the role of exotic locale and symbol. (Arguably, "Heia, Heia" has already provided the requisite major exotic production number in Act 1.) The satiric elements, however, emerge more clearly in No. 10, a musically similar waltz that is a quartet of a distinctly bitter character for the leads, who have found themselves in a *Così fan tutte*–like situation (ex. 4.4). All four are unhappy with each other: Sylva believes Edwin and Stasi are engaged, and Edwin believes Sylva and Boni are married. (Both beliefs are false.) This rage is expressed in an outwardly refined waltz in a nineteenth-century style, exhibiting the fast tempo, hemiolas, and many of the rhythmic patterns identified by Max Schönherr as typical of the nineteenth-century danced waltz.[75] The number is seemingly an

EXAMPLE 4.4. Kálmán, *Die Csárdásfürstin*, No. 10, Quartett, first verse, second strain

(Tempo di Valse)

BONI (*zu Sylva*)

Mut - zi mich reißt es, Put - zi, mich schmeißt es juk - kend, zuk - kend zu dir!

Hupf' mit mir du sü - ßes Mop - si! Mach' mit mir ein klei - nes

Hop - si, Zuk - ker weib gib ei - nen Wal - zer

SYLVA

zu! Kei - ne tanzt Pol - ka wie du! Lieb - ling

example of Kraus's "fossilized forms" but one that has been deliberately turned on its head.

Again, the distance between appearance and reality is revealed through dramatic irony. The characters are paired incorrectly, yet sing, in a fast and bright Viennese-style waltz, about how much they love their respective partners. But the language quickly descends into nonsensical endearments and contradictions:

Mutzi, mich reißt es	Mutzi, it seizes me,
Putzi, mich schmeißt es	Putzi, it throws me,
jukkend, zukkend zu dir!	Itching, twitching to you!
Hupf' mit mir du süßen Mopsi!	Hop with me, my sweet puppy!
Mach' mit mir ein kleines Hopsi!	Make a little leap with me!
Zukkerweib, gib einen Walzer zu!	Sweet women, give me a waltz!
Keine tanzt Polka wie du!	No one dances a polka like you!

Why is anyone hopping during a waltz? The refrain, sung in unison, becomes increasingly frantic: "Hurrah, hurrah! One lives only once and once is nothing, one lives only once, yes!" While the sentiments are not far from those of Budapest, all are aware that the situation is entirely wrong. The Viennese waltz here symbolizes social hypocrisy and the artifice of etiquette, whereas the unconstrained style hongrois found not in the high society ballroom but in the lowly Orpheum is the real utopia of romance. (A similar disjunct between text and music can be found in the Offenbachian No. 8, the "Schwalbenduett" [Swallow Duet] for Stasi and Boni.)

Sylva and Edwin's two duets, No. 3, "Sylva, ich will nur dich," and No. 9, "Heller Jubel," stand outside this opposition.[76] Both are slow waltzes, Kálmán's preferred form for wistfulness and remembrance (as heard in the Prologue to *Gold gab ich für Eisen*), whose texts recall the good old days; the music of the second, Vienna-set number even recalls the Budapest setting of the first. Both employ a similar neighbor-note figure in the verse section. Additionally, the words of the second waltz explicitly recall the events of the first act as Sylva and Edwin describe their bygone romance as a "lustiger Roman" (happy fiction), not reality. Yet the libretto finds a way to make it true: in Act 3, Orpheum regular Féri recognizes Edwin's mother as a former nightclub singer, revealing her condemnation of Sylva as hypocrisy and immediately rendering it invalid.

This abrupt collapse of the old social order recalls the apocalyptic thread running through the song texts: "who knows how much longer the world will turn," "one lives only once and once is nothing," "yes, those were dear times, they are now gone forever." Genuine joy is found only in the memory of the past or the delirious present. The operetta endorses the latter. The social distinctions of Edwin's Viennese family are founded on hypocrisy (and Sylva does not view joining the family as social advancement). Nor does the operetta advocate for the Orpheum as the future—at no point does *Die Csárdásfürstin* seem to provide a vision of any future at all. Rather, *Die Csárdásfürstin* is dedicated to the enjoyment of the present, uncertain and insecure as it might be.[77]

That insecurity was not lost on contemporary audiences. *Die Csárdásfürstin* was a smash hit, running for 533 performances, until May 1917. But contra Richard Traubner's assessment of the operetta's "genial high spirits," almost all the critics commented that it was very serious. The *Neue Freie Presse's* Ludwig Hirschfeld wrote, "One might perhaps only mention in passing that the piece's concept and realization isn't comic enough. The mixture of social oppositions and psychological problems is portrayed with too much righteous seriousness, and the smiles of the audience, sympathetically following along, dissolve into tears."[78] In the *Neue Wiener Journal* Alexander Engel concurred but extended the description of seriousness to include the second act as well, writing, "In the first two acts the authors avoid almost all opportunities for situation comedy... giving the work a certain gravity."[79] *Die Zeit* agreed but casts a more positive light on the development:

> The contents opera, the form operetta. Tragic developments with a happy ending, that still suffers no lack of tempestuous scenes or melancholy music.... Yesterday's success was, however, a distinctly theatrical and dramatic one, that above all belongs to the librettists, who took advantage of all the proven devices as well as many new comic and tragic ones.[80]

The *Wiener Abendpost's* critic perhaps came up with the best description of the operetta's mixture of comedy and sadness: "smiling through tears."[81]

The reviews for Kálmán's score were nearly universally positive; most commented on his penchant for Hungarian national music, which was now recognized as his trademark. Engel wrote that "the most worthwhile numbers are the national ones,"[82] while Hirschfeld proclaimed his Hungarianisms uniquely authentic: "Kálmán's Hungarian music is not faked; much of it, like the opposing rhythmic movements of the instrumental voices, the embellishments, and rubato tempos, seem to be taken from real Gypsy music."[83] Unlike some of his previous efforts, his waltzes also received good reviews. In the *Fremden-Blatt*, Julius Stern noted, "Melodically and rhythmically, he is devoted to his homeland's genius—one hears it gladly. But then he remembers that there is also life outside Hungary and lets out waltzes of various temperaments: melancholy, easygoing, jubilant, lyrical, created only for dancing, but no ordinary 'sensational' ones."[84] Ludwig Karpath of the *Neues Wiener Tagblatt* cannily said, while mixing his metaphors, "Kálmán is, if one can say this, the proper Compromise composer [*Ausgleich*, referring to the Compromise of 1867, which established Austria-Hungary], always standing with one foot in the Hungarian scale and the other on the dance floor, where a Viennese waltz is playing."[85] Most of all, critics agreed that the music worked with the subject. Stern noted, "everything has color—and well chosen—and it fits every scene, even every word."[86]

THE WRECKAGE OF WAR

For Karl Kraus, *Die Csárdásfürstin*'s promise of apocalyptic liberation was unforgivably irresponsible, part of a conspiracy to mollify a population that should have been outraged at the massive crimes perpetuated upon them. But operetta creators were not a function of the state, and their work not a product of it. While at times, as in *Gold gab ich für Eisen*, they worked in coordination with the state's goals, their work was also a product of the same confusion and powerlessness being experienced by the rest of Austria-Hungary's citizenry. By 1915 the war was not to be stopped, and *Die Csárdásfürstin* articulates a very real powerlessness and confusion felt among the general population, as well as an endorsement of operetta itself as the solution for their woes.

Kálmán and the operetta industry as a whole were loyal to the state throughout the war. But were they, as portrayed by Kraus, part of it? As discussed in chapter 2, operetta operated both inside and outside the mainstream. As Jews, the creators of operetta held a particular loyalty to the Austro-Hungarian state scorned by Kraus. For many Jews, World War I was an opportunity to demonstrate patriotism and service to a state that had offered them a remarkably secure home.[87] Kálmán and Léon's tribute to Germanic patriotism in *Gold gab ich für Eisen* is, in this light, nothing less than a bid to be considered worthy citizens of a Germanic state, and *Die Csárdásfürstin* evinces the early premonitions of an identity crisis that would engulf Austria after the war's end.

While the creators of operetta may not have been as representative of a malignant establishment as Kraus often suggested, his portrayal raises other questions regarding an operetta's status as a musical work. As described, Kraus shuffled operetta excerpts fairly indiscriminately and intentionally fragmented his source material. Like most of the music of *Die letzten Tage der Menschheit*, Kraus's vision of an operetta is less a work encompassing score, libretto, and staging than snatches of music he may have heard in a café—the very place most of the operetta music in *Die letzten Tagen von Menschheit* occurs. But which experience should take precedence: Kraus's decontextualized excerpts or the comparatively prestigious performance inside a theater? What can properly be called operetta? Operetta advocates portrayed their works as carefully composed, individual entities and yet simultaneously pursued this easy and lucrative trade in fragments. For critics, operetta's life in the street—and its composers' enthusiastic pursuit of this fame and reputation—overshadowed and even invalidated its creators' plea for consideration as a musical work equal to an opera or a symphony.

But the meaning of *Die Csárdásfürstin*'s individual musical numbers is found only in the context of its larger story. Peter Konwitschny's bombs in Dresden, discussed at the outset of this chapter, are in a way an expansion of the work's context and history, the recovery of an experience written into the operetta's reception. While Konwitschny amplified these fault lines, other productions have attempted to erase them altogether. In 1987 the Volksoper endeavored to produce *Die Csárdásfürstin* in the light, entertaining style favored by the theater. Robert Herzl's production moved the Act 2 quartet to Act 3 and rearranged it. Originally portraying the lovers paired incorrectly, in the new version they appear in their final configuration—Edwin and Sylva with Stasi and Boni—and the number's bitterly sarcastic tone, set to falsely triumphant music, is made entirely sincere. The original text, it seemed, had proved too equivocal, too difficult in tone for a contemporary entertainment. As the changes were unnoted in the program (and several were probably already familiar to audience members from the ultra-kitsch 1971 German TV film version starring René Kollo and Anna Moffo), few were likely aware that this *Csárdásfürstin* had been methodically de-ironicized.[88]

Exotic Liaisons

Reizend war der erste Akt,	The first act was charming
Spannend und exotisch,	Exciting and exotic,
Endlich was, das wirklich packt,	Finally something really thrilling
Und so hübsch erotisch!	And so nicely erotic!
Die Musik, Sie warden seh'n	The music, you will see
Mach noch Karriére [sic],	Will make careers,
Auch der Title, wunderschön klingt	The title also sounds gorgeous:
"Die Bajadere"!	"The Bayadere"!
Reizend finden wir das Milieu	We find the setting charming,
Die Kostüme stilvoll,	The costumes stylish
Ganz entzükkend ist die Idee;	The whole thing is enchanting;
Heiter und gefühlvoll!	Funny and expressive![1]

It could be a review in verse. But these lines were sung by a chorus onstage. They summarize the appeal of exotic music: eroticism, beauty, enchantment, thrill. As suggested by this description, Emmerich Kálmán's 1921 operetta *Die Bajadere* is conventionally exotic. The heroine is first heard offstage, her voice tracing a sinuous melisma. There is an oft-reprised love duet entitled "Lotusblume, ich liebe dich" (Lotus flower, I love you). The text also encapsulates what audiences sought in postwar operetta, including excitement, emotional twists and turns, stylish costumes, and the arrival of a new star—in this case, the composer. But this isn't a review at all; rather these verses are drawn from the opening scene of *Die Bajadere* itself.

The operetta's plot concerns the production of the titular operetta-within-the-operetta whose leading actress, playing an Indian priestess, so enchants actual Indian prince Radjami that he falls in love with her. *Die Bajadere* thus frames itself as an operetta about the pleasures of operetta, a reflexivity even more concentrated than that of *Die Csárdásfürstin*. Prominent among these pleasures is exoticism, but, like Sylva Varescu's "Heia, heia," this is not an exoticism that claims to represent another culture. Instead, it seeks only the thrills of extravagant, fantastic visuals and distance from the quotidian—wrapping those thrills in self-aware exotic clichés. The self-proclaimed artificiality of *Die Bajadere's* Indian priestess— whom we soon meet as Odette Darimode, Parisian actress and exemplary New Woman—does nothing to diminish her charms. It is precisely this self-conscious fakeness that is characteristic of operetta exoticism, which surged in popularity in the postwar period.

After World War I the Viennese had to come to terms with the Austro-Hungarian Empire's dissolution and the city's attendant loss of status. The new Austrian First Republic was beset with enormous economic and political instability, which necessarily had an impact on commercial theater. In addition, operetta now had to compete with the novelty and cheap ticket prices of film, as well as opulent revues. One of the responses to this competition was to increase operetta's visual appeal with ever more spectacular productions. Operettas of this period often featured extravagant exotic settings, juxtaposed with an act set in Vienna or another familiar location in Western Europe. Yet the desire to put strange lands on display was also political: it was symptomatic of a nation and people struggling to come to terms with their place in Europe and the world, negotiating new relationships with foreign powers, and simultaneously reasserting their own greatness. The exotic music heard in many works of this period was also frequently understood as a retreat from difficult modern social realities into a timeless, sensual world of feeling.

This chapter considers the prominence of these exotic spaces within the new realities of life in Vienna during and after the war. The works under discussion are Leo Fall's Turkish fantasy, *Die Rose von Stambul* (1916); *Die Bajadere* (1921, already introduced); and Franz Lehár's tragic journey to China, *Das Land des Lächelns* (1929), all of which portray a young male heir struggling to modernize his old-fashioned empire and contending with that greatest of threats, the modern woman. The exotic settings of operetta represent a conscious attempt to map Austria's changing place in the world order. These operettas offered a postwar and post-imperial alternative to the intra-imperial juxtapositions of *Die lustige Witwe* (discussed in chapter 1). Now the Viennese had to contend with the whole world: foreign people whose ways were mysterious and whose attractions were irresistible. The drastic changes in Vienna's fortunes necessitated negotiation and adjustment in a genre whose identity was closely bound to the city's own glories. In fact, the exotic absolute states included in operettas may not have been foreign at all, frequently recalling the Austro-Hungarian police state that had been abruptly signed out of existence. At the same time, these operettas conjure up

a kind of sentimental universalism. Beneath cultural differences, operetta composers and librettists insist that all people are basically the same. The result is a
strange mélange of distancing and the unexpectedly familiar, of masks assumed
and removed.

AUSTRIA AND OPERETTA IN TRANSITION

In the aftermath of World War I, operetta continued to thrive even as Austria
starved. As the *Arbeiter-Zeitung* noted in 1918, "Perhaps the Viennese operetta is
the apocalypse itself. The liquidation of the Austrian world is carried out alongside
operetta premieres and the opening of new operetta theaters."[2] (A coal shortage
shut down theaters that year, but only briefly.) Indeed, the empire, the Habsburg
regime, and its political apparatus had all seemingly vanished overnight.

Unlike other new postwar states, the Republic of Austria was created not by
nationalism but by diplomatic demands. The resulting German-speaking Austria
did not measure up to nineteenth-century nationalist ideals. Cultural leaders such
as Hugo von Hofmannsthal tried to create a new anti-nationalist Austrian culture
that would serve a moderating, neutral function, but ultimately most Austrians felt
a stronger allegiance to Germany than they did to their new state.[3] The economy
was also left in shambles. After a period of hyperinflation, the schilling replaced
the krone in 1925, but unemployment remained high. Politics was factionalized,
anti-Semitism rose sharply, and a great deal of civil society revolved around German nationalist groups and their militias.

Eventually theaters suffered too. While they had initially continued to proliferate, in the 1920s even the most established stages went through rough patches.
The Carl-Theater and Neue Wiener Bühne closed permanently, and the Johann-
Strauss-Theater was converted into a cinema in 1931.[4] (Silent film was a serious
threat to operetta; sound film proved an existential one.) The immediate cause was
the debilitating luxury taxes (*Lustbarkeitssteuer*) imposed on theaters by the city
government. In 1918 the tax rate was set at 4 percent for spoken theater, 8 percent
for opera and operetta, and 10 percent for film and variety theater. In 1920 the
rates were raised to 5, 10, and 15 percent, and in 1921 raised again to double the
1920 rates, with a ceiling of 20 percent for longer runs.[5] The Socialists considered
operetta ideologically suspect and found in its popularity a source of income for
the city's social improvement projects. (The rates were lowered in 1927.)

Following the war, camaraderie within the industry seems to have disappeared.
The 1920s witnessed a constant succession of temporary and permanent closures;
strikes; conflicts between major composers, librettists, and impresarios both public and private; and accusations of corruption, plagiarism, nepotism, and all manner of dirty dealing. The Theater an der Wien remained preeminent. Intendant
Wilhelm Karczag died suddenly in 1923, and the theater was taken over by his

son-in-law, actor Hubert Marischka. Marischka eventually bought the enterprise outright from the remaining shareholders, making him a rare sole owner. He eventually presided over a shaky empire of three theaters and a publishing company with stakes in film, radio, and records.[6]

To cope with the taxes, theaters raised ticket prices and, because they were operating on narrower margins, became risk averse. More operettas ran for much longer than they had before the war—many for hundreds of performances in a row—and once interest dropped, a production would sometimes be transferred to a smaller theater under the same management. Moreover, even though overhead was low, it became difficult to consistently fill seats, and theaters began to give out more and more free tickets. In 1928 Marischka took the extreme measure of renting the Theater an der Wien out to director Max Reinhardt, giving up on his own productions, a controversial decision.[7] Operetta would continue to attract audiences in droves for the next decade, but Vienna began to share its status as operetta epicenter with Berlin, a more prosperous city with different theatrical traditions (and during this period many Viennese composers wrote for and spent time in Berlin's increasingly lucrative market). Many of the works that were successful—Franz Lehár's opera-like operettas for Richard Tauber, Emmerich Kálmán's jazz-influenced operettas, and the revue-operettas of Ralph Benatzky and Paul Abraham, such as *Im weissen Rößl* and *Viktoria und ihr Husar*—were very different from the Kakanian creations of the previous decade. The exoticism of the 1920s, which opposed the familiar Austria with the novel spectacle of a distant land, provided a bridge from the imperial visions of the Dual Empire era to the revue operettas of the genre's final flowering.

OPERETTA'S EXOTICISM

Exoticism in Viennese operetta was not new, but, as already seen in *Der Zigeunerprimas* (chapter 3), it was not an easy fit for traditional musicological models. Typically, scholars interrogate the representation of the non-Western culture with regard to authenticity and consider the power relations involved.[8] But the exotic realms of operetta composers and librettists are often explicitly marked as fake from the start. The division between East and West is ultimately revealed to be illusionary or unimportant; the main characters share a common humanity. "My love and your love, they're the same, I love you and you love me, and that is all," sing the Viennese Count Gustl and the Chinese princess Mi in *Das Land des Lächelns*. While exoticism is seemingly predicated on the notion of difference, in operetta that difference is frequently subverted. In his study *Musical Exoticism: Images and Reflections*, Ralph Locke argues for a "Full-Context" paradigm, which can find exoticism in moments lacking in many of the conventional musical markers of such.[9] Analyzing operetta's exoticism, however, requires something more like the opposite: one must suspect that not all that appears exotic actually is. Ex-oticism was an attraction but did not run so deep as to penetrate actors' customary star images, nor did a novel setting prove any impediment to operetta's most conventional dramaturgical moves. Its deployment is partial, sometimes ambivalent, and often less than skin deep.

Operetta's exotic spaces represent, more explicitly than in opera, psychological rather than physical zones. In this, operetta has much in common with other Austrian culture of its time, which, Robert Lemon has argued, often takes the form of self-critique, "invoking the oriental 'Other' not to bolster Occidental imperialism but rather to express concerns about their own troubled empire."[10] The East of Austrian literature, Lemon argues, is a relativistic place that is both East and West at once, located not in a distant colony but rather in the Austrian subject's own mind, and acts as a metaphor for Austro-Hungarian relations. Such is also the case in operetta. Many of these operettas transmit, at least at points, a message of universalism and tolerance perhaps typical of their Jewish creators.[11] But they should not be mistaken for a transcultural experience. Exotic people appear within the norms of the genre, and usually in full recognition of their stagy fakeness.

Operetta exoticism followed the same fads of literature and film, and the plotlines recall contemporaneous novels and films like *The Sheik* and *The Prisoner of Zenda*. The problems that afflict operetta's foreign lands are often familiar. Many concern the role of women. Unlike opera, many prominent exotic operettas feature a Western woman paired with an exotic man, allowing librettos to explicitly engage with the role of women in European society.[12] Just after the imperial house abruptly exited the public stage, most postwar exotic operettas conspicuously fixate on those exotic lands' crises of succession. Their central conceit of a young heir struggling to modernize his outmoded state was thus both nostalgic and newly timely, now existing in an age when change in Austria was no longer hypothetical or optional. Their engagement with the crumbling world around them varies, but the divisions between the self and the non-self are rarely as simple as the straightforward musical dualism of Silver Age operetta may suggest.

DIE ROSE VON STAMBUL: TURKISH DELIGHT

The first of the new exotic operettas was Leo Fall's *Die Rose von Stambul* (1916), which takes on the unusual subject of women's rights in modern Turkey, ensconced in the usual marriage plot. Although it was written at a time when Turkey was both accessible and an important wartime ally of Austria-Hungary, Fall and his librettists Julius Brammer and Alfred Grünwald rely largely on old-fashioned *alla turca* clichés whose music and text occasionally even evoke *Die Entführung aus dem Serail*. This approach was seen by some critics, perhaps for the first time, as inappropriate. Fall and his librettists' efforts to simultaneously meet the genre expectations of a modern operetta, indulge in exoticism, and conform to the censor's prohibition against disparaging a war ally produced strange results. Is the Istanbul of *Die Rose von Stambul* intended to be, as one critic wrote, Vienna with a fez? Or is Fall's wartime operetta a genuine effort at cross-cultural understanding or even musical diplomacy?

During World War I, Turkish culture became a matter of great importance to the Viennese. The Ottoman Empire's two sieges of Vienna had a prominent place in the city's historical memory, extending even to a legend regarding the arrival of coffee in the city. But when the Ottoman Empire joined the Central Powers in August 1914, the Austro-Hungarian state launched a major public relations campaign to convince its citizenry that the Turks were now their friends—usually portraying the relationship explicitly in warm and personal terms of friendship. Books were published on Turkish culture, religion, and customs, mostly in the spirit of understanding.[13] The goal was to humanize the long-demonized Turkish state and people to the Viennese so they would be seen as a valuable and reliable ally. Operetta, seen as a local product, might seem an unusual venue for such an effort, but the creators of *Die Rose von Stambul* were known for their unusual interests. Fall specialized in operettas dealing with socially progressive or scandalous women, such as the daughter of an American industrialist in *Die Dollarprinzessin*, suffragettes in London (*Jung-England*), and Lola Montez (*Die Studentengräfin*).[14] Librettists Brammer and Grünwald would go on to write a string of hits for Emmerich Kálmán in the 1920s, including *Die Bajadere*, *Gräfin Mariza*, *Die Zirkusprinzessin*, and *Die Herzogin von Chicago*.[15]

Die Rose von Stambul is set in modern Istanbul (the "Stambul" of the title). The protagonist is a determined young Turkish woman named Kondja Gül, the daughter of politician Kamek Pascha. Westernized, tennis-playing Kondja doesn't want to submit to an arranged marriage. She would rather elope with André Léry, a French author popular among the women of Stambul, with whom she has carried on a passionate correspondence. Little does Kondja know that André Léry is actually eligible Turkish bachelor Achmed Bey, coincidentally also the fiancé chosen by her parents (this plot recalls Lehár's 1909 hit *Der Graf von Luxemburg*). The secondary plot deals with Kondja's friend Midili and her romance with Fridolin Müller, a German tourist who is also facing an enforced betrothal imposed by his Hamburg industrialist father (a parallelism that suggests that Europeans should not feel too superior).

Brammer and Grünwald's libretto evokes a variety of Orientalist clichés, even noting in a stage direction, without further explanation, that the servants appear "more Indian than Turkish in style."[16] Istanbul is visible through the windows, but, tellingly, the only things the authors can imagine the Turkish skyline to contain are "mosques and minarets." The original title in the libretto typescript is not *Die Rose von Stambul* but the geographically dubious *1,001 Souper* (*1,001 Suppers*, as in

Arabian Nights, preserved as the final line of Achmed's entrance song), perhaps an indication of the operetta's shaky claim to authenticity. Furthermore, the contemporary press did not think much of Brammer and Grünwald's research. As the *Neues Wiener Journal* put it, "They are less up on customs and usage in Turkey then they are on the Occidental *Schwank*, operetta, and joke book."[17] The stage descriptions of the first act read in part, "like the rooms of a young European woman, and yet it is immediately apparent that this salon is found in the Orient," naming the requisite ornamental screens.[18] It is simultaneously exotic and not.

But if the visuals of the operetta relied on clichés, the characterization shows that the librettists had at least some awareness of modern Turkish politics. The name of Kondja's father, Kemal Pascha (given as Kamek Pascha in some texts[19]) was presumably intended to evoke that of Mustafa Kemal, known at the time as Kemal Pasha (*Pascha* in German), the future Atatürk. At the time of the operetta's composition, he was known as one of the Young Turks, associated with Westernization and modernization. As for the operetta's Achmed, Fall's biographers point out that the image of a Western-oriented Turkish character may have also been based on Enver Pasha, another Young Turk who commanded Turkish forces during the Balkan Wars and World War I and had served as a Turkish envoy to Berlin and Vienna.[20] The Viennese had a long history of imagining Turkey—and in the Viennese vision of Istanbul, Europe was inevitably a beacon of enlightened modernity set against local prejudice and backwardness.[21]

Critics immediately read *Die Rose von Stambul* as an attempt at a kind of one-sided musical diplomacy, but they did not agree on its message. The *Österreichische Volks-Zeitung* asked, "Are the brave, gallant Turks not close enough to us that we can portray their milieu only through false, erotic operetta effects?"[22] On the other side, *Die Bombe* called the operetta a product of the alliance: "Our alliance with Turkey, so generous for all parties, has as a side effect spawned an operetta by Leo Fall."[23] Simultaneously, some elements of the onstage Turkey can be easily seen as representations of Austrian concerns, and modern scholars have read the operetta largely in such a light. The opposition between Turkey and an enlightened Western Europe could just as easily be set entirely in Western or Central Europe (indeed, variations on the arranged-marriage plot are common in Europe-set operettas such as *Ein Walzertraum* and *Die Csárdásfürstin*, and the conflict between old and new mores is central to the plots of *Die Csárdásfürstin*, *Der Zigeunerprimas*, and *Die lustige Witwe*). The operetta specifically references common wartime problems of hunger, flour shortages, and cigarette shortages, as well as exemplifying the "message of multinational harmony" Steven Beller considers characteristic of wartime works.[24]

But while the librettists' engagement with Turkish culture was limited, the setting was more than window dressing and less friendly than it may appear in summary. The compositional process of *Die Rose von Stambul* is unusually well documented, and examining drafts of the libretto gives a rarely seen perspective on how the work changed, particularly in response to concerns by the police censor. Three drafts survive: an early typescript of Act 1 only, the complete script submitted to the censor, and the printed *Regiebuch*.[25] The earlier versions of the work promote a more traditional Orientalized, threatening Turkey; by the end of the process the setting was a bit more ambiguous, mixing East and West. (Not scrutinized by the censor, the score practices a more straightforward division.) The libretto's basic subject posed several obvious censorial pitfalls. The denigration of another nation—as the censor understandably interpreted most of Brammer and Grünwald's evocations of the savage Turk—was against the censor's rules in peacetime, and during wartime any insult of one of Austria-Hungary's allies was certainly not to be permitted.

The Turkish angle, particularly references to Turkish culture that could be considered derogatory (most of them about women's rights), recedes in each successive version. For example, in the early drafts, the operetta began with a song by Kondja's friend Bül-Bül, sung to a text that was pronouncedly exotic and sexualized in its images, even threatening (and a somewhat unexpected opening for what is otherwise a harmless, not particularly dark operetta). No music survives.

DIE ROSE VON STAMBUL, CUT VERSION OF NO. 1

BÜL-BÜL:	BÜL-BÜL:
Tanze, tanze schlanke Odaliske,	Dance, dance, slim odalisque
Bis sein Auge trunken wird	Until your eyes are drunken
Von dem Glanze deiner Schönheit,	With the light of your beauty
Bis dein Blick sein Herz verwirrt	Until your glance bewilders his heart
Tanz – du Liebchen des Kalifen,	Dance—you beloved of the caliph,
Wecke seine wilde Lust,	Awaken his wild lust,
Wenn dein Herz vor Angst auch zittert,	If your heart also shakes with fear,
Tanz! Daß du nicht sterben mußt.	Dance! So that you may not die.[26]

It is unclear exactly why this text was cut, but it is difficult imagine that it would pass the censor. It was replaced by a much less intense, brighter song sung directly to Kondja ("May your dreams be blissful, may your awakening be sunny!"). Other lines ruled out by the censor included Fridolin's "Of course he has two wives, he's a Turk!" and Kondja's father's on-the-nose speech: "Around here, the only thing we recognize is a done deal! Achmed Bey, the son of the minister, offered her his hand. He doesn't know her, she doesn't know him, the wedding is in five days."[27]

Absent the opportunity for the expected villainy, *Die Rose von Stambul* becomes, like many operettas, self-reflexive. What the women of Turkey seem to long for is the experience of a conventional Viennese operetta heroine. The women's desired reforms amount to Westernization, including typical operetta activities such as dancing the waltz, kissing, and courtship, as described in a song text that was struck both in the draft and in the censor's script but appears in all of the published texts and appears to have been reinstated (No. 3, "Von Reformen, ganz enormen"). The romance offered to Kondja by "André Léry"—Achmed's nom de plume—similarly includes libretto standbys of writing love letters and dancing the waltz. As a piece of war propaganda, the operetta suggests that a closer relationship between Turkey and Austria-Hungary will benefit both parties and that the Viennese have nothing to fear, but this is represented as a one-sided assimilation of the Turkish characters to operetta's culture and values.

Fall's score, however, faced no comparable censorship (only librettos were submitted to the police) and leans more obviously on traditional exotic idioms. The composer adopted the dualistic style of operetta to juxtapose *alla turca* scene-setting with the marketable and expected Viennese forms of waltz and march. The Turkish elements of the score fit neatly into a preexisting Viennese discourse of exotic and *alla turca* music: jangling percussion, static repetition, and ostinatos as well as more broadly exotic musical characteristics like wordless melismas and whole-tone scales (it lacks the rubato that marks "Gypsy" music operetta, which it otherwise resembles). Thus, while the libretto blurs lines between West and East, the score imposes clearer barriers, using Turkish music to establish Kondja's restrictive world and setting her and Achmed's modern, Westernized romance in the modern, Viennese operetta music. (The prevalence of waltzes is explained diegetically: Achmed Bey spent time as a diplomat in both Berlin and Vienna, where he learned to dance.) The result is a score in which the exotic has an unusual function: for Kondja, the alluring foreign sound is that of Western operetta, not Turkey. At the same time, Fall's music portrays a Turkey that is threatening and violent in traditional ways—in fact in the simple terms that the censor resisted in the libretto.

The operetta opens with a blaring theme associated with the totalitarian and conservative aspects of Turkish society, in which the winds outline a whole-tone scale, and an *alla turca* ostinato accompaniment of drums and tambourines (ex. 5.1).[28] This is immediately juxtaposed with the languid, female-gendered ex-oticism of the revised opening chorus, with a cello accompaniment in open fifths, strumming harps, and a narrow, sinuous melody. Like the orchestra in *Ein Walz-ertraum*, the women are first heard offstage and not seen.

Yet this exoticism is complicated in the first scene when Kondja, now onstage with the women, narrates her life story. She begins by repeating the music from this chorus to describe how she spent her early childhood in the country. But when she moved to Istanbul, she says, she needed to become more cultured and worldly. As she describes her education in Western pursuits such as tennis and flirting, the music moves into a section marked "Im Walzertempo." When she turned fourteen, Kondja says, she was told she now needed to wear a veil (ex. 5.2), and the Turkish theme from the opening bursts in from the orchestra, fortissimo and with a gong for good measure. The musical message is simple and obvious:

EXAMPLE 5.1. Leo Fall, *Die Rose von Stambul,* No. 1, Introduktion und Lied, opening

EXAMPLE 5.2. Fall, *Die Rose von Stambul,* No. 2, Auftritt, after rehearsal figure 8

Turkish society (as represented by the whole-tone scale) maintains an oppressive hold on women's lives.[29]

Kondja is forced back into *alla turca*, as she is forced to wear a veil, but Achmed's dual identity as French writer André Léry and Turkish man allows him to switch voices freely. In the early draft of the libretto, he is described as being "dressed in the modern style according to the latest European fashions...only the fez recalls the Ottoman."[30] Except for an easily removed hat of exoticism, he appears European, though "dark-colored," indicating blackface, relatively rare in operetta but certainly not on the stage in general. In the final, published libretto, this description is altered to "a consummate gentleman in demeanor and appearance, he wears a modern Turkish uniform with Persian collar, monocle."[31]

Achmed's first two songs, "O Rose von Stambul" and "Ein Walzer muß es sein," are both waltzes. The first, his entrance song (ex. 5.3), begins in a low vocal register in the minor with an exotic ostinato accompaniment of a tambourine as he describes, in context somewhat inexplicably, what Western Europeans think of Turkish men: "They say of us, that when it comes to ladies we are true to one principle: love *en gros*." But, he says, this is no longer the case, and as he makes this point he briefly modulates to major and ascends to a series of high notes, making this sentiment sound literally brighter and freer. The refrain is a waltz, a declaration of love to his unknown epistolary sweetheart, in pure E major and frequently ascending to the upper register of the voice. This particular use of the high register of the male voice will be seen again in *Das Land des Lächelns*.

In Act 2, he teaches Kondja how to waltz in the number "Ein Walzer muß es sein." This song was evidently the operetta's crowning achievement and was mentioned by all the critics: "a *Tanzwalzer*, one that is surely one of the best and most beautiful that [Fall] has obtained for a long time. That's the high point of the operetta."[32] The *Neues Wiener Tagblatt* went as far as to refer to it as the operetta's *Hauptwalzer* (main waltz).[33] The number is indeed an *echt*-Wiener waltz, full of the traditional nineteenth-century rhythmic figures of Johann Strauss II, and the text self-reflexively describes the amorous effects of the dance. While the opening women's chorus shows a sexualized East, the sound of romance, in both songs, is explicitly marked as Western. Like the French name of Achmed's alter ego, the operetta posits romance as the domain of Europe (and in Act 3 Kondja eventually escapes to Switzerland). The operetta's Turkish characters are sympathetic and not terribly foreign, but its values demonstrate traditionally bifurcated Orientalism.

Critics were more generic in their description of the exotic music, writing that Fall "draws on the melancholy minor scale of the Orient" and that the score "naturally has an Oriental tone in many songs."[34] A reviewer for the *Fremden-Blatt* praised *Die Rose von Stambul* for making the most of "the charming opportunities afforded by the setting, such as the contrast between East and West."[35] But the anonymous reviewer for the *Neues Wiener Journal* suggested that Fall's "colorful"

EXAMPLE 5.3. Fall, *Die Rose von Stambul*, No. 5, Lied des Achmed Bey, opening

use of percussion instruments and winds merely provided him with an exotic foreign mask of "noises," which "sometimes hinders him" but gradually slides away to reveal his true Viennese face:

> The first chords that mount from the orchestra already show a thoroughly characterized color that completely suits the milieu; a refined mixture of woodwinds, xylophone, and sparingly utilized jingle bells. But everywhere, twisted and covered by distant-exotic noises, though shy and only perceptible to the trained ear, the Viennese melody, until it suddenly, tired of modesty, pulses up, triumphantly soaring.[36]

Similarly, Ludwig Karpath wrote, "Without regard to the heavy air of the magic garden of the end of an Oriental fairy tale, he considers, with a spirited haste, his Viennese-ness."[37] The *Fremden-Blatt* was most straightforward, describing *Rose* as a Viennese operetta wearing a fez.[38] This is not wrong, but it is limited: while the libretto promises that the power of operetta could create a culturally colonial rapprochement between Austria and its traditional foe, Fall's score suggests that the Austrians still had farther to go before seeing the Ottoman Empire as something more than a conventionally exoticized Other. It is telling that Fall's Viennese voice emerges only when his characters are acting sympathetically and vanishes when they are not.

Die Rose von Stambul was one of the greatest successes of the war years, rivaled only by *Die Csárdásfürstin* (discussed in chapter 4), and was also a great hit in Berlin, where it starred Leo Fall's favorite diva, Fritzi Massary. As Pyka points out, it served as first-rate wartime entertainment, imagining a luxurious and comfortable world without borders (one critic even pointed out that the Act 3 trip to Switzerland was probably chosen only because the traditional operetta choice of Paris was enemy territory[39]). While the operetta's West represents all that is victorious and just, these virtues are attractive to all, Turk and German alike.

DIE BAJADERE: STAGING INAUTHENTICITY

Librettists Brammer and Grünwald took on exoticism again in 1921, this time with a more obvious choice of composer: Emmerich Kálmán, whose "Gypsy operetta" exoticism (discussed in chapter 4) was still considered his signature asset. According to Kálmán, he first met with the librettists without any particular theme in mind, but they discovered a mutual "predilection for exoticism and mysticism." Before any idea of the plot, the librettists had "the visual conception of one of the main characters ... a young prince, fashionable and elegant, but one who wears instead of a top hat a silk turban with a diamond clasp," a description that strikingly recalls Achmed Bey's fez.[40] A hat is proverbially mutable, suggesting that their characters are not fundamentally different from European gentlemen and that the hat-wearing actors retained their usual star images. The women surrounding tur-

FIGURE 5.1. *Die Bajadere* cast, with Louis Treumann, Christl Mardayn, and Ernst Tautenhayn. Bildarchiv Austria, Österreichische Nationalbibliothek.

ban-wearing Louis Treumann might as well be the women of *Die lustige Witwe*'s Maxim's and he might as well still be playing similarly lazy playboy Danilo, or Octave in *Eva*—and indeed, Treumann's exotic Prince Radjami is similarly idle and in thrall to the women of the Parisian entertainment industry. The *Neues Wiener Journal* critic wrote that the librettists relied on the "beloved Danilo motive, but with a new nuance"[41] (fig. 5.1; Treumann appears in the center holding hands with Christl Mardayn as Odette; second lead Ernst Tautenhayn wears a tuxedo).

In fact, it is unclear whether the women in the photograph are meant to represent costumed Parisian performers or Indian women, because the plot asks the same chorus to represent both groups in different acts. The operetta embeds its exoticism in a complex metatheatrical frame of multiple performances and audiences that deconstructs Silver Age operetta even as it enacts it. While *Die Rose von Stambul* had a fraught relationship with the real Turkey, the librettists of *Die Bajadere* embraced their composer's flexible attitude regarding authenticity and created an elaborate metatheatrical frame. It is not set in India at all but rather around a Parisian theater, the Châtelet, a leading operetta stage and the city's equivalent to Vienna's own Carl-Theater, where *Die Bajadere* premiered in late 1921.

The titular bayadere (temple dancer) is actually Odette Darimonde, a Parisian actress playing a bayadere onstage, while male protagonist Radjami is a homesick Indian prince. The heir to the throne of Lahore, he has just reached his thirtieth birthday and is thus told (by a British colonel!) that he must return to India to immediately marry an Indian girl, or several—the inevitable specter of polygamy appears again—or he will be disinherited. Radjami wants to bring Odette to India and marry her instead, but she refuses. When the captain of the theater's claque installs Radjami as Odette's partner in the Châtelet's operetta, their romance is finally all but consummated on the Châtelet's stage. In the end it is unclear whether they will be leaving for India or not, and they are left happily together on the stage within the stage. Thus the operetta's exotic India is less a literal place than operetta's familiar longing for a realm where sensory stimulation will overpower rational thought, an exoticism without nationality.

Kálmán, Brammer, and Grünwald's collective interest in an Indian setting can probably be ascribed to an instinct for commercial appeal. In 1921 India was a popular setting for silent films, many of which centered on temple ceremonies and other spectacular events, often with bayaderes.[42] The *Neue Freie Presse* noted, "At present India is taking its turn as the land about which hazy imaginings—like rajas, bayaderes, and lotus flowers—are being disseminated."[43] The plot even vaguely echoes the cross-cultural romance of *The Sheik*, the Rudolph Valentino film released only a few months before the operetta's premiere (Edith Maude Hull's novel, the film's source, was published in 1919). Kálmán claimed he was uninfluenced by his predecessors, writing that he began the score by studying "relevant works out of the literature" but quickly threw these aside to search for what he called a "personal kind of foreign rhythm for the setting."[44] (This was in part disingenuous; Odette's first vocal appearance is an offstage cadenza that is transparently modeled on the opening of the famous "Bell Song" from Leo Delibes's *Lakmé*.) But even within the operetta, the music is first heard as diegetic, within the space of a Parisian operetta theater, not as a genuine attempt to evoke Indian music.

The first act of *Die Bajadere* is set in a theater lobby. As the Viennese audience settles into their seats in the Carl-Theater, their minds still occupied with tickets and coat checks, the curtains open to reveal another lobby, its stage only glimpsed through a few upstage doors. *Die Bajadere* has only just begun, but the operetta beyond this onstage lobby (confusingly also entitled *Die Bajadere*) has reached its first intermission, and another audience (the Carl-Theater's chorus) bursts out and tells them about the operetta they have not seen, praising it with the text quoted at the beginning of this chapter. An apparent tastemaker, Count Armand, proclaims that the operetta contains one big hit, which he then proceeds to sing himself: "Lotusblume, ich liebe dich" ("Lotus flower, I love you").

(Throughout Act 1, the invisible operetta-within-the-operetta is playing just off-stage, and the characters' appearances in the lobby correspond with a traditional three-act structure.)

This is a sly move by Brammer and Grünwald, a novel way to introduce what might seem to be a major song and include its marketing hype within the text of the operetta itself. On the one hand, it indicates the stratified connoisseurship of operetta reception—it is one fan who indicates what will become the operetta's greatest hit, and by proclaiming its hit status in front of the crowd, he helps assure that this will come to pass. Later in the operetta, Radjami sings the song to Odette, introducing it as "the song the prince sings to his bayadere onstage" (No. 5). It turns out, however, that the lotus flower is not *Die Bajadere's* main feature: the song is never developed beyond the short phrases heard at the beginning of the operetta and only forms the introduction to a slow waltz duet in the style for which Kálmán was now known, in this case beginning "Rosen aus Djeipur"(Roses from Jaipur).

The sight of Odette as a bayadere is similarly distanced. She is first encountered as a disembodied voice as she performs on the Châtelet's invisible stage, her visual splendor withheld for as long as possible and mediated through Radjami's description and reaction to it. This first non-appearance seems to reference the titular actress heroine of Cilea's *Adriana Lecouvreur,* whose first performance is similarly offstage and refracted through an onstage observer, her stardom made more glamorous through its mediation by another character's reaction.[45] Odette begins with a cadenza seemingly lifted directly out of *Lakmé's* "Bell Song," making Odette an unusually virtuosic coloratura role (it was presumably within actress Christl Mardayn's capabilities; she had performed Blonde in *Die Entführung aus dem Serail* and the similarly demanding title role of Franz von Suppé's *Die schöne Galathée,* both at the Volksoper).[46] Radjami is apparently unable to bear her presence and remains in the lobby—that is, on the real stage—and sings along with her distant voice. They sing a highly eroticized but disconnected love duet, her undulating lines juxtaposed with his commentary. The offstage operetta's chorus—also invisible—helpfully adds, "Hört Ihr das Liebeslied?" (Do you hear the love song?) (ex. 5.4).

While Radjami is only a spectator, he is able to enter Odette's unseen world and sing along. His Indian identity makes him fit right in, and he identifies Odette's singing as "the song of my homeland"—the operetta broaches no authenticity debate of its own, and, for Radjami, Odette's performance is preferable to a trip home to see the real thing. Despite his own status as an exotic subject describing "his own" music, he keeps it at a literal distance. Moreover, he articulates the erotic attraction of exoticism in specific terms (she is "like I saw her in my dreams"), making him a bridge between the offstage voice and the audience—just like the

EXAMPLE 5.4: Kálmán, *Die Bajadere*, No. 3, Ensemble und Lied, Radjami's entrance

EXAMPLE 5.4. (continued)

sein,   komm und trink' mei ner Küs - se   e wig glü hen den   Wein!

tönt mei-ner Hei mat Ge sang,   mei-ner son-ni-gen Hei - mat   Ge sang

Ach   dein,   Hört Ihr das

stage space he occupies, situated in between the real Viennese audience and the invisible Parisian stage.

The "Indian" spectacle returns in Act 2, which takes place at a party at Prince Radjami's house. The performers are, according to the *Regiebuch*, no longer Parisians but "genuine Indian dancers" (who appear after a short hymn to champagne, already heard in Act 1 and similar to that of Act 2 of *Fledermaus*[47]). While the Odette's first appearance in Act 1 had been set within with the Parisian operetta in which she is performing, this dance is meant to be authentically Indian. Yet there is no discernable difference in style, perhaps in an acknowledgment that neither group of ersatz Indians is to be taken as a serious attempt to represent Indian culture. In fact, much of the exotic scoring was immediately recognized as, in short, rather Hungarian. The Act 2 number proper begins with a melismatic, free introduction with a solo clarinet playing a long descending chromatic scale. The fast dance section's sequential scalar figures, ornamented with mordents (ex. 5.5), closely recalls the fast section of "Heia, heia" from *Die Csárdásfürstin*. Finally, most blatantly, the B section of the tertiary dance music includes a cue for a *táragató*, a Hungarian folk instrument that sounds similar to a saxophone—and the cue indeed includes an alternative orchestration for a saxophone.[48]

This Hungarian tone was noted by many critics, and they took it in stride—not

EXAMPLE 5.5. Kálmán, *Die Bajadere*, No. 8, Introduktion, Tanz, und Liedfoxtrot, Allegretto

only, one suspects, because *Die Bajadere* makes a point of its inauthenticity but also because Kálmán was still seen as a composer whose native musical language was itself exotic. "Declared or not, the lotus flower has here and there a pinch of paprika," said the *Neues Wiener Tagblatt*. "Kálmán has solved the problem of making Indian music in the best way: he makes his own music. He has not set the very distant East but rather the much closer Hungary," said the *Neue Freie Presse*. "Kálmán's music has real Hungarian fire, thrilling verve and drive," wrote the *Illustrirtes* [sic] *Wiener Extrablatt*.[49]

MARKETING SPECTATORSHIP

Odette's first appearance onstage, shortly after Radjami sings along with her off-stage, further complicates the operetta's discourse of authenticity. Though the operetta-within-the-operetta is still in progress—it is the second intermission—she appears not as the bayadere but as a chic, worldly Parisian actress greeting her fans (No. 4, Ensemble und Entrée Odette). The *Regiebuch* suggests that her appearance is fashionable and modern, with the glitter of the bayadere only barely visible. The traces she bears of an exotic image are once again worn on her head:

> She perhaps still wears the costume in which she played the second act—but with a large, magnificent evening cloak thrown over it, so one can only see the costume's headdress . . . a spirited, hot-blooded woman, externally temperamental and puts up with nothing, also does not let it be forgotten for a second that she is a genuine and utter lady.[50]

While her disembodied voice suggested mysterious pleasure, in person she describes herself in unusually self-conscious language. The emphasis that she is a "genuine and utter lady" who "puts up with nothing" evokes both the perils of her exotic performance—while she appears in the provocative costume of a (sexually available, it is implied) bayadere onstage, the libretto names her as something more respectable, one of independent, plucky woman usually found at the center of operettas of this era. Intriguingly, these characteristics extended even to exotic characters such as Kondja in *Die Rose von Stambul* and Li, second lead in *Das Land des Lächelns*. Nonetheless, in *Die Bajadere* the more negative aspects of exoticism are not entirely absent. While Radjami is sure he understands Odette from seeing her onstage, in the opening of her entrance song she begins by proposing that her audience does not in fact have any idea of what she is "really" like—saying "if you had any idea what I feel, when I fearfully step onto the stage in the evenings." And while she proudly describes her ability to hypnotize an audience, she rather remarkably describes that relationship as a commodified one, a transaction and nothing more: "The stage belongs to the world, only go to the ticket office and pay your money/buy our fluttering heart, buy our happiness").[51] Her music similarly suggests a different personality from her stage character: she leaves the bayadere's exotic melismas behind in favor of a conventional march and waltz, both of which have a brisk, unsentimental character.

In contrast, Odette's performance in the exotic number, despite its underlined fakeness and kitschy aesthetic, represents something internal and mysterious, and for Prince Radjami even something fervent. In the world of *Die Bajadere*, this divide between conventional and exotic will persist: exoticism promises sensuality and irrationality; European music is self-aware, clever, and external. Predictably, in the tragic second-act finale, Odette attempts to unmask her bayadere persona to Radjami as only that, a performance, singing to the theme of her own exotic operetta, "I was never enchanted, I was never bewitched," but the third act of the operetta suggests otherwise.

The self-reflexive material, as well as the dancing, is concentrated mostly in the material of the secondary couple—actually, in this case, a trio—who are linked to Radjami and Odette's tale in a perfunctory manner. The situation provided is a love triangle centering on a capricious Parisian woman named Marietta. At the outset Marietta is married to bon vivant Louis-Philippe and having an affair with similar bon vivant Napoleon, but by the third act she has married Napoleon, has already tired of him, and is having an affair with Louis-Philippe. While Radjami and Odette's story provides a distanced form of exoticism and sensuality, the secondary plot provides the bubbly frivolity of modern dances and the self-conscious acknowledgment of operetta genre conventions. The irrelevance of the secondary characters is signaled not only in the men's comic names, alluding to French monarchs, but also in the text—upon seeing the operetta-within-the-operetta, Marietta and Napoleon comment on the actors playing their doubles, soubrette and comic, on the invisible stage:

Napoleon: Ah, it's better for us to stay here [in the theater's lobby], now the comic
              has a scene with the soubrette. I can't stand the fellow, he overacts so
              much!

Marietta: Yes, the comic—he overacts!

Napoleon: Yeah, and the soubrette? She perhaps doesn't overact?

Marietta: Yes, I can't stand the soubrette either!

Napoleon: Nobody can stand her! [52]

These characters receive an unusual wealth of numbers, seven in all, most of them modern, American-influenced dances including a "slowfox" (slow foxtrot) and, most memorably, a shimmy.

The two spheres represent a familiar dualism between timeless traditions (India, like Pontevedro) and fashion (always Paris). The shimmy is pointedly timely and modern, "the newest creation." (It was not the first in a Viennese operetta; Robert Stolz had included one the previous year in his *Der Tanz ins Glück*.[53]) The song explicitly describes the dance as something new: "If one wants to be chic and modern/If one wants to be one of the finer gentlemen,/One must do all the fashionable dances.... Shimmy is today vital in the salon/Shimmy is the height of aesthetics/Shimmy is the very latest creation!" Marietta swaps her lovers (at the beginning she is married to one and cheating with the other, by the end it is vice versa) with a determined lack of consequence, making her plot nothing more than a vehicle for shimmying.

The operetta's simultaneous embrace of demystification (Odette's entrance song, Marietta's dialogue) and mystification (the exotic elements) recalls what Jane Feuer has termed the self-reflective musical film's "myth of entertainment":

> Art musicals are structurally similar to myths, seeking to mediate contradictions in the nature of popular entertainment. The myth of entertainment is constituted by an oscillation between demystification and remythicization…the ostensible or surface function of these myths is to give pleasure to the audience by revealing what goes on behind the scenes in the theater or Hollywood—that is, to demystify the production of entertainment. But the films remythicize at another level that which they set out to expose. Only unsuccessful performances are demystified. The musical desires an ultimate valorization of entertainment; to destroy the aura, reduce the illusion, would be to destroy the myth of entertainment as well.[54]

And even if Odette repeatedly demystifies her own performance, by the end of the operetta, her aura is ultimately restored and remythicized. In other words, we end not with her disillusioned view but with Radjami's enchanted one. The operetta does not close with Radjami renouncing his position as Prince of Lahore, nor with Odette resolving to leave Paris, nor with their separation due to irreconcilable cultural differences, nor any other finale that would have offered a tidy closure to their adventures. Rather, Prince Radjami takes the male lead in the fictional operetta, and the operetta and its operetta-within-the-operetta collapse into each other. The leader of the Parisian claque, Pimprinette, introduces this finale not only to the Châtelet audience but also outward to the Viennese audience as "Voilà, the third act of *Die Bajadere*," and it is no longer clear of which *Bajadere* he is speaking. Odette and Radjami step into the operetta-within-the-operetta, and it is there that the librettists and the audience leave them, content. Odette, who had earlier proclaimed her total independence from her role, is left in that character onstage. This finale's resolution is determinedly theatrical, aware of its own artificiality. An important letter passed around by Pimprinette is even proclaimed "a prop à la Sardou!," alluding to operetta's historic reliance on well-made plays as sources and models. *Die Bajadere*'s well-made play "devices" do not perform their usual function of preparing the next well-timed plot twist. (Another convention dictates that the plot often will turn on a revelation from the characters' pasts. In this case, the twist results from an outrageous lie told by Napoleon, which Radjami later finds convenient.) Indeed, the operetta rejects most aspects of a linear narrative in favor of a succession of moods.

Die Bajadere thus ends as an endorsement of itself. In Adorno's formulation, the audience of *Die Bajadere* is not enjoying the operetta at all, but rather the money that they have paid to see it. Of a concertgoer who has bought his ticket, Adorno writes, "he has literally 'made' this success which he reifies and accepts as an objective criterion, without recognizing himself in it. But he has not 'made' it by liking the concert, but rather by buying the ticket."[55] *Die Bajadere* methodically invites the audience members to see their roles in the operetta food chain, underlining the commodity status of the transaction at every opportunity. And the operetta never gives the audience the opportunity to make up their own minds. Even the cynical Pimprinette, the claque leader who manufactures audience reaction for profit, proposes no audience response other than delirious delight. As Adorno argues of popular music, "to like it is almost the same thing as to recognize it."[56] This is not, however, a critical mode: *Die Bajadere* is a celebration of exotic consumerism and of the superficial pleasures the theater can bring—all you need to do, as Odette sings in her entrance song, is buy a ticket to happiness.

This self-conscious commodification was embedded in the operetta's marketing scheme, as is evident in a January 1922 issue of the magazine *Komödie* devoted entirely to the operetta. *Komödie*, subtitled *Wochenrevüe für Bühne und Film* ("weekly revue for stage and film," suggesting a succession of delights), provided glowing promotion for current stage and entertainment events. The magazine appeared to be directed at self-styled connoisseurs who had discerning taste but also wanted to hear an authorized version of salacious backstage gossip. Occasionally, as in this case, it would publish an issue devoted to a single new work (a similar issue was published for Lehár's *Clo-Clo*). Articles in the special issue examine *Die*

Bajadere's production process and the people who work both on and behind the stage: it includes interviews with and anecdotes from critics, composers, librettists, and actors as well as some polemical and personal essays credited to these figures themselves.

As *Die Bajadere* itself reveals operetta's means of production in the service of a myth of entertainment, *Komödie* created a larger myth surrounding the production itself. Published a few weeks after the operetta opened, the special issue already refers to the work as a huge success. It methodically introduces its creators and performers but includes more than straightforward interviews. One jokey article describes the process in which Carl-Theater intendant Siegmund Eibenschütz decided he needed to hire actress Christl Mardayn from the Volksoper in order to sing the vocally challenging role of Odette. Librettists Alfred Grünwald provides the punch line, saying to Eibenschütz, "You should be like Bismarck. If Mardayn is not successful, you are guilty and it costs you your job. If she does well, you had nothing to do with it."[57] Those who found this anecdote funny were those who appreciated the insider jokes of *Die Bajadere* itself.

Finally, the operetta is presented as a visual spectacle, with an article about the costumes and shoes. (There are, unfortunately, no stage photographs.) The feature on the costumes describes ways in which the extravagant stage fashions can be adopted by ordinary women: gold and silver dresses are now so in style that "they no longer belong to a children's fairy tale." The article names both dressmaker and shoemaker, presumably as a form of advertising for both the production's attention to fashion as well as their craft, and prominently names the photography studio where the photographs were taken as well.[58]

Such marketing and consumerism sit uneasily with operetta's attempts to proclaim its own artistic worth (though this never a major concern for Kálmán). But the two are intertwined in their aspirational character: the magazine simultaneously provides a model of spectatorship and fandom for readers who wish to imagine themselves in the know and offers a vision of material aspiration by advertising the luxury good providers whose wares adorn the operetta. By reading *Komödie*, readers can acquire a bourgeois sort of cultural capital that tells them where to buy the material signals of wealth and fashion and relates the gossip to inform their conversations.

This marketing plan worked: the exoticism of *Die Bajadere* is not alienating or threatening. It presents a titillating attraction premade for fashion, one already tamed through its narrative frame and whose clothes and shoes could be worn outside the theater. Operetta had long been a marketable product beyond its scores—*Die lustige Witwe* had provoked a marketing frenzy of vaguely related objects. But *Komödie* and *Die Bajadere* represent a *Gesamtkunstwerk* (total art work) of commodification in a way that *Witwe*'s scattered hats and cigarettes did not. The entire theatrical experience was marketed as a socially elevating phenomenon through which audience members could become more fashionable and fabulous people.

Critics similarly acclaimed Kálmán's score for its ability to speak to both connoisseurs and amateurs:

> He is one of the few who through personality, solid ability and artistically self-conscious ambition are justified to win, along with Lehár, great international success.... Every song, every dance piece, that he releases into the operetta world, is well-considered, precisely calibrated and calculated. Thus, each of his operettas, even the weak ones, have strong concentration and musical power of suggestion that can draw in the practiced listeners as much as the laity.[59]

While critics treated *Die Rose von Stambul* with great skepticism, they let Kálmán, Brammer, and Grünwald off the hook, noting that whatever its authenticity, *Die Bajadere* had great charm. If they enjoyed it, that was enough, and that was all that Kálmán sought. Despite his careful craftsmanship, he was not a composer who felt that he was working beneath his station or who heard a higher aesthetic calling. This was not universal: Franz Lehár was different.

RICHARD TAUBER AND *DAS LAND DES LÄCHELNS*

While Kálmán's *Die Bajadere* transformed a depoliticized exoticism into a meta-theatrical reflection on show business, Franz Lehár's *Das Land des Lächelns* (The Land of Smiles) takes its exoticism in earnest. Lehár saw in the musical portrayal of a forbidding China another opportunity to elevate operetta to operatic heights: a chance to write dramatically specific, locally colored music that used a large orchestra and, according to less charitable critics, often turned bombastic. What *Das Land des Lächelns* shares with previous exotic operettas is a fundamental belief that the distance conferred by exoticism conceals a deeper common humanity. The story is another cross-cultural romance, in this instance between a Chinese prince and a Viennese countess who are linked by a deeper affinity that consists of both their attraction to each other and the greater depth of their feeling compared with those who surround them. But, in a stark difference from most operettas, the cultural differences expressed in the exotic music prove too great to overcome.

Exoticism, however, was joined with the celebrity cult of tenor Richard Tauber. By this time the collaboration between Lehár and Tauber had revived the composer's career.[60] Tauber, who had first established a career as a popular opera singer throughout Germany and Austria, sang nearly every role in the tenor repertory. His somewhat throaty voice was reliable, projected well, and boasted bright, ringing top notes.[61] Tauber had first sung Lehár's music in a Berlin production of *Zigeunerliebe* in 1920, and Lehár first heard him sing the same role at the Salzburger Stadttheater in the summer of 1921.[62] The two discovered a mutual love of

Romantic expression and melody and wariness of more modern fare, deemed by Lehár *Tüfteleien,* or "fiddly bits."[63] In the summer of 1922, Tauber took over the leading role in Lehár's *Frasquita* from Hubert Marischka at the Theater an der Wien, and a flagging production was transformed into a major hit. This career transition was not without cost to Tauber's reputation: his pecuniary gains were incessantly mentioned by some critics, who considered him as a sellout.[64]

In Tauber, Lehár had both a powerful singer who could realize the composer's operatic ambitions and a stiff actor whose performances often suggested that the character's expressivity was more audible than visible. For Tauber's outsized celebrity, Lehár wrote a series operettas based on outsized historical figures, beginning with the premiere of *Paganini,* loosely inspired by the life of the violinist. Tauber sang the Berlin premiere on January 30, 1926, and it was here that the Tauber-Lehár legend was born.[65] Their next two operettas, *Der Zarewitsch* (1927) and *Friederike* (1928), both premiered in Berlin. Compared with the inflation-stretched, heavily taxed theaters of Vienna, Berlin was booming, and Lehár found ample interest in the production of his work.[66]

While Lehár and Tauber found lucrative popular success in Berlin, they also found a more skeptical critical establishment, and the composer's turn toward quasi-opera was roundly criticized.[67] He seems to have been undaunted: in this period he proclaimed triumphantly that his success with the public had finally freed him to write his operettas exactly as he wanted, without making any concessions—though he is vague about who had demanded what earlier in his career.[68] The fact that this purported newfound freedom led him to become more famous and popular than he had been since *Die lustige Witwe* was, presumably, merely a bonus.

Das Land des Lächelns, which followed *Friederike,* marked Tauber's Berlin comeback after an attack of angina or possibly a stroke.[69] It was a revision of an older piece, *Die gelbe Jacke,* which had had only a short run at the Theater an der Wien in 1923 and had never been performed in Berlin. It has often been suggested that the Chinese subject was proposed because of Tauber's lingering health problems—namely, facial disfigurement and a labored walk. The former could have been concealed by the requisite makeup, and the latter by the long robes worn by Prince Sou-Chong, Tauber's character. But this account has been disputed by biographer Otto Schneidereit, who dates the start of the work's development to 1928, before Tauber's collapse.[70]

The revision is credited to new librettists Ludwig Herzer and Fritz Löhner-Beda "after" the work of *Gelbe Jacke* librettist Victor Léon, but until the third act the changes are not dramatic, consisting of a few shuffled numbers and renamed characters (in this chapter, all characters are referred to by their names in *Das Land des Lächelns* to reduce confusion).[71] Both versions are set in 1912. At the start of the operetta, Countess Lisa, in search of romance and adventure, turns down a marriage proposal from the Viennese count (and lieutenant), Gustl, and instead falls in love with visiting Chinese prince Sou-Chong.[72] When Sou-Chong is recalled to China to take up the position of prime minister, Lisa decides to go with him. In China, Sou-Chong is inaugurated to great fanfare with the ceremonial yellow jacket worn by prime ministers (which gave the first version of the operetta its title) but insists that this will not affect his relationship with Lisa. Gustl travels to China to rescue Lisa but is waylaid by Mi, Sou-Chong's attractive younger sister. It is then revealed that Sou-Chong must, in a now-familiar twist, marry four Chinese women. In the original *Die gelbe Jacke,* Lisa then flees back to Vienna, where Sou-Chong eventually joins her, and they live happily ever after. But the revised *Das Land des Lächelns* made drastic changes to the third act, in which the unwilling Lisa is imprisoned in Sou-Chong's palace, where she is rescued by Gustl. Sou-Chong catches the pair as they make their escape. In an opera seria–like act of clemency, he gives Lisa and Gustl leave to return to Vienna, and both pairs of lovers are separated.

Lehár thought he had found in Tauber's voice the instrument that would justify the pathos of his sad ending. Sou-Chong claims that his self is hidden behind his "smiling face." While his ornamental exotic exterior charms the Viennese, his emotional side escapes only when he is alone or with Lisa, and only in music. Sou-Chong's singing voice becomes an intimate mode of address that resonated both with Tauber's performance style and the changing dynamics of operetta production and dissemination. The libretto pushes its characters to unusual extremes, allowing Lehár to compose music full of the kind of drama and tension he had sought for years. Aided by the strong voices of Tauber and soprano Vera Schwarz, he and the librettists created a cathartic, highly charged version of operetta.[73] The focus is relentlessly on the two protagonists: the librettists methodically reduce the role of the chorus, eliminating them from both act finales and keeping the focus on the main characters' interior emotional worlds.

The score includes a good deal of traditional, pentatonic exotic music, which at first seems to simply indicate Sou-Chong's exotic identity and Lisa's fascination with it. At the very opening of the operetta, Lisa arrives having just won an equestrian competition, and she expresses her love of life and adventure in a rousing entrance song (No. 1, Introduktion und Lied). Like her predecessors Odette and Kondja, she describes herself a modern woman and is admired by the chorus. The nature of her desired escapades is indicated in her music: her vocal line in the verse section is entirely pentatonic, emphasized in the orchestra by a straightforward pentatonic scale. But her refrain, a straightforward and not pentatonic waltz, reveals that she is also a fine Viennese lady.

Sou-Chong's entrance song is also heavily pentatonic, but from the start his music suggests that he transcends its limitations. He enters to an imposing motive containing a prominent tritone in the bass. (ex. 5.6a, measures 1–4). The vocal line

EXAMPLE 5.6. Lehár, *Das Land des Lächelns*, No. 3, Entrée des Sou-Chong, opening

of the verse, as in Lisa's entrance song, is pentatonic, but like Lisa, he does not stay there long. In the second phrase of the refrain, he moves from a G to an F sharp on "immer zufrieden" (ex. 5.6b, measure 3). The timing is canny. Restricted to his middle register for the rest of the number, Sou-Chong's voice—and, in the later version, Tauber's true tenorial self—bursts out in a shift that is both harmonic and vocal, finally revealing high notes and vocal strength as emblematic of his true self. By insisting in the private space of a solo song that the world does not see his "wahres Gesicht" (true face), Sou-Chong declares himself to be, beneath the smiling mask of exotic China, a lonely person with "Sehnsucht" and "Schmerz" (longing and pain). The slide out of the pentatonic implies that that true face is the one unmarked by the exoticism imposed by China, a musical move that recalls Achmed Bey's entrance song in *Die Rose von Stambul*. (This song was unchanged from its earlier incarnation in *Die gelbe Jacke*, where it was sung by Hubert Marischka, who was also the first Achmed Bey.)

In this first act, the exotic thus performs its customary function of depicting the foreign culture that is embodied in Sou-Chong and desired by Lisa, as well as binding Sou-Chong and Lisa together through a common musical idiom. But the pentatonic is Janus-faced, as is revealed in the second act, when Sou-Chong and Lisa journey to China. The exotic land that Lisa imagined is now all too real,

EXAMPLE 5.6. (continued)

and threatening. The roles of exotic and non-exotic music are reversed: the exotic music portrays the external setting, while the character's private feelings are expressed using non-exotic music. Lisa leaves her pentatonicism behind in favor of a nostalgic, homesick Wiener-Lied (No. 12, "Ich möcht' wieder einmal die Heimat seh'n"), and, most spectacularly, Sou-Chong abandons the exotic entirely in his climactic love song.

Das Land des Lächelns was often compared to two strongly pentatonic, Asia-set operas by Puccini, *Turandot* and *Madame Butterfly*.[74] Critics described the score as "operatic" (*opernhaft*) and dramatic. The anonymous critic for the *Neues Wiener Journal*—this was a rare case in which a Viennese paper printed a review of a Berlin premiere, such was Lehár's fame—wrote, "It is a thoroughly serious affair, and Lehár accentuates this with subtle, dramatic music."[75] The Berlin newspaper

Vossische Zeitung referred to the work's "operatic features." In the *Berlin Börsen-Courier*, Oscar Bie noted something similar, only framed it in less complimentary terms: "Lehár involuntarily approaches a certain operatic style, but, between us, it becomes a little boring."[76] The "operatic features" were also considered incompatible with humor. "But it remains an operetta with opera scenes, with very sentimental operetta, from which humor, or what we take as such, is nearly entirely banned,"[77] wrote the critic of *Der Tag*. Similarly, Edmund Kühn in *Germania*: "A kingdom for a good joke, for any joke at all! How should I reconcile so much 'quality'—and that is the glory of today's Metropol-Theater—with the duty to entertain the Berliners in the birthplace of 'Hoppla trallalla.'"[78] Bie wrote, alluding to the title, "Perhaps smiles, but not laughs [das Lächeln, aber nicht das Lachen]."[79] There is, however, comic material, relegated to the second couple of Mi and Gustl, who also are responsible for most of the operetta's dancing. Their characters, according to Karl Westermeyer of the *Berliner Tageblatt und Handelszeitung*, sat uneasily with the very serious parts:

> At all events, *Das Land des Lächelns* remains dramatically weak, and moreover the pseudo-tragedy of the plot of the dramatically exaggerated *Singspiel* gets out of the light operetta realm. The deep Buddhist thoughts of smiling self-conquest for the sake of the good of the collective are not made clearly enough; the characters remain stuck in cliché.[80]

According to Westermeyer and others, the operetta relied too heavily on the talents of Tauber for its dramatic effect, and despite its composer's ambition to write a comic opera, he had produced something more like a Tauber vehicle.

TECHNOLOGICAL REPRODUCIBILITY ONSTAGE

Richard Tauber made an unlikely hero. Most operetta actors were triple threats—that is, actors, dancers, and singers, often in that order—while Tauber's gifts were above all vocal. In contrast, his rivals Hubert Marischka and Louis Treumann, whose physical attractions and stage comportment were much more frequently described in print, Tauber favored a vocal delivery that tended toward *Sprechgesang*, following the rough contours of the pitch and rhythm but without a particularly resonant or beautiful vocal sound.[81] Tauber's vocal palette, in contrast, was much larger, and he could put a classically cultivated sound and a dazzling range of vocal effects to work on Lehár's music. He was frequently praised for his precision; as one Berlin critic put it, "The technique with which Tauber treats this exceptional instrument has no compare among German tenors."[82]

The numbers Lehár wrote for Tauber became their own genre. The "Tauber-Lied" was a climactic solo sung by Tauber, appearing somewhere in the middle of Act 2, and was usually an effusive declaration of love to an offstage woman.

Tauber's soprano object of affection was rarely afforded the opportunity to properly respond to this declaration; the real relationship was between Tauber and his audience. For most critics and audience members, the "Tauber-Lied" stood out as the most important moment in the performance, prompting a fervent reaction. Yet the song served a dual function: it was not only the operetta's most cathartic and memorable moment but was also destined to be famous outside of its dramatic context. As Erich Urban wrote in *BZ am Mittag* about the "Tauber-Lied" in *Das Land des Lächelns*, "The hit for the winter of 1929–1930, the successor to 'O Mädchen, mein Mädchen' [from *Friederike*] is born!"[83] Similarly, the *Vossische Zeitung* critic noted, "Yesterday, this tenorial eroticism of the big solo hit ravished the receptive audience; it will reach the popular distribution of the tenor numbers from *Frasquita* and *Paganini*."[84]

The Tauber-Lied of *Das Land des Lächelns*, "Dein ist mein ganzes Herz," appears midway through Act 2, exactly as anticipated. It is based on a short section sung by Sou-Chong in the Act 3 finale from *Die gelbe Jacke*, an act that was cut and entirely replaced in *Das Land des Lächelns*. The theme's appearance in *Jacke* was deemed by Lehár to fall too late in the piece: he described the location as "three minutes before the curtain's fall, when people already are thinking of the coat check."[85] Lehár moved the melody into Act 2 of *Das Land des Lächelns* and expanded it into a new Tauber-Lied, composing a new B section and setting the entire thing to a new text by the *Lächelns* librettists. It follows the model of previous Tauber-Lieder. Unlike the conventional verse-chorus form of most operetta songs, they are in ABA ternary form. Tauber summarized the form: "The main melody [comes] at the beginning and ending [rather than as a refrain following the verse], as a middle section [introduces] a whole new melody."[86] (Subsequent Tauber-Lieder include "Freunde, das Leben ist lebenswert" [Friends, life is worth living] from *Giuditta* [1934] and "Du bist die Welt für mich" [You are the world to me] from Tauber's own operetta, *Der singende Traum* [1934].)

Tauber-Lied trademarks can also be seen at the local level. Consider the openings of several Tauber-Lieder: "Gern hab' ich die Frau'n geküßt" from *Paganini* (a paean to women in general rather than any particular one), "O Mädchen, mein Mädchen" from *Friederike*, and "Du bist meine Sonne" from *Giuditta* (which followed *Das Land des Lächelns*).[87] Each song begins with a surging, effusive declaration of love sung at a moderate tempo, containing long notes in the middle register (usually around B in the middle of the staff) for Tauber to display his beautiful tone, usually followed by a few eighth notes to be sung with rhythmic freedom, often containing an unexpected fermata, allowing Tauber to seize control of the musical pulse and simultaneously giving the audience a sustained moment to bask in his sheer vocal sound and assert his agency over the performance. Most of the songs have a high tessitura for operetta and sustained high notes (usually As or A-flats).

"Dein ist mein ganzes Herz" (ex. 5.7) has the trademarks of the Tauber-Lied: the long note in the middle register, the fermata, and the eventual ascension to the upper register. It is also notable for what it lacks: exoticism. The first section, in fact, could belong to any Lehár operetta of any setting. The middle section promises a return to pentatonic on "Wohin ich immer gehe," and the parallel movements of the woodwinds in sixths and strumming open fifths in the bass line resonate with the use of the woodwinds in "Immer nur lächeln." But after these two measures, Lehár returns to the major. This brief moment seems to acknowledge Sou-Chong's background only to almost immediately forget it; the rest of the section avoids penatonicism. It seems doubtful that the two measures of pentatonicicsm would register as bluntly exotic without the context of the rest of the operetta. This nearly unmarked quality was both dramatically appropriate and commercially convenient. Like Sou-Chong's slide out of the pentatonic in "Immer nur lächeln," it suggests that he is, at heart, not foreign but the same as his European audience. It places him in opposition to the public oppressions of Chinese culture seen elsewhere in this act.

Simultaneously, the relative lack of exoticism prepares it for distribution outside the operetta, where its perceived unmarked universality becomes a commercial asset and it will not require any context to be understood. Distribution of a song independent of its context was hardly new, and even some of the methods—sheet music, performances by salon orchestras—were old. But the Tauber-Lied's rapid spread in the form of recorded sound on radio and record, far beyond the popularity and lifespan of the operetta it came from, marked a break with earlier practice.[88] Distribution was now not in the form of a musical text to be reinterpreted by other performers but rather a sound object, namely Richard Tauber's voice. In the operetta it was a climactic number; outside of it, it was a *Schlager*, a hit song.

TEXT, "DEIN IST MEIN GANZES HERZ"

Dein ist mein ganzes Herz!	My entire heart is yours!
Wo du nicht bist, kann ich nicht sein.	Where you are not, I cannot be.
So, wie die Blume welkt,	As the flower wilts,
wenn sie nicht küsst der Sonnenschein!	when it does not kiss the sunshine!
Dein ist mein schönstes Lied,	Yours is my most beautiful song,
weil es allein aus der Liebe erblüht.	because it alone blossoms from love.
Sag mir noch einmal, mein einzig Lieb',	Say to me once more, my only love,
oh sag noch einmal mir:	Oh, say once more to me:
Ich hab dich lieb!	I love you!
Wohin ich immer gehe,	Wherever I may go
ich fühle deine Nähe.	I feel your presence.
Ich möchte deinen Atem trinken	I would like to drink your breath
und betend dir zu Füssen sinken,	And sink in prayer at your feet
dir, dir allein! Wie wunderbar	You, you alone! How wonderful

EXAMPLE 5.7. Lehár, *Das Land des Lächelns*, No. 11, Lied, opening

ist dein leuchtendes Haar!	Is your shining hair!
Traumschön und sehnsuchtsbang	Beautiful as a dream and full of longing
ist dein strahlender Blick.	Is your radiant gaze.
Hör ich der Stimme Klang,	When I hear the sound of your voice
ist es so wie Musik.	It is like music.
Dein ist mein ganzes Herz!, etc.	My entire heart is yours, etc.

Schlager were portable, disposable, adaptable, and broadcast into many contexts. The moniker was first applied to the cabaret songs of the early twentieth century; by the 1920s the word entailed songs heard on the radio and on records, no longer necessarily linked to the collective theatrical experience that defined an operetta. Schlager, even more than operetta, sought to enter listeners' daily lives, a principle described by Peter Wicke as "success through the avoidance of distance," in which the affective space between the song and the hearer is made as narrow as possible.[89] The Schlager was often condemned in these exact terms: its ubiquity and intrusion into the private sphere of the home represented a destruction of *Gemeinschaft* and, in the views of Marxist and later Frankfurt School critics, was intended to dissuade class-consciousness and prevent critical thinking among the petite bourgeoisie.[90] The Schlager's portability and infinite reproducibility would seem antithetical to the communal theatrical experience and fervor that defined a Lehár operetta in Berlin. What is more, and as already seen, Lehár aspired to the immortal status of high art, not disposability.

But several of the essential characteristics of the Schlager—portability, repetition, and the intimacy of individual and private address—were intrinsic to the song's performance in operetta itself, as is evident in the staging of the numbers and the descriptions of Tauber's performance of them. As in "Immer nur lächeln," Sou-Chong entrusts the audience with a revelation of his otherwise-hidden inner world. The Chinese minister Tschang has just insulted Lisa and forced Sou-Chong to accept the "4,000-year-old" tradition of marrying four Chinese women. He leaves, and Sou-Chong is alone onstage. He begins with a solo speech:

> Prince (*alone, lifts arms towards the sky*): Thou eternal gods, what I do *cannot* be
> wrong!…Thou put in humankind's breast a heart, thou hast made the heart
> into a vessel for love and my love and my heart belong to this one, this woman
> alone![91] (emphasis in original)

He then sings. His declarations are addressed to the intimate "du," meaning Lisa, but no one else is present onstage, and he sings directly to the audience. Tauber the star thus addresses each member of his public individually, as if they have a close relationship. In Adorno's analysis of the Schlager, such intimacy was crucial to the song's effect: when the listener recognizes the theme of a popular song, that person "become[s]…the subject for whom the Schlager ideally speaks.…He feels at once his isolation ameliorated, joined to a community of fans."[92] In live performances those fans were actually present and together, and this created an electric effect, but it seems also to have laid the way for the wide distribution of the Schlager, where Tauber's voice would resonate in private spaces to individual listeners.

The repressed emotions Sou-Chong had described in "Immer nur lächeln" are finally released in "Dein ist mein ganzes Herz." Tauber's limitations as a physical performer were here put to productive use: his acting was as stiff as ever, and his face and gestures were concealed by a long robe, thick makeup, and smiling mask he adopted to "look Chinese" according to the operetta's exotic terms.[93] In contrast to the palette afforded by his vocal skill, his character deliberately rejected visual expression. The static nature of the stage picture tightened this focus. There are no stage directions for the aria that would indicate Tauber moving around the stage or doing anything other than standing still. The page of the *Regie- und Soufflierbuch* where the diagrams indicating the staging of the song would appear, is entirely blank, not even indicating where Sou-Chong will exit (the text specifies that he exits left). The next diagram indicates the beginning of the next scene, in which Mi and Gustl enter the stage from the right.[94]

The song itself is dispensable in the larger trajectory of the drama. But Tauber's performances, by all accounts, stopped the operetta in its tracks, prompting prolonged applause, cheering, and shouting from the audience, and then "dacapos" (encores, rendered in one word in German). Tauber frequently sang "Dein ist mein ganzes Herz" and other Tauber-Lieder five, six, or more times in a single performance. One critic commented on the premiere, "I don't how many times Tauber sang the main Schlager, but surely more than a dozen times."[95] Other critics counted five or six encores. While accounts of earlier operettas often record up to two or three encores of popular numbers, Tauber's numbers were unprecedented. Moreover, they served as a disruption of the work, particularly discordant with Lehár's purported high art aims. Critic Oscar Bie, none too enchanted with *Das Land des Lächelns* in general, said of the endless encores, "It costs too much patience and has something shameful in it."[96] Several critics noted the song was already ready for distribution as a record; *Germania* commented on the "many pungent melodies, which will create a magnificent onslaught of new Tauber records."[97] The song was itself arguably a dacapo of previous Tauber-Lieder, a familiar variation on a well-established theme (as noted by Urban's comment quoted above).

Even in live performance, then, the song became a Schlager. Like a record player, the audience could wind Tauber up and listen to him again. Tauber's performances can be read as a repudiation of the Benjaminian aura, the determined commodification of the Tauber-Lied even before such commodification was enforced by recording and infinite distribution. The song was endlessly repeated, both "Dein ist mein ganzes Herz" and the larger Tauber-Lied phenomenon from operetta to operetta. The Tauber-Lied was no longer, in Benjamin's terms, "embedded in the context of a tradition,"[98] able to be played whenever it was demanded.

But despite their adoption of the tropes of the Schlager, Tauber's encores reacquired a sense of liveness through the singer's interpretive abilities: he was famous for never singing the song the exact same way twice. This was, according to fans, his true mark as an artist of insight and integrity as well as a popular performer and a singer of great technical skill. He would sing the entire song piano, he would switch the phrasing, he would sing it in falsetto. He is described as singing "small variations before the roaring of the house."[99] Such variations made the encores more than a series of near-mechanical reproductions, and critics considered it his mark as a true artist:

> Besides, Tauber is truly the unique standing virtuoso of the encore. He sings his number differently every time, with new vocal nuances and so makes out of every encore a delicacy for the musical listener. And at the same time every encore entices the audience to demand another encore, because they are curious what Tauber will offer now.[100]

In his pianissimo variations—where he self-consciously renounced the bombast of a large, operatic sound for more technically difficult and supposedly tasteful soft singing—he forced audiences to listen carefully to his voice, requiring them to remain still and silent in his presence. He made his audience connoisseurs as they practiced fine distinction between his various interpretations. His variations refuted the near-mechanical nature of his encores, restoring to the performance both linearity and mystery (how will he sing it the next time?) and rooting it in the present moment, making it more than a performance by Tauber on the radio. Tauber's variations prevented the depreciation of value brought on by repetition, making each rendition a new work.

Tauber's salvo at artistic legitimacy was matched by Lehár's. The operetta's sad ending proclaims not only Lehár's status as a "serious artist" but also the irreconcilable conflict between the inner romantic self and the cruelties of the external world. Operetta's shift from *Die gelbe Jacke*'s reconciliation—one might add the happy ending of *Die Rose von Stambul* as well—to *Das Land des Lächeln*'s separation is symptomatic of an art form seeking higher emotional stakes, in Lehár's view. (Such endings were already commonplace in American musical theater.) On an aesthetic level, the ending marked *Das Land des Lächelns* as something bigger and more original than a tidy, formulaic operetta marriage comedy. For Martin Lichtfuss, the new irreconcilability between Sou-Chong and Lisa reflected what he delicately calls the growing *Rassenkonflikt* (race conflict) in Central Europe. The operetta, he points out, never proposes that Sou-Chong and Lisa should not be together; the plot's tragedy is that under present conditions they cannot be.[101] *Das Land des Lächelns*, he says, is Lehár's plea for tolerance in a precarious world. (For

Lehár, a Catholic with a Jewish wife, these concerns would become timelier in the following decades.[102])

If Sou-Chong and Lisa were left in despair,. Lehár, the great composer, triumphed as an artist. The success was in part one over critics and industry norms that would confine him to narrow genre expectations. To Lehár, the success of the sad ending proved that he was more in touch with his audiences than were his critics. This attitude reflects a contradictory relationship with the high art establishment that was already present in Lehár's relationship with modern music. He longed for the prestige and immortality accorded to the composers whose busts decorated opera houses and made definable steps toward this sort of serious status. But he simultaneously sought popular success and frequently positioned himself as an advocate for audiences against those same critics, and he viewed modern opera as inaccessible and overly difficult. In the rapidly changing world of popular culture, Lehár wanted historic, enduring success on his own terms. In a way, he would get this in 1934 with the premiere at the Wiener Staatsoper of *Giuditta*, his final major work.

Operetta in the Past Tense

The end of the Austro-Hungarian Empire marked the beginning of the end of Viennese operetta. Despite popular and lucrative successes during the 1920s (foremost among them the Kálmán- Brammer-Grünwald collaborations at the Theater an der Wien such as *Die Bajadere, Gräfin Mariza*, and *Die Zirkusprinzessin*), operetta's hold on the present loosened, and plots, productions, and theatrical calendars became increasingly fixated on an idealized imperial past. As Austrian society struggled to recover from the war, large-scale commercial theater underwent regular crises. Vienna faced increased competition from Berlin as a popular culture center. But perhaps even graver than these material threats were the more nebulous concerns of operetta's place in the Viennese cultural ecosystem. Operetta had come to embody the particularly diverse world of late Habsburg Vienna, both ethnic and musical. It was unclear what it had to say to the new Austrian republic. The most successful operettas of the 1920s either embodied this search for a new place in the world—the exotic operettas examined in the previous chapter—or worked to summon a world gone by, often in increasingly nostalgic terms. When operetta authors sought to be modern, they imitated other genres, most often revue and film. But this assimilation ultimately served it poorly. This chapter addresses two interlocking problems: The first is operetta's increasing historicism and imitation of other genres. The second is the economic collapse of the theater system, which deprived the industry of the vertical integration and defined boundaries of genres that had previously regulated operetta's identity. Then I consider operetta performance today and how it continues to play out the aesthetic debates of the early twentieth century.

Operetta's gradual retreat can be charted in entertainment magazines such as

Die Bühne (The Stage) and *Komödie* (Comedy), where revues and film occupy an increasingly central position and operetta, while still celebrated, is a more occasional subject. Many of operetta's biggest late successes came when composers and librettists embraced the anti-modern and exploited its close relationship with a retrospectively golden past. Such nostalgic operettas became a stage for the cultivation of a new, *gemütlich* Austrian identity, one that appealed to domestic audiences as well as tourists and was suitable for export.[1] Older operettas were given prestige revivals and reworkings, usually with extravagant productions, a few new songs, a chorus line, or some kind of extra spectacle number.[2] The juxtaposition of past and present in these revivals would seem to invite nostalgia, as defined by Linda Hutcheon: "Nostalgia is not something you 'perceive' *in* an object; it is what you 'feel' when two different temporal moments, past and present, come together for you and, often, carry considerable emotional weight."[3]

Those writing about operetta also increasingly turned toward the past. Many of the newspaper features written about operetta composers and librettists in this period do not concern new works but tell nostalgic stories about earlier hits. Sometimes revivals even reached back to the nineteenth century: In the 1920s an influential series of revivals of lesser-known Johann Strauss II operettas spearheaded by director Max Reinhardt and the young Erich Wolfgang Korngold reorchestrated the sound of the Golden Age for the richer tastes of Silver Age ears, and many works of this period similarly reference a premodern, ethnically homogenous, nineteenth-century Vienna or a comfortably noble aristocracy.[4]

Not everything looked to the past, however. The leading composers of the later 1920s and 1930s belonged to a new generation: Berlin-based composers such as Ralph Benatzky and Paul Abraham, who wrote loosely plotted works whose appeal rested primarily on visual spectacle, *Schlager* (hit songs), and, in the case of Abraham, more Hungarian color.[5] Kálmán took Abraham's success as a personal affront, writing to composer and orchestrator Nico Dostal that "this Abraham stole all my music."[6] For those in operetta scholarship who have adopted Lehár's own middlebrow aspiration, this later generation was without integrity; Andrew Lamb's Grove article on Abraham claims, conflictingly, that "Abraham's operettas pandered openly to the popular musical idiom of the time, but contained strikingly effective numbers which have remained justly popular."[7]

Even some of the more innovative operetta creators tried on a nostalgic guise.[8] In 1928 Julius Brammer and Alfred Grünwald broke off their collaboration with Kálmán to work with composer Edmund Eysler on *Die gold'ne Meisterin*, a sweet love story set in sixteenth-century Vienna that harkens back to the nineteenth-century world of the *Volksstück*.[9] Kálmán's own works of the 1920s carried nostalgia as well, most notably *Gräfin Mariza* (1924), in which the musical dualism of *Die Csárdásfürstin* is revived to portray a Hungarian count fallen on hard times. The post-imperial fate of Tassilo, the formerly artistocratic protagonist, is a job as an estate manager. In one of Kálmán's most popular csárdás numbers, "Komm, Zigány," Tassilo finds himself among a sympathetic group of operetta-typical Gypsies and sings, "once I was also a fine Csárdáskavalier, I commanded Gypsies just like you."[10] Now he has been demoted to the status of servant; his genuine lament is mistaken by his employer for a pleasant evening's entertainment, and he is outraged and insulted.[11] He intended, like Rosalinde in *Fledermaus*, only to appropriate the emotional depth of the "Gypsy style" but instead was taken for the servant he has in fact become. In Kálmán's *Die Csárdásfürstin*, this old hierarchy was joyfully dissolved, but only a few years into Austria's interwar troubles it is a subject for nostalgia. By the end of the operetta, Tassilo is restored his social position and place in a conventional hierarchy through marriage to Mariza. More provocatively, Tassilo's rival is one Koloman Zsúpan, a character whose name pays tribute to the pig farmer of Johann Strauss II's *Der Zigeunerbaron* and who proclaims himself a descendent of that same character. This dual face of operetta as lament and entertainment sustained it through most of the First Republic.

The more sentimentally escapist operettas had always been ready for nostalgic readings—of the works examined in this book, this is most prominent in *Ein Walzertraum* (chapter 2). But after the war, operetta as a whole, both new and old, more actively sought to summon this world that now was forever gone. Ironically, many celebrated the imperial pomp that had, in an earlier era, been prohibited from Dual Empire stages: Kálmán's *Kaiserin Josephine* (1936; following *Giuditta* it was planned for the Wiener Staatsoper but because of theatrical crises eventually premiered in Zurich); Fritz Kreisler and the Marischka brothers' *Sissy* (1932), which includes the Emperor Franz Joseph and Empress Elisabeth as main characters; and Oscar Straus's *Drei Walzer* (1935), which traces the lineage not of royalty but of the music of the "Waltz King" through multiple generations of theatrical families. But the operetta ends with not an apotheosis of operetta but with the final generation's turn to the film industry.[12]

DIE HERZOGIN VON CHICAGO AND DISSOLUTION

Such concessions to the film industry's supremacy can be found in other late operettas as well. Emmerich Kálmán's *Die Herzogin von Chicago* is a work that looks both forward and backward, an example of the negotiations between operetta's traditions and new realities. Kálmán might appear to be the composer with the most to lose after the loss of the empire: he was operetta's representative of Hungary, and the dissolution made his "Dual Empire" style anachronistic. Yet Kálmán proved able to adapt, incorporating elements of new, American-inspired dance music and the tableau dramaturgy of the revue along with a fond look back at the glory days of the empire. Freed from geopolitical realities, Kálmán's already fantastical Hungary was elevated to purely symbolic status. While he wrote some works in which Hungary as such did not feature—most prominently *Die Bajadere*, analyzed in chapter 5—in others his style hongrois took on a warm and inviting nostalgic tone that, as seen previously in *Die Csárdásfürstin*, deconstructed operetta even as familiar tropes played out.

But the legibility of these deconstructions—as well as more conventional, simpler operetta formulations—depended on a particular audience from a particular cultural sphere, one that in *Die Herzogin von Chicago* appears to be in crisis. Written to a libretto by Brammer and Grünwald, the operetta seems to open new pathways but was ultimately more of a fond farewell than a new beginning. The plot is familiar in its outlines, elements of which are borrowed from Thomas Mann's 1909 novel *Königliche Hoheit*.[13] A small and bankrupt state, Sylvania, is ruled by a debauched king who spends most of his time on the Riviera. Governing instead falls to Prince Sandór Boris, an old-fashioned cultural conservative who sees newfangled dance and music as a threat to his anachronistic kingdom. But the real threat is that Sylvania is, like every operetta state before it, bankrupt. Sylvania has a potential savior in Mary Lloyd, a Chicago millionaire's daughter who makes a bet with her friends that she can buy the most expensive and difficult-to-obtain thing in Europe.[14] Mary arrives and bails Sylvania out by proposing to buy the castle but brings her offensive jazz music with her. She and Sandór begin to fall for each other as well, despite his prejudice against her and her music. But when Sandór finds out about Mary's bet, he is outraged and thinks that he himself has been bought. The decrepit king of Sylvania, a seeming symbol of a bygone entitled aristocracy, returns from Monaco and attempts to seduce Mary himself, without success. Finally, a movie producer arrives from the United States and announces that he wants to make a movie about Mary and Sandór, but he cannot do so unless they provide him with a happy ending. In a concession not to operetta but rather to Hollywood, they somewhat inexplicably decide to marry.

Control of the plot has been ceded to the deus ex machina of the film producer. Operetta itself can no longer promise a happy ending, but Hollywood can force one upon the diffident protagonists. According to the *Regiebuch*:

> In the closing song, the star banner girls from the second act dance out from the first entrance left and right and bow to the audience. On their top hats are letters that spell out the words [in English] "Happy – end!" All throw paper streamers into the auditorium.[15]

The ending is proclaimed to be happy in English words that are revealed to the audience when the chorus girls bow their heads, breaking the fourth wall. The words are not legible to the characters onstage but visible only to the audience, and the streamers thrown into the auditorium are for the benefit of the audience alone. This ending speaks only in terms external to the rest of the work.

The conventions of operetta have been subordinated to those of another form as well, the theatrical revue. Instead of the conventional three acts, the operetta is in four parts: an extensive prologue, two acts, and a *Nachspiel*, epilogue. The traditional spectacular production number at the beginning of Act 2 has become redundant because the entire score is littered with such numbers (such as No. 15, "Rose der Prairie"). While some moments register as more or less traditional operetta features, other numbers are unmotivated by the plot and exist solely to provide visual spectacle and appearances by the chorus line of "girls."

Die Herzogin von Chicago's juxtaposition of Mary's American and Sandór's European music is perhaps the swan song of the dualistic operetta score. Yet it never takes these differences seriously, undermining them nearly every time they are invoked and complicating them with a variety of valences of each style. While the basic split between Europe and America is clear enough, Kálmán and his librettists evoke a dizzying array of music from each continent: Beethoven, American jazz, Hungarian csárdáses, and Viennese songs all make appearances in the prologue alone. Ernst Krenek's *Jonny spielt auf* is even evoked with the suggestion of a Hungarian in blackface (whom Sandór points at while singing, "Jonny, spielt auf"). The work is less a drama than montage, a sequence of popular sounds arranged into a pleasing pattern.[16]

Kálmán's Austro-Hungarian works had juxtaposed a socially mediated Vienna with a visceral and soulful Hungary. In *Die Herzogin von Chicago*, this is reconfigured to contrast a soulful, idealistic, traditional Europe with a materialistic, forward-looking America. (This framework has a history in Viennese operetta, particularly in Leo Fall's 1907 *Die Dollarprinzessin*.) The Habsburg state's chaotic mix of nationalities have been retroactively united in Sylvania: Prince Sandór Boris has a Hungarian first name, a Slavic last name, and a purportedly independent state of the Pontevedro variety whose cultural identity turns on both Hungarian music and Viennese waltzes.[17] Played by Hubert Marischka, one of the biggest stars of operetta for over a decade and the owner of the Theater an der Wien, he is a living symbol of operetta as well. At the same time, he also represents more contemporary politics: in Act 1, Marischka's costume reportedly resembled that of archconservative Hungarian regent Miklós Horthy.[18] Sylvania represents the entire Habsburg legacy in miniature, a miniaturization that is even foregrounded visually with a soldier puppet prop resembling Sandór appearing in the first act.[19] Marischka's personal politics were not public during this era, but after a 1933 appearance of a swastika flag on the Theater an der Wien's stage in the revue *O du, mein Österreich!*, Kálmán at least was highly suspicious. Marischka would join the Nazi Party in 1938 and stay in the Viennese entertainment business throughout the Third Reich era, directing a number of *Wiener Filme* (Vienna-themed films).

The plot presents an economic conflict—American Mary's infinite funds will rob Sylvania of its sovereignty—dramatized as a competition between American and European music. Yet for all its complexity, the contest is rigged: it is obvious from the outset that America has already won. The operetta opens in a Budapest *Tanzbar* to a chorus of dancers proclaiming, "Charleston! Charleston! Tanzt man heut'" (Charleston! Charleston! That's what one dances today). The dancers proclaim that the "Herren von morgen" (lords of tomorrow) are named Bobby and Yimmy (i.e., Jimmy). The café-style Gypsy band members, wielding jazz instruments, even offer a foxtrot arrangement of Beethoven's Symphony No. 5, an opportunity for Kálmán to indulge his fondness for musical parody (previously heard in the *Zigeunerkapelle* arrangement of Mendelssohn's Wedding March in *Die Csárdásfürstin*). But the band's modernity also suggests that—in a fulfillment of *Der Zigeunerprimas's* prophecy—the age of the traditional Gypsy folk musician has passed. At the same time, American music is presented less as an original creation than as a fun but cheapened version of European art and folk music. The Beethoven foxtrot would not exist without Beethoven. Not only is American music derivative, but Sandór also attacks it as spiritually empty. The Charleston, Sandór explains, is danced with the feet, but the waltz is danced with the heart. In response to the Charleston, Sandór convinces the Gypsy band to switch back to their traditional instruments of violin and cimbalom. They offer snippets of the Rakoczi March and the "Donauwalzer."

Then Sandór sings a waltz with them, describing "Wiener Musik" as the sound of a more humane, lost world (ex. 6.1). The waltz salutes itself as the music that "kehrt uns zurück" (brings us back) to presumably happier times. This Viennese music now includes both "Lieder von Schubert" and "Walzer von Strauß"; the *E*- and *U*- genres of Vienna have been united in opposition to the foreign invader. The chorus of *Tanzbar* patrons—who had just proclaimed the supremacy of the Charleston—is not immune to the charms of this music, first humming along and finally singing the refrain as Sandór whistles the melody. Not content to commemorate Vienna only, Sandór follows this up later in the scene with a csárdás celebrating traditional Hungarian music in similar terms, "I hear your fiddle again/ that you once played and felt once in May," evoking the same May-themed retrospection as "Leise, ganz leise" from *Ein Walzertraum*.[20]

But while Sandór initially finds the Europe and America styles irreconcilable, he soon learns otherwise. The prologue ends with Mary's dramatic entrance into the club and an extended alternation of his and her music. Finally, half of the chorus dances a csárdás while the other half simultaneously dances a foxtrot. Despite their competition, they can be performed to the same music.[21] The implications of this overlap become more obvious in Act 2, where Sandór learns what this finale in the prologue had already suggested: that the Charleston is only the "American csárdás." As Kálmán had showed through his previous operettas, Hungarian dances could be as concerned with the body as American ones. The confluence of modern dance music and Hungarian folk style, something Kálmán had explored since the Hazazaa of *Der Zigeunerprimas* (see chapter 3), is now made thematic.

EXAMPLE 6.1. Kálmán, *Die Herzogin von Chicago*, No. 2, Wienerlied, refrain

Valse lento
PRINZ

Wi-ner Mu-sik, Wie-ner Mu-sik, konn-test die Welt einst be-tö-

pp

nen! Lie-der so reich, Wal-zer so weich, will euch denn nie-mand mehr

rit.   rhythmisch

hö-   ren? Lie-der von Schu-bert und Wal-zer von Strauß klan-gen einst

mf   rhythmisch

EXAMPLE 6.1. (continued)

ju - belnd hin - aus...   Du schö - ne Wie - ner Mu - sik,   du hol - des, klin - gen - des

Glück,   Du kehrst ja doch einst zu - rück!

The operetta even offers a rare plot centered on American immgration in the second male lead: Mary's secretary, James Bondy, is described as "born Myslowitz,"
with a family hailing from "Kokotnitz bei Brünn," an amusingly fictional location in Moravia whose name is an appropriately Habsburgian amalgamation of
languages. (When offered a cross of honor, he exchanges it for a Star of David, a
rare open acknowledgement of Judaism in late Silver Age operetta.) The operetta
ultimately concludes that all entertaining music is worthwhile—as second couple
Bondy and Princess Rosemarie say, "Im Himmel spielt auch schon die Jazzband"
(in heaven, the jazz band is already playing too).

Kai Marcel Sicks argues that the American elements of *Die Herzogin von Chicago* are superficial: after all, there is still a large, European theater orchestra in
the pit, a composed, fully notated score without improvisation, and a series of
European-style arias and scenes.[22] While the "jazz" of an operetta like *Die Herzogin von Chicago* indeed has little in common with Louis Armstrong, neither did
that of most of Tin Pan Alley, the material to which this work is more appropriately compared (which also included a large orchestra, though perhaps not on

Kálmán's scale). Marischka favored Paul Whiteman; George Gershwin famously met Kálmán and saw *Die Herzogin von Chicago* when visiting Vienna. And the song-dialogue format was standard for musical theater on either side of the Atlantic.[23] More broadly, the specters haunting *Die Herzogin von Chicago* are less those of nationality than those of genre. The conventions of operetta have receded in favor of those borrowed from film and revue.

For Theodor Adorno, this melting of operetta into the montage of revue was, while not exactly progress, at least less pretentious than some alternatives. While Viennese operettas have the appearance of autonomous dramatic form (like many others, he identifies "tragic second act finales" as their key characteristic), he writes, revues drop this appearance of pseudo-individualized personality and "deceptive interiority." Instead, the chaos and fragmentation of the revue acknowledges its own status as a fetish object.[24] (Interestingly, even in 1932 he already identifies recent operetta as "late Viennese operettas," implying that they are over.) While the operetta had ambition to be considered as art, the revue's lack of shame has a certain honesty. For Kálmán in *Die Herzogin von Chicago*, adopting these new styles was a way to stay modern, even as other elements of the operetta signal nostalgia. Critic Ernst Decsey referred to the result as "demagoguery" and chaos. Kálmán, he wrote, allowed both nostalgia and Charleston to triumph, a cacophony without meaning.[25]

"VULGARIZED GENRE"

While Kálmán moved toward mass culture in *Herzogin*, Franz Lehár continued in the opposite direction. In 1934 Lehár's youthful dream of operatic fame was fulfilled: he had a premiere at the Wiener Staatsoper. The work, *Giuditta*, carried the genre designation of "musikalische Komödie," skirting the decision between opera and operetta. A *Carmen*-like tale of romance and tragedy between an army officer and the titular Italian lady, its score represents nothing more or less than the continuation of *Das Land des Lächelns*. Yet when thrust into the Wiener Staatsoper, it profoundly disrupted the boundaries of genre. The title role was played by opera singer Jarmila Novotná; the tenor was, naturally, Richard Tauber, still the only performer who could convincingly bridge the opera-operetta divide. (Novotná had practiced this on a smaller scale, appearing in Max Ophüls's filmed *The Bartered Bride* in 1932; she later starred in several Hollywood films.) Operettas had, in fact, been frequently performed at the Staatsoper, their popularity bolstering the theater's box office during the difficult years of the early 1930s.[26] Yet the theater's all-out investment in the Tauber and Lehár circus of *Giuditta* marked, for some, artistic bankruptcy.

The most vociferous condemnation came from, again, Ernst Decsey. He was a regular operetta critic and playwright and enjoyed a close relationship with

Lehár—he had even written an authorized biography of the composer in 1924—making this not a simple external critique of the genre but a condemnation of what it has become from someone with a real stake in its existence.[27] Given unusually prominent feuilleton real estate in the *Neues Wiener Tagblatt*, he condemned *Giuditta* as evidence of a "vulgarized genre."[28] It is never entirely clear whether the debased genre in question is operetta or opera; because of their dilution, both are afflicted. *Giuditta*, Decsey makes clear, was popular with audiences, bringing in 40,000 schillings for the premiere alone (or so he claims).

Decsey notes, however, that the premiere did not attract the usual Staatsoper audience, but rather the "Lehár audieince that one usually sees in the Theater an der Wien." Clemens Krauss, the conductor and the theater's general director, sat in his box but was, Decsey projected, "intellectually absent." Decsey fails to note that the Staatsoper regularly produced works like *Die Fledermaus* and *Der Opernball* and instead compared the operetta's reception to that of *Wozzeck*. He notes that *Giuditta*'s premiere had displaced the more Staatsoper-appropriate but less lucrative *Karl V* by Ernst Krenek (whose *Jonny spielt auf* had been referenced in *Die Herzogin von Chicago* only a few years earlier).

In a belated outburst of liberal compartmentalization that recalls nothing less than Eduard Hanslick, Decsey cannot help but find *Giuditta* all wrong.[29] Brought out of its appropriate home, an operetta no longer makes sense.

> It's operetta theater, it's Theater an der Wien, it isn't Staatsoper, and can only be brought there by force. Each space has its laws, and they shall be respected. Where is the musical comedy? *Giuditta* is an operetta, an amorous, large-scale, numbing, ambitious, occasionally charming, occasionally dumb operetta. Vulgarized genre. But "musical comedy"? Why didn't he write a proper one?[30]

An operetta in the Staatsoper violates the laws of the space, promoting a kind of spectatorship and pleasure inappropriate to the dignity and gravity of the Staatsoper's surroundings. *Giuditta* would be appropriate for the Theater an der Wien (indeed Hubert Marischka was the stage director), but in the Staatsoper it embodies reflexive genre conventions inappropriate for the "musical comedy" genre it claims to be. It brings with it an inappropriately loud and flashy audience, and its stellar box office prompts unwelcome avariciousness. He then diverts his criticisms, however, to attack operetta genre conventions themselves: the nonsense sprouted by the "second couple," whose plot barely intersects with that of the principals, the absurdity of a waltz playing out in an opera set in Benghazi.

Yet Decsey is fixated on a genre distinction whose meaning had lost common currency among theater audiences. *Giuditta*'s enshrining of operetta in a pantheon of high art and *Die Herzogin von Chicago*'s dissolution of operetta signifiers reflect the same problem: a genre without a clear identity. Operetta was no longer Vienna's favorite. As in previous eras, operetta composers sought to stay on top by incorporating the latest musical trends. But the more operetta relied on jazz or contemplated opera, the more its association with Vienna was diluted.

The rise of Austrofacism would seem to bode well for backward-looking operetta; as Ulrike Petersen writes, "the internationally preferred image of the nostalgic, backward homeland of 'wine, women, and waltzes' matched the new regime's idealized image of an idyllic agrarian, deproletarianized country with cultural traditions between the baroque and Biedermeier."[31] But ideological alignment was no substitute for a lack of cash. After the ascension of Engelbert Dollfuß as chancellor of Austria, the situation deteriorated dramatically: between 1933 and 1934, the Raimund Theater, Bürgertheater, and Theater der Komiker all closed, and the Theater an der Wien's Karczag Verlag faced a devastating loss in royalty revenue after Jewish composers were prohibited in Germany. As Petersen relates, operetta began to move to smaller venues, taking on new guises, and after the *Anschluss* in 1938 was subject to Nazi ideological control.[32]

These institutional and political changes fundamentally altered Viennese theatrical culture and, with the exception of a few distant echoes, marked the end of large-scale new operetta in Vienna. The Third Reich eliminated the possibility of any revival. By the mid-1930s, most of the artists of the operetta industry had turned to other pursuits; the Nazis destroyed what community remained. A few figures who were not Jewish continued to prosper: Franz Lehár, the rare non-Jewish operetta composer, remained popular throughout the war, but on the strength of his old works only; Hubert Marischka and his brother Ernst wrote and directed a number of lighthearted films under Nazi sponsorship. Meanwhile, Emmerich Kálmán, Alfred Grünwald, Oscar Straus, Paul Abraham, and many others fled to the United States and sought employment on Broadway and in Hollywood with varying degrees of success.[33] Richard Tauber took up residence in London, where he was as popular as ever. Julius Brammer died in 1943 on the Côte d'Azur even as Alfred Grünwald and other colleagues struggled to secure his passage to the United States. Béla Jenbach, librettist of *Die Csárdásfürstin,* hid in a basement in Vienna for three years and died of untreated stomach cancer in 1943. Fritz Löhner, librettist of *Das Land des Lächelns* and *Giuditta,* was murdered in Auschwitz. Critic and librettist Leopold Jacobson and Louis Treumann, the Silver Age's perennial lazy gentleman, both died in Theresienstadt.[34]

Yet even as their world was shattered, their work played on. Works by Jewish composers were off limits, but works with Jewish librettists simply had the offending names removed and were programmed as often as before.[35] For audiences—both during the war and after it—operetta was a reminder of simpler, happier times. If some of its final works, such as *Die Herzogin von Chicago,* had revealed a world in transition, the revival of old operettas served to remind audiences of a time they remembered as whole, even if they had not been there to see it themselves. In 1949 Arthur Maria Rabenalt posited that "today's operettas sidestep [the present] in phantasmagorias distant from reality.... They produce fantasies (not by the fireplace, which no longer exists) in a vacuum, they believe they can avoid the wreckage and ruins of our time."[36]

OPERETTA'S PAST AS OPERETTA'S PRESENT

Since the middle of the twentieth century, operetta has come to embody an old-fashioned alternative to more current musical and theatrical styles. Today operetta performances in German-speaking areas are known for attracting older patrons, often accompanied by their grandchildren. Operetta has acquired a corresponding reputation among theater-goers as charmingly retro camp at best and antiquated and politically reactionary at worst, but it remains a solid box office draw. As Viennese music critic Wilhelm Sinkovicz wrote in 2011, "Operetta is dead, of that commentators have long been certain. The audience, however, does not play along.... Where operetta is played, the houses are full."[37] But while many productions present operetta in a cozy traditionalist vein, some theaters have explored more aggressive and often updated productions, most prominently a series of stagings of Berlin operettas overseen by Barrie Kosky at the Komische Oper Berlin. These visions were contrasted in the title of a 2016 special issue of the journal *Österreichische Musikzeitschrift*, which asked, "Is operetta dusty, anarchic, kitschy, provocative, hopelessly reactionary, or an exciting social critique?"[38] At times, both production styles claim a mantle of authenticity—the traditional approach harkens to a more comforting world of yesterday; the updates appeal to operetta's fragile but persistent satirical vein. Both are, of course, fundamentally contemporary practices whose origins are better located in German television films and German *Regietheater*, respectively. (An analogy to the authenticity debates around early music already has been explored by Kevin Clarke.[39]) But it is remarkable the extent to which contemporary performance practices continue to play out operetta's age-old debate between sentimentality and satire.

Operetta venues, few as they are today, are varied in their repertoire choices, performance practices, and audiences. In Vienna the Volksoper is a leading venue for operetta productions and produces a variety of both popular and unusual works. But one telling transformation is the movement of many Viennese operetta productions in Austria from urban theaters to specialist summer festivals and theaters located in idyllic spa and resort towns such as Mörbisch, Baden bei Wien, and Bad Ischl, the latter of which has historical status as the summer home of the operetta industry's elite as well as the Lehár-Villa museum, located in the composer's house.[40] Operetta, once the most metropolitan of genres, has become part of a pastoral retreat. In Germany operetta productions are found at urban state theaters such as the Komische Oper Berlin, Staatsoperette Dresden, and Munich's Staatstheater am Gärtnerplatz as well as scattered throughout the programs of numerous non-specialist opera houses. Many of the most interesting productions hail from smaller theaters and festivals. While small theaters and local cultures are appropriate for operetta, from a scholarly perspective their short runs and paucity of videos make them sadly inaccessible to those outside their immediate geographical area.[41] The German record label Classic Produktion Osnabrück (cpo) also produces an ever-growing series of recordings based on many of these theaters' productions (including an ongoing complete Lehár edition), which present scores in as much anachronistic operatic and orchestral glory as possible.[42] Internationally, Viennese operetta can also frequently be found in translated form at the Budapest Operetta Theater and the Ohio Light Opera.[43]

In Austria in particular many theaters cultivate a production aesthetic commensurate with operetta's reputation as nostalgia product. Unlike most operas in German-speaking theaters, operettas are often produced in a conservative style featuring period costumes, straightforward storytelling, and sympathetic, predictable characterization. Dialogue is delivered in an old-fashioned, mannered style; the entire aesthetic is high kitsch and, compared with most local opera, thoroughly middlebrow, something suggested by Sinkovicz's implication of a divide between "commentators" and audiences. (DVDs produced by the Seefestspiele Mörbisch provide many examples.[44]) Interpretively, the majority of these productions are what David Levin would term weak readings, "embrac[ing] the prevailing understanding of the work's meaning, seeking to reproduce the work's prevailing aesthetic identity, and often presenting itself as a nonreading, one that does not consciously venture an interpretation but instead merely seeks to present the work in its most familiar form."[45]

The most familiar form and understood meaning, for operetta, is one of old-fashioned entertainment detached from the world. Or, as a critic for the magazine *Applaus* wrote of a 2004 production of *Gräfin Mariza* at Mörbisch, in prose that in translation retains its purple hue but loses its alliteration, "Here you know what you have: entertainment at the highest level, a trace of nostalgia (but with the old freshness), alternating fiery Gypsy sounds and sweet floating in familiar-dreamy [*vertraut-verträumt*] music...and notions hardly common nowadays: elegance and the good life."[46] Sinkovicz's 2011 article was even headlined "In Bad Ischl, the world is as it should be." Yet these productions rarely stop to interrogate: what should operetta be, and how did it come to be this?

The traditional production style's timeless appearance belies its relatively recent origin. It is, in fact, an invented tradition, a product not of the early twentieth century but most immediately of West German television films of the 1960s and 1970s (as well as the stage performances of that same era), which many of today's elder patrons remember fondly. Starring opera singers like Anna Moffo and Rudolf Schock, these productions, according to a recent DVD reissue, "faced direct competition from live broadcasts such as *Der goldene Schuß, Dalli-Dalli,*

ZDF Hitparade, Erkennen Sie die Melodie, and *Anneliese Rothenberger gibt sich die Ehre"*—that is, programs specializing in the art of the Schlager, akin to the American *Lawrence Welk Show.*[47] Operetta historians have often criticized these films for their textual interventions and soupy musical stylings; for example, Richard Traubner considers a film of *Die Zirkusprinzessin* to be "about as close to the original operetta as *Ma and Pa Kettle,*" citing the "vulgar, ping-pongy arrangements" as well as drastic changes in the libretto.[48] It is notable that Traubner seeks *Urtext* fidelity in a way never particularly valued by operetta in its own time, a dilemma that recalls Philip Gossett's work on nineteenth-century Italian opera.[49] But perhaps more relevantly, these productions' wide dissemination means that they hold their own form of authenticity in their audiences' memories. While Traubner is aware how far these productions diverge from the styles of the works' premieres, most audiences are not, and when operetta is conceived of as "pure entertainment," it is unclear why they should care. A demand for *Werktreue* (fidelity to the "work") transforms operetta into a historicized text, not something these productions claim to offer. Librettist Victor Léon had identified bridging the gap between expert and amateur audience members as the most challenging aspect of operetta composition (see introduction); it remains a crux of operetta production.

But there is a more important charge against the traditional style than false authenticity and a more compelling reason to recover original practice than the spectral principle of *Werktreue.* The earlier roots of the TV film style, historians such as Kevin Clarke and Clemens Risi have argued, must be traced back another step, to the Third Reich, where the enforced Nazi aesthetic of operetta as bland entertainment effaced its Jewish creators and transformed it into a wartime morale booster. As Risi writes, "That operetta's label as unserious has, long into the postwar period, remained coupled to watered-down harmlessness lies largely in this cleansing of operetta through Nazi cultural politics and the trimming of its repertoire."[50] From this perspective, recovering an earlier practice is not merely a matter of historical interest but an act of reconciliation. Clarke produces a succinct list of five values that must be recovered to return to an earlier operetta practice: sexual innuendo, ironic distance or stylization, "crude but effective" effects, virtuosic dancing, and glamorous personalities.[51] He also urges against the casting of opera singers (as is the usual practice in nearly all larger theaters and many smaller ones) in favor of performers with distinctive, often not classically trained voices as well as more experience delivering spoken dialogue and dancing.

Clarke's recommendations are tied more particularly to the repertoire of Weimar Berlin than to Vienna. They are closely aligned with the work of director Barrie Kosky at the Komische Oper Berlin. Since 2012 at the Komische Oper, Kosky has directed or (as intendant of the theater) programmed productions of a number of largely forgotten Berlin operettas such as Paul Abraham's *Ball im Savoy* (Ball at the Savoy, 1932) and Oscar Straus's *Die Perlen von Cleopatra* (The Pearls of Cleopatra, 1923) and *Eine Frau, die weiß, was sie will!* (A Woman Who Knows What She Wants!, 1932). Stylistically, Kosky tends to emphasize slapstick humor, sexual innuendo, gender fluidity and drag, and elaborate dance numbers, drawing an analogy between Weimar Berlin and the city's present.[52] Crucially, Kosky recruited a new ensemble of performers for these productions which is mostly distinct from the Komische Oper's usual operatic ensemble, including the cabaret trio Geschwister Pfister and the actors Dagmar Menzel and Max Hopp. Kosky defines his project both as emphatically Jewish and in the same terms as Clarke: operetta, "the unruly, illegitimate sibling [of opera], was, during Nazism and also in the postwar period, domesticated and reduced to mere entertainment.... Operetta became staid, dutiful entertainment, disciplined into order."[53] Kosky's intervention should not be reduced to staging style; the operettas he has programmed are a rather different group of works than those favored by more traditional theaters. (Franz Lehár is conspicuously absent, ironic considering that the theater the Komische Oper currently occupies was once the Metropol-Theater, the site of some of the composer's greatest Berlin triumphs.) But, considering that the productions are promoted under the umbrella of operetta as a whole, Kosky presents a strongly contrasting aesthetic and political vision of what that can mean.

Yet it is striking the extent to which Kosky's and Clarke's critiques—that traditional operetta is too prim, too bourgeois, insufficiently taboo-breaking—replicate a much older vein of operetta discourse, one found throughout this book. From Karl Kraus's criticisms of operetta's coziness with power to Erich Urban's 1903 declaration that operetta should return to its Dionysian, Offenbachian roots, operetta chaos has always been privileged by critics and, in performance, relatively scarce. In Germany's state-supported, urban theater system, satirical operetta has perhaps finally found its haven, which is not to suggest that Kosky's productions lack an audience but rather that even in today's small world of operetta the Komische Oper occupies a different habitus than the Seefestspiele Mörbisch, and neither performs the same role that operetta did in 1905 or 1925. Both, however, present a vision of operetta as camp, Mörbisch usually unintentionally and the Komische Oper by design.

While Kosky rejects operetta conservatism, other directors have turned it against itself, deconstructing operetta's jolliness into violent *Regietheater* mayhem. Such provocations are not unusual in German-language opera houses, but when applied to operetta they sustain the power to shock.[54] One example is Hans Neuenfels's production of *Die Fledermaus* at the Salzburg Festival in 2001, which found a different avenue for critiquing the shadow of National Socialism through operetta staging. Conceived as a bitter farewell by Gerard Mortier in his final year as intendant of the festival, it took direct aim at the conservative power structure of Austrian society, many of whose members were conveniently gathered in Salzburg to see this national icon.[55] Neuenfels's production featured a dense assemblage of

Nazis, masturbation, drugs, incest, and, perhaps most transgressively, a Prince Orlofsky who did not sing Strauss's music melodiously. Like much *Regietheater*, Neuenfels cited his sources, including texts by Karl Kraus in the spoken dialogue, and, in case it was not clear that the festival's audience was meant to be complicit, the jailor Frosch scolded them directly. The production succeeded in generating widespread outrage, including a statement from the far-right Freedom Party (FPÖ), which warned that "once again the question arises as to what damage is done to the Salzburg Festival by such productions that completely antagonize and mislead the audience and how much [Salzburg's] reputation as a serious festival city is put at risk."[56] One audience member put Werktreue to a legal test, suing for his money back under the argument that he had not been given the *Fledermaus* he had been promised; he lost.[57]

Neuenfels posed *Fledermaus* and operetta in general as a mirror held up to Austrian society. A 2017 production of *Das Land des Lächelns* at the Opernhaus Zürich, directed by intendant Andreas Homoki, was comparatively a salvage mission, attempting to streamline and rescue operetta from its reputation as old-fashioned kitsch and present it to its best, most flattering advantage. Far more elegant than the average Mörbisch or Baden production, it featured a glossy black minimalist set, a limited color palette, tastefully restrained conducting, and internationally famous opera singers in the main roles (including tenor Piotr Beczala, who has recorded a Richard Tauber tribute album), all of which elevated the performance's cultural capital to a level appropriate for the Opernhaus Zürich, one of the most elite and exclusive of European opera houses (fig. 6.1).[58] (The aesthetic recalled Anthony Minghella's production of *Madama Butterfly*, produced at the English National Opera and Metropolitan Opera.) The spoken dialogue, meanwhile, was drastically cut, leaving only slightly more than a medley of famous songs and some revue-like dance numbers. The production rejected the yellowface still common in productions of this operetta, but its highly aestheticized presentation of Chinese exoticism remained unexamined and uncritical.[59] What was worth preserving, this production seemed to propose, was primarily the score, sung by world-class operatic voices, secondarily a sense of style and exotic charm, and virtually nothing else, leaving an emotional vacuum under its glamorous surface.

Unfortunately, relatively few productions have embraced the dualism and self-reflexivity of operetta texts themselves or taken the opportunity to ground their interpretations more firmly in operetta's own reception histories. As the operetta world continues to play out the debate between sentimentality and satire, most productions seem to choose one at the exclusion of the other. This is particularly notable considering the current popularity of reception narratives within opera stagings.[60] Peter Konwitschny's Dresden *Csárdásfürstin*, discussed in chapter 4, arguably performs this historicized role, placing the work within its wartime reception. But perhaps the best example is Claus Guth's 2018 production of *Die lustige*

FIGURE 6.1. *Das Land des Lächelns,* Opernhaus Zürich. T+ T Fotografie Toni Suter, Opernhaus Zürich

Witwe at the Oper Frankfurt.[61] Guth's production used another popular *Regietheater* device, a theater-within-a-theater, in which the cast comprised a group of actors making a film of *Die lustige Witwe* (the setting was moved up several decades, and much of the spoken dialogue was new). The Parisian hijinks were, for the most part, played within the film, while the protagonists' personal histories were staged as the lives of the actor-Hanna and actor-Danilo (given the names of the real singers playing them, in this case Kirsten and Christoph), in a naturalistic style, a conceit likened by critic Manuel Brug to Cole Porter's *Kiss Me, Kate.*[62]

While occasionally confusing, the production brilliantly deconstructed the dualistic score, balancing the artifice and performance of spectacular dances with sincere feeling. The austere latter-day setting conferred an elegiac tone, suggesting that both the cheerfulness of the filmed material and Hanna and Danilo's love are located in an inaccessible past. The film ended with film-Hanna and film-Danilo together in "Lippen schweigen," but, in a rewritten ending, the following brief reprise of "Ja, das Studium der Weiber ist schwer" broke up Kirsten/actor-Hanna and Christoph/actor-Danilo's relationship. This suggests that the perfunctory third acts of most operettas do not, in fact, bridge the gap between the dueling social spheres established in the first two acts nor the melodramatic fissure of the tragic second-act finale. Dramatically speaking, this new ending solves one of operetta's dramaturgical weaknesses in much the same way that Lehár would himself in many of his later works. It also suggests that operetta's very optimism remains a sticking point in its reception, and that after the horrors of the twentieth century and the tragic fates of many operetta artists it can be difficult to sustain such a hopeful vision of 1905 Vienna. The ambivalent, wistful postmodernism of Guth's *Regietheater* is not the native language of operetta, but what was remarkable about the production was how its double plot could hold happiness and sadness side by side without invalidating either. The comic and folkloric elements of the score were ironically distanced but not mocked or parodied; their pleasures were real even though their reality was not. It is this pleasure that Viennese operetta promised its audiences: three acts in which the mechanics of an operetta plot could briefly vanquish homesickness, work, social inequality, or money troubles, even as the real world awaited their return.

Studying operetta means taking these mechanics and their potential seriously. Operetta promised both simple joys for the fans and sophisticated allegories and meta-narratives for the fanatics. Studying it requires requires attention to both, and to the ways composers and librettists incorporated, remixed, and instrumentalized the debates surrounding its own instabilities; it demands and sharpens awareness of liminality, of the discursive power (and limitations) of Vienna's mania for taxonomies of cultural prestige. Operetta's emotional generosity, inextricably linked to the demographics and society of late Habsburg Vienna, was its greatest asset and its biggest critical hurdle. Operetta forces us to confront a repertoire that, even within a relatively small theatrical sphere, sought to be everything: pleasure, serious art, satire, fairy tale, anarchy, bourgeois entertainment, old-fashioned, up-to-date, heartbreaking, provocative, affirmative, absurd, and nostalgic. Ultimately, operetta thrived on these conflicts, which power the dramaturgical machinations of operettas themselves and continue to define its reception. Operetta's stubborn tendency toward idealism meant that in the space of an evening all these self-contradictory impulses could be reconciled onstage, and with them came a fragile happy ending. When it convinced, operetta promised nothing less than a more harmonious, more beautiful, and happier life.

NOTES

ABBREVIATIONS USED IN NOTES

Newspaper Theater Critics

Newspaper critics most often signed their reviews with a nickname, usually their initials or a few letters from their last name (such as "rp" for Ludwig Karpath and "D.B." for David Josef Bach). I have identified most of the regular critics and their full names are included in brackets; a question mark indicates some conjecture. Many of the less regular authors, however, remain unidentified and some reviews are unsigned.

Newspapers

AZ	Arbeiter-Zeitung
FB	Fremden-Blatt
NFP	Neue Freie Presse
NWJ	Neues Wiener Journal
NWT	Neues Wiener Tagblatt
RP	Reichspost

Libraries and Archives

ADK	Akademie der Künste, Berlin
NÖLA	Niederösterreichisches Landesarchiv, St. Pölten, Austria
NYPL	New York Public Library
ÖNB	Österreichische Nationalbibliothek, Vienna
ÖNB MS	Österreichische Nationalbibliothek, Musiksammlung, Vienna
ÖTM	Archive of the Theatermuseum, Vienna
WB	Wienbibliothek im Rathaus, Vienna

PREFACE

1. "'Wiener Blut': Grüne werfen FPÖ 'Nazi-Jargon' vor," *Die Presse*, August 16, 2010, https://www.diepresse.com/587895/wiener-blut-grune-werfen-fpo-nazi-jargon-vor. "Wiener Blut" is also the title of a 1988 song by Falco, whose racy subject matter is not typical of Freedom Party rhetoric.

INTRODUCTION: OPERETTA IN VIENNA

1. The protagonist is based on Cankar himself. The text used here is Köstler's German translation from the Slovenian; the original title is "Pred ciljem." Ivan Cankar, "Vor dem Ziel," in *Vor dem Ziel: Literarische Skizzen aus Wien*, trans. Erwin Köstler (Klangenfurt, Austria: Drava Verlag, 1995). The story was first published in Ivan Cankar, *Knjiga za lahkomiselne ljudi* (Ljubljana: L. Schwentner, 1901).

2. The description of the theater as near the center of the city suggests that it is likely the Theater an der Wien, located just south of the center city. Jereb's walk might trace the path between the outer districts of Ottakring or Rudolfsheim through the Vorstadt's Neubau or Josefstadt, through Mariahilf, arriving in the fourth district, Wieden. Another possibility is the Carl-Theater, located in the Leopoldstadt, north of the city center and across the Donaukanal, placing Jereb's home in Alsergrund or Brigittenau. See map on page xii.

3. Cankar, "Vor dem Ziel," 64.

4. The term "Silver Age" did not come into wide use until after World War II. Today, "Silver Age" conventionally refers to all Viennese operetta between *Die lustige Witwe* and World War II, for example in the histories of Richard Traubner and Volker Klotz. Volker Klotz, *Operette: Porträt und Handbuch einer unerhörten Kunst*, rev. ed. (Kassel: Bärenreiter, 2004); Richard Traubner, *Operetta: A Theatrical History*, rev. ed. (New York: Routledge, 2003).

5. Carl Dahlhaus, *Nineteenth-Century Music*, trans. J. Bradford Robinson (Berkeley: University of California Press, 1989), 228. (The German original dates from 1980.)

6. For arguments for various sorts of authenticity see, Bettina Brandl-Risi and Clemens Risi, eds., *Kunst der Oberfläche: Operette zwischen Bravour und Banalität* (Leipzig: Henschel, 2015); Volker Klotz, *Es lebe: Die Operette: Anläufe, sie neuerlich zu erwecken* (Würzburg, Germany: Königshausen & Neumann, 2014).

7. William Weber, *The Great Transformation of Musical Taste: Concert Programming from Haydn to Brahms* (Cambridge: Cambridge University Press, 2008); Lawrence W. Levine, *Highbrow/Lowbrow: The Emergence of Cultural Hierarchy in America* (Cambridge, MA: Harvard University Press, 1988); Andreas Huyssen, *After the Great Divide: Modernism, Mass Culture, Postmodernism* (Bloomington: Indiana University Press, 1986).

8. Derek B. Scott, *Sounds of the Metropolis: The Nineteenth-Century Popular Music Revolution in London, New York, Paris, and Vienna* (Oxford: Oxford University Press, 2008), 4.

9. These debates preoccupy the writers collected in Marion Linhardt's two source anthologies dealing with operetta. Derek Scott traces the distinction back to the term *Trivialmusik* in the 1830s. Marion Linhardt, ed., *Stimmen zur Unterhaltung: Operette und Revue in der publizistischen Debatte (1906–1933)* (Vienna: Lehner, 2009); Marion Linhardt, ed.,

"'Warum es der Operette so schlecht geht': Ideologische Debatten um das musikalische Unterhaltungstheater (1880–1916)," special issue of *Maske und Kothurn*, 45, no. 1–2 (2001); Scott, *Sounds of the Metropolis*, 87–92.

10. Adam Müller-Guttenbrunn, *Wien war eine Theaterstadt* (Vienna: Graeser, 1885), 8. As cited and translated in W. E. Yates, *Theatre in Vienna: A Critical History, 1776–1995* (Cambridge: Cambridge University Press, 1996), 168.

11. The foremost advocate for this position is Viennese gadfly Karl Kraus, whose critique will be examined in detail later in this study, but it is also evident in Siegfried Kracauer's study of Offenbach, *Jacques Offenbach and the Paris of His Time*, trans. Gwenda David and Eric Mosbacher (New York: Zone Books, 2002).

12. Carolyn Abbate, "Offenbach, Kracauer, and Ethical Frivolity," *Opera Quarterly* 33, no. 1 (Winter 2017): 62–86.

13. This elision of production and product is examined, in terms of later work, in Bernard Gendron, "Theodor Adorno Meets the Cadillacs," in *Studies in Entertainment: Critical Approaches to Mass Culture*, ed. Tania Modleski (Bloomington: Indiana University Press, 1986), 18–36.

14. Hermann Broch, *Hugo von Hofmannsthal and His Time: The European Imagination, 1860–1920*, ed. and trans. Michael P. Steinberg (Chicago: University of Chicago Press, 1984), 65; Carl E. Schorske, *Fin-de-Siècle Vienna: Politics and Culture* (New York: Knopf, 1979).

15. Scott, *Sounds of the Metropolis*, 9–12. Marion Linhardt examines this phenomenon in Vienna-specific terms in *Residenzstadt und Metropole: Zu einer kulturellen Topographie des Wiener Unterhaltungstheaters (1858–1918)* (Tübingen: Niemeyer, 2006).

16. Victor Léon, "Bittere Operettenwahrheiten," *Komödie: Wochenrevue für Bühne und Film*, January 9, 1923.

17. Pierre Bourdieu, *The Field of Cultural Production*, ed. Randal Johnson (New York: Columbia University Press, 1993), 126.

18. Franz Lehár, "Die Zukunft der Operette," *Die Wage*, January 10, 1903.

19. Franz Hadamowsky and Heinz Otte, *Die Wiener Operette: Ihre Theater- und Wirkungsgeschichte* (Vienna: Bellaria-Verlag, 1947), 298.

20. Adorno's most specific writing on operetta is "Arabesken zur Operette," in *Gesammelte Schriften*, vol. 19, Musikalische Schriften VI (Frankfurt: Suhrkamp, 2003), 516–19.

21. Arthur Maria Rabenalt, *Operette als Aufgabe: Aufsätze zur Operettenkrise* (Berlin: Heinz Menge-Verlag, 1948), 13.

22. For more on formulas and production systems, see Micaela Baranello, "The Operetta Factory: Production Systems of Silver-Age Vienna," in *The Cambridge Companion to Operetta*, ed. Derek B. Scott and Anastasia Belina (Cambridge: Cambridge University Press, 2019), 189–204; Heike Quissek, *Das deutschsprachige Operettenlibretto: Figuren, Stoffe, Dramaturgie* (Stuttgart: Verlag J.B. Metzler, 2012).

23. The power of operetta in the multinational era is considered in Moritz Csáky, *Ideologie der Operette und Wiener Moderne: Ein Kulturhistorischer Essay zur österreichischen Identität* (Vienna: Böhlau, 1996). Operetta's final years are examined in Matthias Kauffmann, *Operette im "Dritten Reich": Musikalisches Unterhaltungstheater zwischen 1933 und 1945* (Neumünster, Germany: von Bockel Verlag, 2017); Ulrike Petersen, "Operetta after the Habsburg Empire" (PhD diss., University of California, Berkeley, 2013).

24. The happy ending was close to universal in operetta until Lehár's experiments in the late 1920s, a subject of much contention. See Manfred Angerer, "Zorikas Traum von der silbernen Operette: Lehárs originelle Konzeption des Sowohl - Als auch," *Studien zur Musikwissenschaft: Beihefte der Denkmäler der Tonkust in Österreich* 36 (1985): 111–22; Alexander Engel, "Der Schrei nach dem Happy end," *NWJ*, March 24, 1929.

25. David Brodbeck, *Defining Deutschtum: Political Ideology, German Identity, and Music-Critical Discourse in Liberal Vienna* (Oxford: Oxford University Press, 2014), 6.

26. The topographical hierarchy of Vienna is discussed in detail in Wolfgang Maderthaner and Lutz Musner, *Unruly Masses: The Other Side of Fin-de-Siècle Vienna*, trans. David Fernbach and Michael Huffmaster (New York: Berghahn Books, 2008), 31–43.

27. Statistische Central-Commission, *Spezialortsrepertorium der österreichischen Länder* (Vienna: Verlag der K. K. Hof- und Staatsdruckerei, 1915).

28. Maderthaner and Musner, *Unruly Masses*, 23–25.

29. A general history of the city is Peter Csendes and Ferdinand Opll, eds., *Wien: Geschichte einer Stadt*, vol. 3, *Von 1790 bis zur Gegenwart* (Vienna: Böhlau, 2006). An excellent study of the era considered in this volume is Brigitte Hamann, *Hitler's Vienna: A Dictator's Apprenticeship*, trans. Thomas Thornton (Oxford: Oxford University Press, 2000). The subaltern experience is examined in detail in Maderthaner and Musner, *Unruly Masses*.

30. William J. McGrath, *Dionysian Art and Populist Politics in Austria* (New Haven, CT: Yale University Press, 1974); Allan Janik and Stephen Toulmin, *Wittgenstein's Vienna* (New York: Simon and Schuster, 1973); Maderthaner and Musner, *Unruly Masses*, 1.

31. Schorske, *Fin-de-Siècle Vienna*. Some important responses to Schorske are Pieter M. Judson, *Exclusive Revolutionaries: Liberal Politics, Social Experience, and National Identity in the Austrian Empire, 1848–1914* (Ann Arbor: University of Michigan Press, 1996); John W. Boyer, *Political Radicalism in Late Imperial Vienna: Origins of the Christian Social Movement, 1848–1897* (Chicago: University of Chicago Press, 1981); John W. Boyer, *Culture and Political Crisis in Vienna: Christian Socialism in Power, 1897–1918* (Chicago: University of Chicago Press, 1995); Steven Beller, *Vienna and the Jews, 1867–1938: A Cultural History* (Cambridge: Cambridge University Press, 1989); Steven Beller, ed., *Rethinking Vienna 1900* (New York: Berghahn Books, 2001).

32. Christopher Chowrimootoo, *Middlebrow Modernism: Britten's Operas and the Great Divide* (Berkeley: University of California Press, 2018), 8.

33. Dana Gooley, "Hanslick on Johann Strauss Jr.: Genre, Social Class, and Liberalism in Vienna," in *Rethinking Hanslick: Music, Formalism, and Expression*, ed. Nicole Grimes, Siobhán Donovan, and Wolfgang Marx (Rochester, NY: University of Rochester Press, 2013), 92.

34. Otto Keller, *Die Operette in ihrer geschichtlichen Entwicklung: Musik, Libretto, Darstellung* (Leipzig: Stein Verlag, 1926).

35. Karl Westermeyer, *Die Operette im Wandel des Zeitgeistes: Von Offenbach bis zur Gegenwart* (Berlin: Drei Masken Verlag, 1931); Hadamowsky and Otte, *Die Wiener Operette*; Traubner, *Operetta*.

36. Linhardt, *Residenzstadt und Metropole*; Stefan Frey, *Was sagt ihr zu diesem Erfolg: Franz Lehár und die Unterhaltungsmusik des 20. Jahrhunderts* (Frankfurt: Insel, 1999); Stefan Frey, *"Unter Tränen Lachen": Emmerich Kálmán: Eine Operettenbiographie* (Berlin: Henschel, 2003); Stefan Frey, Christine Stemprok, and Wolfgang Dosch, *Leo Fall: Spöt-*

tischer Rebell der Operette (Vienna: Edition Steinbauer, 2009); Camille Crittenden, *Johann Strauss and Vienna: Operetta and the Politics of Popular Culture* (Cambridge: Cambridge University Press, 2000). Frey's earlier, briefer study of Lehár also has valuable insights; Stefan Frey, *Franz Lehár oder das schlechte Gewissen der leichten Musik* (Tübingen: Niemeyer, 1995).

37. Petersen, "Operetta after the Habsburg Empire"; Kevin Clarke, *"Im Himmel spielt auch schon die Jazzband": Emmerich Kálmán und die transatlantische Operette, 1928–1932* (Hamburg: von Bockel, 2007); Kauffmann, *Operette im "Dritten Reich"*; Barbara Denscher, *Der Operettenlibrettist Victor Léon: Ein Werkbiographie* (Bielefeld, Germany: Transcript, 2017). There are a few other studies of librettists with a more biographical slant, such as Henry Grunwald, *Ein Walzer muß es sein: Alfred Grünwald und die Wiener Operette* (Vienna: Überreuter, 1991); Brigitte Dalinger, Kurt Ifkovits, and Andrea Braidt, eds., *"Gute Unterhaltung!": Fritz Grünbaum und die Vergnügungskultur im Wien der 1920er und 1930er Jahre* (Frankfurt: Peter Lang, 2008); Barbara Denscher and Helmut Peschina, *Kein Land des Lächelns: Fritz Löhner-Beda, 1883–1942* (Salzburg: Residenz, 2002).

38. Laurence Senelick, *Jacques Offenbach and the Making of Modern Culture* (Cambridge: Cambridge University Press, 2017).

39. Marie-Theres Arnbom, Kevin Clarke, and Thomas Trabitsch, eds., *Welt der Operette: Glamour, Stars und Showbusiness* (Vienna: Brandstätter, 2012).

40. Clarke, *Im Himmel spielt auch schon die Jazzband*; Tobias Becker, "Globalizing Operetta before the First World War," *Opera Quarterly* 33, no. 1 (November 11, 2017): 7–27; Derek B. Scott, *German Operetta on Broadway and in the West End, 1900–1940* (Cambridge: Cambridge University Press, 2019); Len Platt, Tobias Becker, and David Linton, eds., *Popular Musical Theatre in London and Berlin: 1890 to 1939* (Cambridge: Cambridge University Press, 2014); Tobias Becker, *Inszenierte Moderne: Populäres Theater in Berlin und London, 1880–1930* (Berlin: De Gruyter, 2014).

41. Pierre Bourdieu, *Distinction: A Social Critique of the Judgement of Taste* (Cambridge, MA: Harvard University Press, 1984), 170.

CHAPTER 1. *DIE LUSTIGE WITWE* AND THE CREATION OF SILVER AGE VIENNESE OPERETTA

1. Lehár hinted at the incident in "Vom Schreibtisch und aus dem Atelier," a biographical essay published in *Velhagen & Klasings Monathefte* (February 1912), but it is not made into the centerpiece of *Witwe*'s genesis until Ernst Decsey described it in "Franz Lehár," a profile in *Komödie: Wochenrevue für Bühne und Film* (May 25, 1924), 11, as well as his biography of Lehár, published the same year: Ernst Decsey, *Franz Lehár* (Vienna: Drei Masken-Verlag, 1924), 83.

2. The most notable entries in the *Die lustige Witwe* memorial genre include Ludwig Karpath, "Das Schicksal der 'Lustigen Witwe,'" *NWJ*, June 26, 1923, by a theatre critic present at the dress rehearsal; Emil Steininger, "Vom unbekannten Lehar und dem durgefallenden Leo Fall," *NWJ*, December 16, 1928, by the Theater an der Wien's business manager; an entry by Karczag's co-director, Karl Wallner, "Die Wahrheit über Lehars 'Lustige Witwe,'" *NWJ*, January 1, 1931; the rebuttal to Wallner by librettist Victor Léon, "Die wahre Wahrheit über 'Die lustige Witwe,'" *NWJ*, January 6, 1931; and actor Louis Treumann's recol-

lection, "Entstehungsgeschichte eines Welterfolges (aus einem Gespräch)," *NFP*, December 30, 1936. Some notable later descriptions of the success immortalized those accounts: Fritz Stein, *50 Jahre Die Lustige Witwe* (Vienna: Doblinger, 1955); Maria von Peteani, *Franz Lehár* (Vienna: Glocken-Verlag, 1950).

3. The first figure is from Anton Bauer, *150 Jahre Theater an der Wien* (Zurich: Amalthea-Verlag, 1952), 459; the second is from Otto Keller's still-authoritative 1926 history. Operetta studies' fetish for statistics—understandable, considering the very real importance of popular success to composers and librettists and thus to the genre's development—is visible in Keller's extensive, ranked lists of performance figures up to 1921. *Die lustige Witwe* is first among operettas composed after 1900; Johann Strauss II's *Fledermaus* (1874) tops the table of 1855–1900 premieres with 11,962 performances, but it had thirty more years than *Witwe* to achieve those numbers. Keller, *Die Operette in ihrer geschichtlichen Entwicklung*, 427.

4. Karl Wallner, "Die Wahrheit über Lehars 'Lustige Witwe,'" *NWJ*, January 1, 1931; Victor Léon, "Die wahre Wahrheit über Die lustige Witwe," *NWJ*, January 6, 1931.

5. Traubner, *Operetta*, 249.

6. Like many of the Silver Age's features, this dualism has its roots in Johann Strauss II's *Der Zigeunerbaron*, but it is deployed more consistently and pointedly in the twentieth century. See Crittenden, *Johann Strauss and Vienna*, 170–209.

7. Felix Salten, "Die neue Operette," *Die Zeit*, December 8, 1906.

8. The overlap between various theatrical traditions is considered in Volker Klotz, *Bürgerliches Lachtheater: Komödie, Posse, Schwank, Operette*, 4th ed. (Heidelberg: Universitätsverlag Winter, 2007).

9. Crittenden, *Johann Strauss and Vienna*, 7–44; Marion Linhardt, ed., *"Warum es der Operette so schlecht geht."*

10. Urbanization is considered in more detail in Jacek Blaszkiewicz, "Writing the City: The Cosmopolitan Realism of Offenbach's 'La Vie Parisienne,'" *Current Musicology* 103 (Fall 2018).

11. Herbert Schneider, "Couplet," in *MGG Online*, ed. Laurenz Lütteken (Kassel, Germany: Bärenreiter, 1995), https://www.mgg-online.com/mgg/stable/12453.

12. This territory is surveyed by Crittenden, *Johann Strauss and Vienna*, especially chapters 6 and 7. See also Linhardt, *Residenzstadt und Metropole*, 54–76.

13. Collected in Eduard Hanslick, *Am Ende des Jahrhunderts, 1895–1899* (Berlin: Allgemeiner Verein für deutsche Literatur, 1899), 27.

14. After the *Gründerzeit*, Graf argued, growth and improvements in public transportation made operetta both more homogenous and more suited to a mass market. Max Graf, "Von den Wiener Operettenbühnen," *NWJ*, October 24, 1905. See also Gooley, "Hanslick on Johann Strauss Jr.: Genre, Social Class, and Liberalism in Vienna."

15. This is often quoted as "politics in a sharper key," a phrase also used by William McGrath. Schorske, *Fin-de-Siècle Vienna*, 119.

16. Adam Müller-Guttenbrunn, *Wien war eine Theaterstadt*. Müller-Guttenbrunn's subsequent work is examined in more detail in Richard S. Geehr, *Adam Müller-Guttenbrunn and the Aryan Theater of Vienna: 1898–1903: The Approach of Cultural Fascism* (Göppingen, Germany: A. Kümmerle, 1973); Yates, *Theatre in Vienna*, 168–77.

17. Dr. Mutus, "Cagliostro in Wien," *Hans Jörgel* 10, no. 1 (1875): 10. Cited in Rudolf

Holzer, *Die Wiener Vorstadtbühnen: Alexander Girardi und das Theater an der Wien* (Vienna: Verlag der Österreichischen Staatsdruckerei, 1951), 298.

18. This terminological issue is further discussed in Scott, *German Operetta on Broadway and in the West End,* 178.

19. "Theater an der Wien," *FB,* October 17, 1897.

20. While in some respects similar to the eighteenth-century form of grotesque dance and the eccentric dance of the 1920s, this music hall–derived style is its own special form. Marion Linhardt examines this style in greater detail in Linhardt, *Residenzstadt und Metropole,* 184–95.

21. Louis Treumann, "Die Wiener Operette und Ich," *Wiener Theater- und Musik-Magazin. Monatschrift für Theater, Konzert, Musik und Musikliteratur* 1, vol. 5 (1928), 1. The perplexing "salto mortadella" is perhaps a hammy malapropism for "tarantella" or "saltarello."

22. Hans Stieber, "Die Wiener Operette," *Wochenschrift für Kunst und Musik* 1 (1903), 245.

23. Built by Emmanuel Schikenader, the theater hosted the premieres of all three versions of *Fidelio* as well as many of the most important Golden Age operettas. The theater's history is documented in Eugen Brixel, "Die Ära Wilhelm Karczag im Theater an der Wien" (PhD diss., University of Vienna, 1966) as well as Bauer, *150 Jahre Theater an der Wien;* Attila E. Láng, *200 Jahre Theater an der Wien: "Spectacles Müssen Seyn"* (Vienna: Holzhausen, 2001); Tadeusz Krzeszowiak, *Theater an der Wien: Seine Technik und Geschichte 1801–2001* (Vienna: Böhlau, 2002); Holzer, *Die Wiener Vorstadtbühnen.*

24. Statistics can be found in Bauer, *150 Jahre Theater an der Wien,* 449. Richard Heuberger's career is examined in Peter Grunsky, *Richard Heuberger: Der Operettenprofessor* (Vienna: Böhlau, 2002).

25. Decsey, *Franz Lehár,* 89.

26. Keller, *Die Operette in ihrer geschichtlichen Entwicklung.*

27. This was followed by a section on *Gegenswartsprobleme* (problems of the present). Westermeyer, *Die Operette im Wandel des Zeitgeistes.*

28. Kevin Clarke, "Zurück in die Zukunft: Aspekte der Aufführungspraxis des 'Weissen Rössl,'" in *Im weißen Rössl: Zwischen Kunst und Kommerz,* ed. Ulrich Tadday, Musik-Konzepte, 133/134 (Munich: edition text + kritik, 2006); Hans-Jörg Koch, "Das NS-Wunschkonzert: Operette als Narkotikum," in *Operette unterm Hakenkreuz: Zwischen hoffähiger Kunst und "Entartung,"* ed. Wolfgang Schaller (Berlin: Metropol, 2003), 119. Christoph Dompke examines the evidence for the term's origin in detail in *Unterhaltungsmusik und NS-Verfolgung* (Neumünster: von Bockel, 2011), 43–46. He cites Marion Linhardt, for example, who locates "Gold" in several prewar texts but has not located a clear origin for "Silver."

29. Hadamowsky and Otte, *Die Wiener Operette,* 297. More recently, Volker Klotz proclaimed the distinction between Gold and Silver to be "worthless." Klotz, *Operette,* 834.

30. Erich Urban, "Die Wiedergeburt der Operette," *Die Musik* (Berlin) 3, no. 3 (1903/4): 176–86; continued in 3, no. 4 (1903/4): 269–81.

31. Ferdinand Scherber, "Die Operette," *Neue Musik-Zeitung,* November 10, 1904, 45–46.

32. Franz Lehár, "Die Zukunft der Operette," *Die Wage,* January 10, 1903, 85.

33. Erich Urban, "Die Wiedergeburt der Operette," *Die Musik*, 3, no. 4 (1903/4): 269.

34. Eugen Thari, "Warum es der Operette so schlecht geht," *Der Kunstwart* 18 (1904/1905): 543–48. Reprinted in Linhardt, *Warum es der Operette so schlecht geht*, 234–39.

35. Theodor Antropp, "Die Wiener Operette," *Die Zeit*, February 11, 1905.

36. Eugen Thari, "Warum es der Operette so schlecht geht." While many critics of Thari's vintage, as well as successors like Karl Kraus and Siegfried Kracauer, described Offenbach's work as explicitly political, modern historians have contended that Offenbach's status as a political subversive was, in the words of Carl Dahlhaus "if not sheer myth, at least grossly naïve," and that Offenbach was comfortable and popular among the Parisian political establishment. More recently, Laurence Senelick writes that Kracauer "overemphasize[d] Offenbach's interest in politics." Dahlhaus, *Nineteenth-Century Music*, 228; Laurence Senelick, *Jacques Offenbach and the Making of Modern Culture*, 7.

37. Urban, "Die Wiedergeburt der Operette," 280. The Berlin composers he names—Paul Linke and Victor Holländer—became far better known internationally as song composers than as dramatic composers. Berlin's real time would come in the 1920s, when the booming Weimar Republic surpassed Vienna as a cultural center and its revue-style operettas came into fashion. Satirical operettas were occasionally written throughout the early twentieth century, but they were always described as the exception rather than the rule. A history of Berlin operetta is Otto Schneidereit, *Berlin, wie es weint und lacht: Spaziergänge durch Berlins Operettengeschichte*, 2nd ed. (Berlin: Lied der Zeit Musikverlag, 1973). Two more recent studies of the city's theater culture are Tobias Becker, *Inszenierte Moderne: Populäres Theater in Berlin und London*; Platt, Becker, and Linton, *Popular Musical Theatre in London and Berlin*.

38. Twentieth-century operetta was not without its satirical moments, most memorably in Oscar Straus's 1904 Wagner parody *Die lustigen Nibelungen* and Franz Lehár's *Die lustige Witwe* self-parody *Mitislaw der Moderne*, but few such works enjoyed the lasting success or influence of more serious works. *Mitislaw*, for example, played in the Theater an der Wien's Hölle cabaret space rather than on its main stage.

39. The investors hired journalist Karczag for the job. Because of Karczag's lack of business experience, the owners of the theater obliged him to hire a co-director with greater financial acumen. The first co-director was Georg Lang, who was replaced by Karl Wallner in 1902. Karczag, however, was the public face of the theater's direction.

40. Albert Kauders, "Die Wiener Operette," *Bühne und Welt* 6 (1904): 970.

41. Most of the major composers of the Silver Age—not only Lehár, but also Oscar Straus, Leo Fall, and Emmerich Kálmán—were conservatory trained, unlike their Golden Age predecessors. Lehár's training is examined in Frey, *Was sagt ihr zu diesem Erfolg*, 30–32.

42. Frey, 68–69.

43. Girardi's career is the major subject of Holzer, *Die Wiener Vorstadtbühnen*.

44. See *Deutsches Bühnen-Jahrbuch*, vols. 15 and 16 (Berlin: F. A. Günther & Sohn, 1904 and 1905).

45. A detailed account of *Der Rebell* is found in Frey, Stemprok, and Dosch, *Leo Fall*, 45–52.

46. For more on *Simplicius*, see Crittenden, *Johann Strauss and Vienna*, 210–56. Léon's career is related in detail in Denscher, *Der Operettenlibrettist Victor Léon*.

47. Henri Meilhac, *L'Attaché d'Ambassade: Comédie en trois actes, en prose* (Paris: Michel Lévy Frères, 1861).

48. Frey, *Was sagt ihr zu diesem Erfolg*, 70–71.

49. bs [Leopold Jacobson], "Theater an der Wien," *NWJ*, December 31, 1905.

50. The mention of Hackländer, a prolific translator and adapter of French plays, is probably an error—Hackländer never wrote a play entitled *Der Attaché*, which was close to the title of Alexander Bergen's adaptation of Meilhac, *Der Gesandtschaft-Attaché*. The description of a libretto as "built" or "constructed" is common in operetta reviews and recalls Scribe and Sardou's concept of the "well-made play." Henri Meilhac, *Der Gesandtschafts-Attache: Lustspiel in drei Acten*, trans. Alexander Bergen (Vienna: Anton Schweiger, 1862); bs [Leopold Jacobson], "Theater an der Wien."

51. st [Julius Stern], "Theater an der Wien," *FB*, December 31, 1905.

52. Victor Léon and Leo Stein, *Die lustige Witwe*, NÖ Reg. Präs Theater TB-K 338/27, NÖLA. Published as rental as Franz Lehár, Victor Léon, and Leo Stein, *Die lustige Witwe: Vollständiges Soufflierbuch mit Sämtlichen Regiebemerkungen* (Vienna: Doblinger, 1906). It seems likely that the operetta's costumes were determined before the censor intervened. Other operettas with Balkan settings are discussed in Christian Glanz, "Das Bild Südosteuropas in der Wiener Operette" (PhD diss., Universität Graz, 1988).

53. Elizabeth Roberts, *Realm of the Black Mountain: A History of Montenegro* (London: Hurst & Company, 2007), 258–59.

54. Sch—r. [Karl Schreder], "Theater an der Wien," *Deutsches Volksblatt*, December 31, 1905.

55. st [Julius Stern], "Theater an der Wien."

56. D.B. [David Josef Bach], "Theater an der Wien," *AZ*, December 31, 1905.

57. Lehár's entry was a one-act opera entitled *Rodrigo*. Franz Lehár, "Mein Werdegang," *Die Zeit*, October 13, 1907; Frey, *Was sagt ihr zu diesem Erfolg*, 36.

58. The source (in this case cited) is Alfred Delacour and Alfred Hennequin's 1884 play *Les dominos roses*, known in German as *Die Rosa-Dominos*.

59. Louis Treumann, "Entstehungsgeschichte eines Welterfolges (Aus einem Gespräch)," *NFP*, December 30, 1936.

60. Considering the contemptuous tone of his dismissal of operetta in *Nineteenth-Century Music* (see note 36), it is ironic that Dahlhaus also wrote this piece. One suspects that, like Hanslick, he harbored some personal affection for the genre. Carl Dahlhaus, "Zur musikalischen Dramaturgie der Lustigen Witwe," *Österreichische Musikzeitschrift* 12, no. 40 (1985): 657–64.

61. The association of folk song and authentic identity is considered in Larry Wolff, *Inventing Eastern Europe: The Map of Civilization on the Mind of the Enlightenment* (Stanford: Stanford University Press, 2010), especially 324–31.

62. Csáky, *Ideologie der Operette und Wiener Moderne*, 129. The number from *Der Opernball* is Nr. 8, marked "Rendezvous-Duettino," the operetta's most popular individual number.

63. The kolo, a folk dance that over the course of the nineteenth century was, like the mazurka, domesticated into a ballroom dance for the aristocracy, is an apt choice. Nancy Lee Chalfa Ruyter, "Dvoransko Kolo: From the 1840s to the Twentieth Century," in *Balkan*

Dance: Essays on Characteristics, Performance, and Teaching, ed. Anthony Shay (Jefferson, NC: McFarland, 2008), 239–49.

64. Dahlhaus, "Zur musikalischen Dramaturgie der Lustigen Witwe," 658.

65. Lehár, "Mein Werdegang."

66. See the modern reprint: *Felix Salten—Wurstelprater: Ein Schlüsseltext zur Wiener Moderne*, ed. Siegfried Mattl, Karl Müller-Richter, and Werner Michael Schwarz (Vienna: Promedia, 2004), 76.

67. Letter in the private collection of Thomas Schulz, Vienna; included in full in Linhardt, *Residenzstadt und Metropole*, 199–200.

68. "Star image" is defined in Richard Dyer, *Stars*, 2nd ed. (London: BFI Publishing, 1998).

69. Felix Salten chose Treumann as his primary example in his essay of this title, "Die neue Operette," *Die Zeit*, December 8, 1906.

70. Lehár would reproduce this strophe in "Er geht links, sie geht rechts" in *Der Graf von Luxemburg*, which also takes place in Paris.

71. Eckhard John, "Es waren zwei Königskinder," in *Populäre und traditionelle Lieder: Historisch-kritisches Liederlexikon* (Freiburg: Zentrum für Populäre Kultur und Musik, Universität Freiburg, 2013), http://www.liederlexikon.de/lieder/es_waren_zwei_koenigskinder.

72. The example is based on a publication contemporaneous to *Witwe*, No. 222 in August Linder, ed., *Deutsche Weisen: Die beliebtesten Volks- und geistlichen Lieder für Klavier (mit Text)* (Stuttgart: Albert Auers Musikverlag, c. 1900), 181. The song can also be found in the important collection Ludwig Erk, ed., *Deutscher Liederhort: Auswahl der vorzüglichern deutschen Volkslieder aus der Vorzeit und der Gegenwart mit ihren eigenthümlichen Melodien*, vol. 1 (Berlin: Enslin, 1856), 65–66.

73. Hadamowsky and Otte, *Die Wiener Operette*, 298; Adorno, "Arabesken zur Operette," 517.

74. Dahlhaus calls the Pontevedran "ahs" (he does not consider the Parisian "zipps") "*tönende Schweigen*," "sounding silence," a quintessentially Wagnerian device (though, he hastens to note, *Witwe* never reaches Wagnerian levels of pathos owing to differences in style level). Dahlhaus, "Zur musikalischen Dramaturgie der Lustigen Witwe," 663.

75. "Theater an der Wien," *NFP*, December 31, 1905.

76. Rudolf Bernauer, *Das Theater meines Lebens: Erinnerungen* (Berlin: L. Blanvalet, 1955), 215.

77. Bernauer, 215–16. Fall, Bernauer, and Welisch had progressed far enough to submit a revised version of their work to the police censor in January, and the mostly revised score is contained in the Austrian National Library's Musiksammlung. Rudolf Bernauer and Ernst Welisch, *Der Rebell*, Reg. Präs Theater TB-214, 255 (first version), TB-1906/16 (revised version), NÖLA; Leo Fall, Rudolf Bernauer, and Ernst Welisch, *Der Rebell*, score draft, revised version, F88 Leo Fall 1–2, ÖNB MS.

78. Critics routinely attended general rehearsals, though the only writer known to have attended that of *Die lustige Witwe* was the influential Ludwig Karpath of the *Neues Wiener Tagblatt*. Léon, "Die wahre Wahrheit über 'Die lustige Witwe,'" Frey, *Was sagt ihr zu diesem Erfolg*, 76.

79. "-rp" [Karpath, Ludwig], "Theater an der Wien," *NWT*, December 31, 1905.

80. Wallner estimated the number of free tickets—given out to "paper" the house and create the appearance of a full audience and a scarcity of tickets—as representing 40 percent of seats, a dangerously high number. Operetta theatres often gave away many tickets early in a show's run. The beneficiaries were generally employees of the theater and their families and friends. See Hugo Poller, "Die ökonomische Bewirtschaftung eines Operettentheaters" (PhD diss., University of Würzburg, 1920); the only copy is available at Staatsbibliothek zu Berlin (MS 20/1052).

81. A comprehensive account of *Die lustige Witwe*'s international reception is found in Frey, *Was sagt ihr zu diesem Erfolg*, 78–103.

82. Theodor W. Adorno, "Lustige Witwe," in *Gesammelte Schriften*, vol. 19, *Frankfurter Opern- und Konzertkritiken* (Frankfurt: Suhrkamp, 1997), 249–51.

83. Lehár expands upon this topic in "Die Zukunft der Operette."

84. Karl Kraus, "Grimassen über Kultur und Bühne," *Die Fackel* 10, no. 270–71 (January 19, 1909): 1–18; Karl Kraus, "Girardi," *Die Fackel* 9, no. 246–47 (March 12, 1908): 38–44.

85. A good example of this narrative in action is Martin Lichtfuss, *Operette im Ausverkauf: Studien zum Libretto des Musikalischen Unterhaltungstheaters im Österreich der Zwischenkriegszeit* (Vienna: Böhlau, 1989), as well as Thorsten Stegemann, *Wenn man das Leben durchs Champagnerglas Betrachtet—: Textbücher der Wiener Operette zwischen Provokation und Reaktion* (Frankfurt: Peter Lang, 1995).

86. Salten, "Die neue Operette."

CHAPTER 2. SENTIMENTALITY, SATIRE, AND LABOR

1. Straus's café, Zum Eisvogel, still exists in the Prater today but now lies in the midst of the amusement park's hustle and bustle rather than in its original, more pastoral location.

2. Franz Mailer, *Weltbürger der Musik: Eine Oscar-Straus-Biographie* (Vienna: Österreichischer Bundesverlag, 1963), 40–41. Mailer interviewed Straus near the end of the composer's life, and some of the anecdotes strain credibility. Mailer is, however, restrained in comparison with the florid Bernard Grun, whose *Prince of Vienna* is full of invented dialogue, including a conversation between Franz-Joseph and the Empress Elisabeth. Bernard Grun, *Prince of Vienna: The Life, the Times, and the Melodies of Oscar Straus* (New York: G.P. Putnam's Sons, 1957).

3. Mailer, *Weltbürger der Musik*, 40–41; Hans Müller, *Buch der Abenteuer* (Berlin: E. Fleischel & Co, 1905). Müller, then an unknown, would later write two librettos for Erich Wolfgang Korngold (*Violanta* and *Das Wunder der Heliane*), a successful comedy for the Burgtheater (*Die Puppenschule*), and screenplays for several film operettas. See Arthur Maibach, "Vergessen und verdrängt," in *Glitter and be gay: Die authentische Operette und ihre schwulen Verehrer*, ed. Kevin Clarke (Hamburg: Männerschwarm, 2007), 140–45.

4. Klotz, *Operette*; see especially 16–17.

5. This is a juxtaposition made explicitly in Dahlhaus, *Nineteenth-Century Music*, 227. I consider this territory in Micaela Baranello, "*Arabella*, Operetta, and the Triumph of Gemütlichkeit," *Opera Quarterly* 31, no. 4 (Autumn 2015): 199–222.

6. Kracauer, *Jacques Offenbach and the Paris of His Time*, 245.

7. There is no scholarly biography of Oscar Straus. Franz Mailer worked closely with the composer near the end of his life to write his memoir-like biography but consulted few

sources beyond his subject (see note 2 for this chapter). Bernard Grun's biography, *Prince of Vienna*, is largely fable, leaning heavily on imagined dialogue. One brief but reliable account is Stefan Frey, "Oscar Straus," in *Lexikon verfolgter Musiker und Musikerinnen der NS-Zeit*, ed. Claudia Maurer Zenck, Peter Petersen, and Sophie Fetthauer (Hamburg: Universität Hamburg, 2017), https://www.lexm.uni-hamburg.de/object/lexm_lexmperson _00002671. On the general unreliability of composer memoirs and their functions, see Eugen Semrau, "Mehr als ein Leben: Konstruktion und Funktion der Robert-Stolz-Legende," in *Operette unterm Hakenkreuz*, ed. Wolfgang Schaller (Berlin: Metropol, 2007), 179–97.

8. Otto Julius Bierbaum, *Stilpe: Ein Roman aus der Froschperspektive* (Berlin: Schuster & Loeffler, 1897), 358–59.

9. Ernst von Wolzogen, *Wie ich mich ums leben brachte: Erinnerungen und Erfahrungen* (Braunschweig: Georg Westermann, 1922), 197.

10. He had obtained the position by frequenting the correct cafés and encountering by chance the journalist Oskar Geller, who as well as writing theater criticism for the *Berliner Lokal-Anzeiger* maintained a parallel career as a cabaret clown known as Luigi Spontelli. Geller also wrote the scenario for Alexander Zemlinsky's "mime drama" *Ein Lichtstrahl*, commissioned by Wolzogen for the Überbrettl. Geller recommended Straus to Wolzogen. Straus was originally charged with writing Spontelli music for a pantomime number. According to the composer's own account, Wolzogen then asked him to fill out the opening program with a setting of Bierbaum's already well-known poem. Mailer, *Weltbürger der Musik*, 24–26; Antony Beaumont, *Zemlinsky* (London: Faber, 2000), 83.

11. An image of the performance appears in Hanns von Zobeltitz, "Aus den Berliner Theatern," *Velhagen & Klasings Monatshefte* 15, no. 2, part 1 (February 1900), 191. The critic describes it as "wahrlich kein himmelstürmendes Werk" (in truth no heavenly work) but when sung "dann will der Jubel kein Ende nehmen" (the cheers never end).

12. Peter Jelavich, *Berlin Cabaret* (Cambridge, MA: Harvard University Press, 1993), 41.

13. Harold B. Segel, *Turn-of-the-Century Cabaret: Paris, Barcelona, Berlin, Munich, Vienna, Cracow, Moscow, St. Petersburg, Zurich* (New York: Columbia University Press, 1987), 125.

14. Ute-Christiane Hauenschild, *Rideamus: Die Lebensgeschichte des Fritz Oliven* (Berlin: Hentrich & Hentrich, 2009).

15. Straus biographer Franz Mailer asserts that it was due to a citywide distaste for the operetta genre, but considering the still-healthy number of operettas produced there at time this seems implausible: "Es handelte sich unbestreitbar um eine Operette neuen Stils. Doch niemand wollte das Stück aufführen. Und schon gar kein Berliner Theater. So lag die Partitur zwei Jahre in Dr. Olivens eleganter Kanzlei." Mailer, *Weltbürger der Musik*, 33.

16. I address this in Micaela Baranello, "'Operettendämmerung': Die Lustigen Nibelungen and the Failures of Wagnerian Operetta," *Opera Quarterly* 33, no. 1 (Winter 2017): 28–48.

17. Wolzogen, *Wie ich mich ums leben brachte: Erinnerungen und Erfahrungen*, 199.

18. Jefferson S. Chase, *Inciting Laughter: The Development of "Jewish Humor" in 19th Century German Culture* (Berlin: Walter de Gruyter, 1999), 18. The landscape of Jewish identity in German cabaret and theater is also considered in detail in Marline Otte, *Jewish Identities in German Popular Entertainment, 1890–1933* (Cambridge: Cambridge University Press, 2006).

19. The extent to which the "fin de siècle Vienna" artistic phenomenon itself was a Jewish one has been the subject of considerable scholarship. See Beller, *Vienna and the Jews*, 14–33.

20. Many Jews did, however, change their names, such as Emmerich Kálmán (born Imre Koppstein) and Louis Treumann (Alois Pollitzer). The only major operetta composer to convert was Edmund Eysler, who became Catholic in 1898 (before he had achieved any significant success). Eysler's choice of subjects and musical style were, for his entire life, more provincial and Viennese-specific than any of the composers considered in detail here, and the audience for these more traditional works would have likely been less friendly to a Jewish composer. Yet conversion did not prevent his operettas from being banned by the Nazis. Norbert Nischkauer, *Edmund Eysler: 12 März 1874–4 Oktober 1949* (Vienna: self-pub., 2000).

21. Jews had been permitted to settle in Vienna starting in 1848, and all geographic restrictions were lifted in 1867. The enormous wave of immigration in late nineteenth-century Vienna (discussed in chapter 1) was in part a Jewish one: the population of Jews in Vienna increased from around 6,000 in 1857 to 175,000 in 1910, at which point they comprised 8.5 percent of the city's population. Marsha L. Rozenblit, *The Jews of Vienna, 1867–1914: Assimilation and Identity* (Albany: State University of New York Press, 1983), 19.

22. Marion Linhardt, "'Wer kommt heut' in jedem Theaterstück vor? Ä Jud'!': Bilder des 'Jüdischen' in der Wiener Operette des frühen 20. Jahrhunderts," in *Judenrollen: Darstellungsformen im Europäischen Theater von der Restauration bis zur Zwischenkriegszeit*, ed. Hans Bayerdörfer and Jens Malte Fischer (Tübingen: Niemeyer, 2008), 191–206.

23. For example, Philip Bohlman, *Jewish Music and Modernity* (Oxford: Oxford University Press, 2008); Otte, *Jewish Identities in German Popular Entertainment, 1890–1933*.

24. L.Hfd [Ludwig Hirschfeld], "Carl-Theater," *NFP*, December 21, 1902.

25. Felix Salten, "Die neue Operette," *Die Zeit*, December 8, 1906, 42.

26. Linhardt, *Residenzstadt und Metropole*, 191.

27. Salten, "Die neue Operette," 43.

28. I address this in much more detail in Micaela Baranello, "Viennese Blood: Assimilation and Exclusion in Viennese Popular Music," in *Watersheds*, ed. Marijeta Bozovic and Matthew D. Miller (Brighton, MA: Academic Studies Press, 2016), 53–69.

29. Walter Dahms, "Die Operette," *Neue Preußische Zeitung: Kreuzzeitung*, June 25, 1914.

30. Erich Eckertz, "Die Wiener Operettenpest," *Die Zeit*, November 23, 1910. The entire talk and responses are included in Linhardt, *"Warum es der Operette so schlecht geht,"* 59–91. Eckertz's University of Rostock dissertation on Heinrich Heine's wit contains a section on the racial composition of humor, referring to Heine's Judaism as being "washed away with baptismal water." Erich Eckertz, *Heine und sein Witz* (Berlin: Felber, 1908). For more on the discourse of race in Vienna, see Julie Brown, "Otto Weininger and Musical Discourse in Turn-of-the-Century Vienna," in *Western Music and Race*, ed. Julie Brown (Cambridge: Cambridge University Press, 2007), 84–101.

31. "Für und gegen die Wiener Operette: Äußerungen auf eine Rundfrage," *Die Zeit*, December 25, 1910. The respondents were operetta artists Lehár, Charles Lecocq, and French actor Felix Galipaux and art music luminaries Eugen d'Albert, Ferruccio Busoni, Karl Goldmark, Lilli Lehmann, Ruggiero Leoncavallo, Max Reger, pianist Moriz Rosen-

thal, and Felix Weingartner. Three more are from theater artists associated with elite culture: actor Bernhard Baumeister, Berlin intendant Graf Georg Hülsen, and "Bernhard Shaw" [sic!]. The remaining respondents are Nietzsche's sister Elisabeth Förster-Nietzsche, author Heinrich Mann, and apparent Polish aristocrat Princess Marie Adam Lubomirska.

32. Hans Joachim Moser, "Die Operettenepidemie," *Der Greif* 2 (1914): 508.

33. Moser, 513.

34. Franz Lehár, "Die Zukunft der Operette," *Die Wage*, (January 10, 1904), 85. Note that "Müh' und Plage" is also the phrase used by Danilo in his entrance song in *Die lustige Witwe.*

35. Franz Gräflinger, "Operettentaumel," *Der Musiksalon: Internationale Zeitschrift für Musik und Gesellschaft* 2, no. 3 (1910), 28.

36. Max Horkheimer and Theodor W. Adorno, *Dialectic of Enlightenment: Philosophical Fragments*, ed. Gunzelin Schmid Noerr, trans. Edmund Jephcott, (Stanford, CA: Stanford University Press, 2002), 107. Adorno is generally credited with sole authorship of this chapter.

37. Dahlhaus, *Nineteenth-Century Music*, 227.

38. These conventions are catalogued systematically in Quissek, *Das deutschsprachige Operettenlibretto.*

39. While the plot is clearly drawn from Müller's novella, it also bears a surprising resemblance to Leo Fall's flop *Der Rebell* (see chapter 1). This similarity is remarked upon in Frey, Stemprok, and Dosch, *Leo Fall*, 49.

40. Margaret Myers, "Searching for Data about European Ladies' Orchestras, 1870–1950," in *Music and Gender*, ed. Pirkko Moisala and Beverley Diamond (Urbana: University of Illinois Press, 2000), 190.

41. For much more on mid-twentieth-century women's bands, as well as some general comments on the phenomenon, see Sherrie Tucker, *Swing Shift: "All-Girl" Bands of the 1940s* (Durham, NC: Duke University Press, 2000).

42. They were not exclusively Viennese—indeed the most in-depth study of the Damenkapelle only considers groups in Germany: Dorothea Kaufmann, *"…routinierte Trommlerin gesucht": Musikerin in einer Damenkapelle; zum Bild eines vergessenen Frauenberufes aus der Kaiserzeit* (Karben, Germany: Coda, 1997). See also Ulrike Keil, "Professionelle Damenkapellen und Frauenorchester um die Jahrhundertwende," in *"Von delectatio bis entertainment": Das Phänomen der Unterhaltung in der Musik: Arbeitstagung der Fachgruppe Soziologie und Sozialgeschichte der Musik in Düsseldorf am 22 und 23. November 1997*, Musik-Kultur 7 (Essen: Die blaue Eule, 2000), 99–110; Myers, "Searching for Data about European Ladies' Orchestras, 1870–1950."

43. George Bernard Shaw, *Shaw's Music: The Complete Musical Criticism in Three Volumes* (New York: Dodd, Mead, 1981), 338–40.

44. Joseph Roth, "Erinnerung an eine weisse Damenkapelle (Frankfurter Zeitung, 20.6.1931)," in *Werke*, ed. Klaus Westermann, vol. 3 (Cologne: Kiepenheuer & Witsch, 1991), 349.

45. The photograph is dated from 1912 and identified by curators of Vienna's Albertina as using Agfa-Farbenplatte technology, which was not publicly available until 1916. Arthur von Hübl had published a treatise on color photography in 1908: Arthur von Hübl, *Die Theorie und Praxis der Farbenphotographie mit Autochromplatten* (Halle: W. Knapp, 1908).

The photograph is reprinted in Michael Ponstingl, *Strassenleben in Wien: Fotografien von 1861 bis 1913* (Vienna: Christian Brandstätter Verlag/Albertina, 2005), 63.

46. Salten, *Felix Salten—Wurstelprater*, 92.

47. Salten, 92. Salten's perception recalls that he remains the leading suspect for the authorship of fin de siècle Vienna's most popular socially conscious pornography: the purportedly autobiographical 1906 work *Josefine Mutzenbacher: Die Lebensgeschichte einer wienerischen Dirne, von ihr selbst erzählt* [Josefine Mutzenbacher: The life of a Viennese whore, told by herself] (Reinbek bei Hamburg: Rowohlt, 1978).

48. Scholarship on all-woman ensembles explicitly prioritizes the recovery of musicians' voices and experiences and thus restores to them some degree of agency over their own performances. See, for example Tucker, *Swing Shift*; Myers, "Searching for Data about European Ladies' Orchestras, 1870–1950."

49. The ensemble's orchestration was tinkered with (possibly owing to casting issues), but in the end included flute, piccolo, two first violins, one second violin, one viola, one cello, percussion, and piano (a trumpet was cut). The published score includes a harmonium as well, but there is no part for it in the manuscript. See Oscar Straus, *Ein Walzertraum,* manuscript score, 1906, MHc 14207, WB. The manuscript contains both a piano-vocal score and an orchestral score, in different hands. Straus generally did not generally orchestrate his own operettas, but in this case there is no indication as to the identity of the orchestrator. The piano-vocal score is in Straus's hand and contains clear indications of which sections of the Damenkapelle numbers are to be played by the stage band and which are to be played by the pit orchestra, and these instructions were faithfully realized.

50. Klotz, *Operette*, 660.

51. Segel, *Turn-of-the-Century Cabaret*, 120.

52. Klotz, *Operette*, 128–29.

53. Traubner, *Operetta*, 277.

54. Siegfried Kracauer, *From Caligari to Hitler: A Psychological History of the German Film* (Princeton, NJ: Princeton University Press, 1947), 141.

55. For example, the *Neue Freie Presse* said that "one can speak of a sort of Viennese *Alt-Heidelberg.*" "Carl-Theater," *NFP*, March 3, 1907. *Die Zeit* described the piece as having "*Alt-Heidelberg* sentimentality." "Carl-Theater," *Die Zeit*, March 3, 1907.

56. Heinrich Reinhardt, "Ein Walzertraum," *NWJ*, March 3, 1907. Unusually, Reinhardt's name is given in full in his byline.

57. S.T. [Julius Stern], "Ein Walzertraum," *FB*, March 3, 1907.

58. D.B. [David Josef Bach], "Ein Walzertraum," *AZ*, March 3, 1907.

59. His most directly parodic work was likely the one that immediately followed *Witwe, Mitislaw der Moderne* (premiered January 5, 1907), a cabaret-scale operetta written for Louis Treumann, largely mocking his turn in *Die lustige Witwe*. His 1903 *Göttergatte* has an Offenbach-esque mythological libretto but, despite being revised twice, failed to find an audience all three times.

60. *Die Haubenlerche* is set in a paper factory near Berlin. The operetta's shift to a Brussels setting allowed for a more plausible move to operetta's favorite setting of Paris in the last act and corresponded with Belgium's high degree of industrialization and strong labor unions. Ernst von Wildenbruch, *Die Haubenlerche: Schauspiel in vier Akten* (Berlin: Freund & Jeckel, 1897).

61. The name suggests an allusion to another young aristocrat, Octavian in *Der Rosenkavalier* (which had premiered ten months earlier).

62. st [Julius Stern], "Theater an der Wien," *FB*, November 25, 1911.

63. This accompaniment pattern, while seemingly novel among operetta's small repertoire, had actually been used by Lehár before, in Camille and Valencienne's first duet in *Die lustige Witwe*, where it features a violin, a flute, and a clarinet (No. 2, "So kommen Sie").

64. Maya Cantu, *American Cinderellas on Broadway Musical Stage: Imagining the Working Girl from* Irene *to* Gypsy (London: Palgrave Macmillan, 2015), 3.

65. Albert Gier, *Wär' es auch nichts als ein Augenblick: Poetik und Dramaturgie der komischen Operette* (Bamberg: University of Bamberg Press, 2014), 190.

66. "Franz Lehars Operette 'Eva,'" *NFP*, November 25, 1911. Reviews in the *Neue Freie Presse* were, during this period, not given any byline.

67. bs [Leopold Jacobson], "Theater an der Wien," *NWJ*, November 25, 1911.

68. Wolfgang Maderthaner and Siegfried Mattl, "'…den Straßenexcessen ein Ende machen': Septemberunruhen und Arbeitermassenprozeß 1911," in *Sozialistenprozesse: Politische Justiz in Österreich, 1870–1936*, ed. Karl R. Stadler (Vienna: Europaverlag, 1986), 117–50.

69. "Franz Lehars Operette 'Eva.'"

70. Wilhelm Karczag, "Operette und musikalische Komödie," *NWJ*, April 12, 1914.

71. D.B. [David Josef Bach], "Theater an der Wien," *AZ*, November 25, 1911.

CHAPTER 3. HUNGARY, VIENNA, AND THE "GYPSY OPERETTA"

1. Frank Berkeley Smith, *The City of the Magyars* (London: T. Fisher Unwin, 1903), 202–3. A photograph shows Rácz Laczi looking quite gentlemanly, dressed in a tuxedo with a bow tie, vest, and watch chain. He sports a luxuriant Austro-Hungarian mustache, hair parted in the center, and slicked back. He looks frankly at the camera, holding his violin (equipped with a modern chinrest) on his shoulder but not against his neck. A photograph of "a nomad gypsy camp" several pages later shows men and women in more traditional folk costume, surrounded by chickens and clustered around houses made of bark and branches.

2. *Primas* conventionally refers to the leader of an ensemble playing "Gypsy music."

3. Stefan Frey, *Unter Tränen lachen*, 126.

4. Radio broadcast excerpt included on recording, Emmerich Kálmán, *Der Zigeunerprimas*, Claus Peter Flor, cond., Münchener Rundfunkorchester with Roberto Saccà (Laczi), Wolfgang Bankl (Pali), Edith Lienbacher (Juliska), et al. cpo 3493256, 2005, compact disc.

5. "Gypsy music" is the preferred term in two major recent studies of this music. Lynn M. Hooker, *Redefining Hungarian Music from Liszt to Bartók* (Oxford: Oxford University Press, 2013); Anna G. Piotrowska, *Gypsy Music in European Culture: From the Late Eighteenth to the Early Twentieth Centuries*, trans. Guy R. Torr (Boston: Northeastern University Press, 2013).

6. "Johann-Strauß-Theater," *NFP*, October 12, 1912.

7. Maurus Jókai, "Gemüthsart und Temperament des magyarischen Volkes," in Crown Prince Rudolf, ed., *Die Österreichisch-Ungarische Monarchie in Wort und Bild*, vol. 5 (Vienna: K.K. Hof- und Staatsdruckerei, 1888), 299.

8. Robert Musil, *The Man without Qualities*, ed. Burton Pike, trans. Sophie Wilkins, vol. 1 (London: Picador, 1995), 490–91.

9. One operetta set in a modern, non-stereotypical urban Budapest is Franz Lehár's *Wo die Lerche singt* (1918). Kálmán's *Die Csárdásfürstin* (discussed in detail chapter 4) mixes elements of a modern city and the expected stereotypes.

10. Lynn M. Hooker, "Hungarians and Hungarianisms in Operetta and Folk Plays in the Late Habsburg and Post-Habsburg Era," in *The Cambridge Companion to Operetta*, ed. Derek B. Scott and Anastasia Belina (Cambridge: Cambridge University Press, 2020), 61–75; András Batta and János Kárpáti, eds., *Music in Hungary: An Illustrated History* (Budapest: Rózsavölgyi, 2011).

11. Traubner, *Operetta*, 331. For a recent and more detailed consideration of Huszka, see Hooker, "Turks, Hungarians, and Gypsies on Stage."

12. The primary source for Kálmán's youth is his autobiographical sketch "Die unverfälsche Wahrheit," found in Julius Bistron's biography; Julius Bistron, *Emmerich Kálmán* (Vienna: Karczag, 1932). As Stefan Frey points out, its title, "The unfalsified truth," is something of a misnomer. Frey's biography does a great deal to fact-check and contextualize Kálmán's mythic narrative. Kevin Clarke has also written a useful overview of Kálmán biographies and sources; see Clarke, *"Im Himmel spielt auch schon die Jazzband,"* 28–46.

13. Uwe Harten, "Koessler, Hans von," *Oesterreichisches Musiklexikon* (Vienna: Verlag der Österreichischen Akademie der Wissenschaften, 2003), http://www. musiklexikon.ac .at/ml/musik_K/Koessler_Hans.xml.

14. "Landes-Musikakademie," *Pester Lloyd*, March 1, 1904. Among the six pieces on the program, the critic rates that of Bartók the highest and Kálmán's just behind.

15. Bistron, *Emmerich Kálmán*, 35.

16. Frey, *Emmerich Kálmán*, 59–61.

17. Laurence Cole, *Military Culture and Popular Patriotism in Late Imperial Austria* (Oxford: Oxford University Press, 2014), 11.

18. The relationship between the military and operetta, particularly the programming of operetta excerpts by military bands, is examined in Eva Slavíčkova, "Militärkapelle und ihre Stellung in dem Musikleben des 19. Jahrhunderts: Einfluss der Militärkapelle auf die Olomoucer Musikkultur bis zum Jahre 1918," *Musicologica Olomucensia* 5 (2000): 144; Friedrich Anzenberger, "Die Strauss-Pflege der 'Hoch- und Deutschmeister' unter Carl Michael Ziehrer: Untersuchungen zur Programmgestaltung einer traditionsreichen Wiener Militärkapelle," in *Straussiana 1999: Studien zu Leben, Werk und Wirkung von Johann Strauss (Sohn)*, ed. Monika Fink and Walter Pass, vol. 1 (Tutzing, Germany: Hans Schneider, 2001), 7–22; Timothy Freeze, "Gustav Mahler's Third Symphony: Program, Reception, and Evocations of the Popular" (PhD diss., University of Michigan, 2010), 151.

19. Curt von Zelau, "Die Wiener Operette: Plaudereien mit Komponisten und Librettisten," *Deutsche Revue über das gesamte nationale Leben der Gegenwart* 10 (1885): 163–73.

20. Walther Kellerbauer, "Gegen die Wiener Operette," *Neue Musik-Zeitung* 32 (November 1910): 189–95; Alfred Wolf, "Die Operettenmoloch," *Die Musik* 9, no. 20 (September 1909): 259–63.

21. r (Ludwig Hirschfeld), "(Theater an der Wien.)" *NFP*, January 23, 1909, 13.

22. bgr, "Ein Herbstmanöver," *Die Zeit*, January 23, 1909.

23. Emmerich Kálmán, "Der Roman eines Operettentheaters," *Pester Lloyd*, August

12, 1928, 3. Despite proclaiming that "a composer should compose, speak little, and write little—only compose," the years Kálmán spent in music criticism are evident in his finely observed, wry prose, quite different from Lehár's emphatic proclamations.

24. See Hooker, *Redefining Hungarian Music from Liszt to Bartók*, 42–45 and 78–84; Jonathan Bellman, *The Style Hongrois in the Music of Western Europe* (Boston: Northeastern University Press, 1993), 178–79; Bálint Sárosi, *Gypsy Music*, trans. Fred Macnicol (Budapest: Corvina Pres, 1978), 141–43. On the relationship between Gypsy music and national music in Hungary, see Judit Frigyesi, *Béla Bartók and Turn-of-the Century Budapest* (Berkeley: University of California Press, 1998), 55–60.

⟩ 25. Hooker, *Redefining Hungarian Music from Liszt to Bartók*, 138.

26. A catalog of this type can be found in Rudolf Angermüller, "Zigeuner und Zigeunerisches in der Oper des 19. Jahrhunderts," in *Die "Couleur locale" in der Oper des 19. Jahrhunderts*, ed. Heinz Becker (Regensburg, Germany: Gustav Bosse Verlag, 1976), 131–60.

27. David E. Schneider, *Bartók, Hungary, and the Renewal of Tradition: Case Studies in the Intersection of Modernity and Nationality* (Berkeley: University of California Press, 2006), 53–55.

28. One example arguing for a geographical division is Ernő Pesovár, "Typen und Entstehung des Csárdás," *Studia Musicologica Academiae Scientiarum Hungaricae* 29, no. 1/4 (January 1, 1987): 137–79.

29. Bálint Sárosi describes the makeup of a typical Gypsy orchestra in *Gypsy Music*, 238–43.

30. These gestures are catalogued by Jonathan Bellman in *The Style Hongrois in the Music of Western Europe*, 93–130.

31. Crittenden, *Johann Strauss and Vienna*, 170–209.

32. This issue is examined at considerable length, with reference to Lehár's later revision of the work, in Angerer, "Zorikas Traum von der silbernen Operette," 111–22.

33. Bellman, *The Style Hongrois in the Music of Western Europe*, 216–17.

34. It should be noted that the most popular excerpt from *Zigeunerliebe*, Ilona's csárdás (No. 16, "Hör' ich Cymbalklänge") was was added to the published edition only in 1938, well after Kálmán had revived the csárdás in operetta.

35. Lehár is variously described as Hungarian and Slovakian. While he was more often described in the Viennese media as Slavic than Magyar, the Hungarian press was, after *Die lustige Witwe*, eager to claim him as their own, even referring to him as Lehár Ferenc. He serves as a prime example of the complexity of national identification in the Habsburg Empire. I am grateful to Lynn Hooker for discussing Hungarian sources with me.

36. While the Johann-Strauß-Theater had a brief but distinguished history as an operetta theater (lasting from 1908 to 1929), its records have been lost, and its institutional history has been hardly studied at all, in stark contrast with the extremely thoroughly documented Theater an der Wien. It was located in the fourth district on Favoritenstraße, near the Theater an der Wien but somewhat farther from the center of the city.

37. His death notice can be found in "Foreign Musical Intelligence," *Musical Standard* 28, no. 1073 (February 21, 1885): 119. "The death is announced, on the 30th ult., of Racz Pali, a well-known Hungarian artist, a violinist, a conductor, and composer of national music. He was seventy-two years of age. He was married four times and had no less than thirty-

four children. His fortune, including a favorite violin and a diamond ring presented by the Prince of Wales, was left to his eldest son, Racz Pali." This is corroborated in "Musical Gossip," *The Athenaeum*, no. 2990 (February 14, 1885): 225. Only the final announcement refers to Racz's band as specifically "gipsy."

38. Rácz Laci cigányzenekara, "De szomorú ez az élet," recorded in Budapest circa 1907, Gramophone Concert Record, 78 rpm, G. C.-70533, 5411 I. In *The City of the Magyars*, published in 1903, Rácz is identified as "in his fortieth year." Smith, *The City of the Magyars*, 203. Considering the number of his descendants, it also seems likely that he was related to Aladár Rácz, the Roma cimbalom player who collaborated with Stravinsky.

39. In a way, this role's historicism can be seen as a prelude to Girardi's 1913 film *Der Millionenonkel*, in which he reprised a number of his most famous roles, including this one. Petersen, "Operetta after the Habsburg Empire," 11–24.

40. "Johann-Strauß-Theater," *NFP*.

41. Frey, *Unter Tränen lachen*, 87.

42. While this might seem like dramatic irony, it actually has considerable basis in truth. Lynn Hooker points out that by 1893, when Hungary conducted a "Gypsy census," the vast majority (more than 95 percent) of Roma were settled rather than peripatetic. Hooker, *Redefining Hungarian Music from Liszt to Bartók*, 37.

43. This impression is backed up by Girardi's recording of the piece. Alexander Girardi, "Meine alte Stradivari" from *Der Zigeunerprimas*, recorded 1912. Grammophon 942550, 78rpm record, digitized by the Österreichische Mediathek (Technisches Museum Wien), https://www.mediathek.at/oesterreich-am-wort/suche/treffer/atom/017452EC-133-07C65 -00000DBC-01733A62/pool/BWEB/.

44. Derek Scott discusses dance music hybridity in operetta more broadly in *German Operetta on Broadway and in the West End*, 34–36.

45. Writing about the Berlin premiere in the *BZ am Mittag*, Erich Urban described it as the best number of the operetta, "which isn't in the [published] score." See Frey, *Unter Tränen lachen*, 90. Both "Hazazaa" and the number it replaced are the fifth number of the score, and both are duets for Sári and Gaston. The original number, the waltz "Sie wüßten eine Braut für mich," is found in the first edition (1912), while a subsequent edition marked 1913 contains "Hazazaa." Slight irregularities in the typesetting of the table of contents of the 1913 edition show that the change was made on the original printing plates, and there is a separate copyright notice on the lower margin of the first page of the number. Both editions are in wide circulation. There are also changes in Act 3, with the later edition featuring an additional duet for Sári and Gaston (No. 14, "Ich tu' das meinige") and a reprise of "Hazazaa" (No. 15½), also for Sári and Gaston, to replace the 1912 version's "musikalische Szene," a reprise of "Laut dringt der frommen Chor" for Laczi, Racz, and Julishka (No. 15, "Du, du, du, lieber Gott"). The second version increases the prominence of Sári and Gaston. *Der Zigeunerprimas* does not precisely fit the operetta *fach* role classification system—it is somewhat unclear whether Sári or Julishka is the female lead, and while Laczi is the male lead, Racz and Gaston also are very important—so some flexibility was possible. The 1912 version can be found online courtesy of the University of Rochester's Sibley Music Library (https://urresearch.rochester.edu/viewInstitutionalCollection.action?collectionId=63).

46. st [Julius Stern], "Johann Strauss-Theater," *FB*, October 12, 1912.

47. "Johann-Strauß-Theater," *NFP*.

48. bs [Leopold Jacobson], "Johann-Strauss-Theater," *NWJ*, October 12, 1912.

49. "Johann-Strauß-Theater," *NFP*.

CHAPTER 4. OPERETTA AND THE GREAT WAR

1. Leo Stein, Bela Jenbach, and Emmerich Kálmán, *Die Csárdásfürstin: Operette in drei Akten: Soufflier- und Regiebuch* (Leipzig: Weinberger, 1916). Descriptions of Konwitschny's production are based on the dress rehearsal video in the Konwitschny collection, Inszenierungsarchiv, Akademie der Künste, Berlin (unnumbered).

2. For two accounts of the performance, the first from the perspective of a critic and the second from Konwitschny, see Manuel Brug, "Die letzten Tage der Operetten-Menschheit," *Die Welt*, December 31, 1999, https://www.welt.de/print-welt/article595737/Die-letzten-Tage-der-Operetten-Menschheit.html; Kai Luehrs-Kaiser, "Oper ist kein echtes Vergnügen," *Die Welt*, July 11, 2007, sec. Kultur, http://www.welt.de/kultur/article1016389/Oper-ist-kein-echtes-Vergnuegen.html.

3. At one point in the ensuing scandal, he was accused of being an informant to the East German secret police of the same name.

4. Note in unnumbered "Csárdásfürstin" folder, Peter Konwitschny collection, Inszenierungsarchiv, Akademie der Künste, Berlin.

5. Traubner, *Operetta*, 266.

6. Translation, slightly edited, from Karl Kraus, *The Last Days of Mankind: A Tragedy in Five Acts with a Prologue and an Epilogue*, trans. Patrick Healy (Amsterdam: November Editions, 2016), 521. The representation of modernity as a performance picks up on the use of "Vorstellung" in the previous sentence, where it means "imagining" but in this context can mean "performance." Such wordplay is what makes Kraus impossible to translate. German original: Karl Kraus, *Die letzten Tage der Menschheit: Tragödie in fünf Akten*, ed. Christian Wagenknecht, Karl Kraus Schriften 10 (Frankfurt: Suhrkamp, 1986), 675.

7. Marion Linhardt, "Mobilization and the Creation of Collective Identities: War and Popular Theatre in 1914," trans. Judith Beniston, *Austrian Studies* 21 (2013): 76.

8. Martin Baumeister, *Kriegstheater: Großstadt, Front und Massenkultur 1914–1918* (Essen: Klartext, 2005).

9. Letter from Wilhelm Karczag to Hubert Marischka, August 5, 1914. The company was dissolved, according to Gertrude Marischka's unpublished memoir. Both are available in the Nachlass Hubert Marischka (unnumbered), ÖTM.

10. This and other chaotic happenings early in the war are documented in Linhardt, "Mobilization and the Creation of Collective Identities."

11. *Komm', deutscher Bruder!*. NÖ Reg. Präs Theater ZA-1914/25, NÖLA.

12. "Eigenhändiger Brief an Alban Berg, [Wien], 18.8.14. 1 Bl. Briefpapier zu einem Doppelblatt gefaltet, 4 Seiten mit schwarzer Tinte beschrieben," F21.Berg.1197/15 ÖNB MS.

13. This operetta's title is given variously as *Gold gab ich für Eisen*, *Gold gab ich für Eisen!*, and "*Gold gab ich für Eisen*," the latter including the quotation marks to indicate the phrase's status as a motto. The simplest option is used here.

14. See Victor Léon and Karl von Bakonyi, *Der gute Kamerad*, NÖ Reg. Präs Theater TB-648/16, NÖLA.

15. The reviews are summarized in Stefan Frey, *Unter Tränen lachen*, 78–79.

16. Victor Léon, *Gold gab ich für Eisen,* NÖ Reg. Präs Theater TB-344/3, NÖLA.

17. "Theater an der Wien," *NWJ,* October 18, 1914. (Unusually, this review is unsigned.)

18. st [Julius Stern], "Theater an der Wien," *FB,* October 18, 1914.

19. Jason Stanley, *How Propaganda Works* (Princeton, NJ: Princeton University Press, 2015), 48.

20. Victor Léon, Karl von Bakonyi, and Emmerich Kálmán, *Der gute Kamerad* (Vienna: Karczag, 1911); Victor Léon and Emmerich Kálmán, *Gold gab ich für Eisen* (Vienna: Karczag, 1914).

21. "Theater an der Wien," *NFP,* October 18, 1914.

22. Stefan Zweig, *The World of Yesterday* (Lincoln: University of Nebraska Press, 1964), 226.

23. Victor Léon, *Gold gab ich für Eisen,* NÖ Reg. Präs Theater TB 344/3, NÖLA.

24. For example, this passage from Act 2, when Xaverl is teased by his father, Vitus (all spellings and emphasis are original):

Xaverl: "Einem Uhlanenrittmeister wurde die Cartousche entrissen"—

Vitus: Na horst, wann ich die Kartusch g'habt hätt', ich hätt' mir's net wegnehmen lassen.

Xaverl: Da man dadurch in den Besitz wichtiger Papiere kam, bedeutet diese Kartusch einen grossen Erfolg auf dem Kriegstheater.

Vitus: Du, was in denn dös eigentlich a Kartusch?

Xaverl: A Patrontascherl.

Vitus: Ah so! I' hab' glaubt, dös bist Du! Also, Xaverl, jetzt komm' zur Schlossfräul'n.

Victor Léon, *Gold gab ich für Eisen,* NÖ Reg. Präs Theater TB 344/3, NÖLA, 52. Kartousch would participate in further meta-theatrical games in *Die Bajadere;* see chapter 5.

25. Maureen Healy, *Vienna and the Fall of the Habsburg Empire: Total War and Everyday Life in World War I* (Cambridge: Cambridge University Press, 2004), 166.

26. Marsha Rozenblit posits that the war offered opportunities for Jewish women in particular to indicate their loyalty and sacrifice to the Austro-Hungarian Empire as a political cause. Marsha L. Rozenblit, "For Fatherland and Jewish People: Jewish Women in Austria during the First World War," in *Authority, Identity, and the Social History of the Great War,* ed. Frans Coetzee and Marilyn Shevin-Coetzee (New York: Berghahn Books, 1993), 199–220.

27. "Theater an der Wien," *NWJ,* October 18, 1914; see also "Theater an der Wien," *NFP,* October 18, 1914.

28. Baumeister, *Kriegstheater,* 13.

29. One highly nationalist 1913 German book detailing the Napoleonic campaigns with an emphasis on the Battle of Leipzig even shared a title with the operetta, along with the colorful subtitle of "Germany's Ignominy and Exaltation in Contemporary Documents, Letters, and Diaries from the Years 1806 to 1815." Ernst Müsebeck, *Gold gab ich für Eisen: Deutschlands Schmach und Erhebung in zeitgenössischen Dokumenten, Briefen, Tagebüchern aus den Jahren 1806–1815* (Berlin: Deutsches Verlagshaus Bong & Co., 1913).

30. Jay Winter, *Sites of Memory, Sites of Mourning: The Great War in European Cultural History* (Cambridge: Cambridge University Press, 2014), 78.

31. The directive is addressed "an die Frauen im preußischen Staate." It begins, "Das Vaterland ist in Gefahr!" and describes that men and boys have gone off to fight, summoning tears from mothers everywhere. By donating jewelry, money, or any "small valuable," women could prove their worth to the fatherland, even if they could not fight. Müsebeck, *Gold gab ich für Eisen*, 216–17.

32. "Gold gab ich für Eisen – St. Veit an der Glan," 1914, poster, 61 × 42 cm, Buchdruckerei Heinrich Schlick & Söhne, St. Veit an der Glan (Kärtnen), KS 16214315, ÖNB Bildarchiv und Grafiksammlung.

33. Bernhard Denscher, *Gold gab ich für Eisen: Österreichische Kriegsplakate 1914–1918* (Vienna: Jugend & Volk, 1987), 6–7.

34. Nicholas J. Saunders, *Trench Art: Materialities and Memories of War* (Oxford: Berg, 2003), 222.

35. The history of the song and poem are discussed in Hans-Peter Zimmerman, "Der gute Kamerad: Ludwig Uhlands freiheitliche Konzeption des militärischen Totenkults," *Zeitschrift für Volkskunde* 95 (1999): 1–13; John Meier, *Das deutsche Soldatenlied im Felde* (Strassburg: Verlag von Karl J. Trübner, 1916).

36. The setting of the Uhland poem is described in many collections as "after a folk song, first published by Friedrich Silcher in 1825." The "Gloria, Viktoria" refrain was added at some point later in the nineteenth century and is frequently cited by Karl Kraus in *The Last Days of Mankind*. Max Friedlaender and Erk, *Deutscher Liederschatz*, 190; Meier, *Das deutsche Soldatenlied im Felde*, 60.

37. Ludwig Uhland, *Werke*, ed. Harmut Fröschle and Walter Scheffler, vol. 1, *Sämtliche Gedichte* (Munich: Winkler Verlag, 1980), 226; Margarete Müsterberg, trans. and ed., *A Harvest of German Verse* (New York: Appleton and Co., 1916).

38. More recently, it makes a historically appropriate appearance in the Weimar Republic–set television series *Babylon Berlin,* where in one instance it is sung by a group of German World War I veterans to memorialize their fallen comrades.

39. The *Regiebuch* (staging manual) indicates that the curtain opens before the male chorus sings, though they are not visible. The words of the chorus are, "Heil, Heil! Gut und Blut dem Kaiser! Heil Vaterland!" The words are paraphrased from the second verse of the "Kaiserhymne": "Gut und Blut für unsern Kaiser, Gut und Blut fürs Vaterland!" It is drawn from the "Kaiserhymne" text that was official from 1854 to 1918 (still set to Haydn's melody, originally beginning "Gott erhalte Franz, den Kaiser"), which did not name the emperor and had official versions in the many different languages of the empire.

40. William A. Everett, *Sigmund Romberg* (New Haven, CT: Yale University Press, 2007), 89. See also Frey, *Emmerich Kálmán*, 107.

41. The published edition bears only Romberg's name. Sigmund Romberg, *Her Soldier Boy* (New York: G. Schirmer, 1916). Composers Clifton Crawford and Felix Powell are also credited with individual numbers. The majority of the lyrics are credited to Rida Johnson Young, but four additional lyricists also contributed.

42. Frey, *Unter Tränen lachen*, 108.

43. These progressive tendencies are considered in Steven Beller, "The Tragic Carnival," in *European Culture in the Great War: The Arts, Entertainment, and Propaganda, 1914–1918*, ed. Aviel Roshwald and Richard Stites (Cambridge: Cambridge University Press, 1999), 126–61.

44. *Die Fackel* is available in its entirety online through an open-access project of the Austrian Academy of Sciences at https://fackel.oeaw.ac.at/. The entire run of the journal from 1899 to 1936 (Kraus's death) consists of 37 volumes, 415 issues, 922 "numbers" (corresponding to the theoretical thrice-monthly publication; however, most issues were assigned multiple numbers), and 22,500 pages.

45. Edward Timms, "Karl Kraus's Adaptations of Offenbach: The Quest for the Other Sphere," *Austrian Studies* 13 (January 1, 2005): 91–108; Volker Klotz, "Cancan contra Stechschritt: Antimilitarismus mit Rückfällen in der Operette," in *Österreich und der Große Krieg*, ed. Klaus Amann and Hubert Lengauer (Vienna: Christian Brandstätter, 1989), 52–60; Georg Knepler, *Karl Kraus liest Offenbach: Erinnerungen, Kommentare, Dokumentationen* (Vienna: Löcker, 1984).

46. Karl Kraus, "Grimassen über Kultur und Bühne," *Die Fackel* 10, no. 270–71 (January 19, 1909): 1–18; Karl Kraus, "Ernst ist das Leben, heiter war die Operette," *Die Fackel* 12, no. 313/314 (November 1910): 13–16. The title of the latter references Schiller's *Wallensteins Lager*, "Ernst ist das Leben, heiter ist die Kunst" [life is serious, art is cheerful], with a key change of tense of the second clause. Many of Kraus's writings have not been translated, but a recent English-language collection of some of his work is Karl Kraus, *In These Great Times: Selected Writings*, trans. Patrick Healy (Amsterdam: November Editions, 2017).

47. *Die letzten Tage* first appeared in *Die Fackel* in 1918 and 1919. It was published as a book in 1922 and again in 1926. There have been two recent complete English translations: Kraus, *The Last Days of Mankind*; Karl Kraus, *The Last Days of Mankind: The Complete Text*, trans. Fred Bridgham and Edward Timms (New Haven, CT: Yale University Press, 2016). The page numbers in this text referring to the German edition use the modern Suhrkamp edition (cited in note 6 above), not the *Fackel* version. It has been more frequently transmitted as a printed text than as a performed play; however, in 2014 the Salzburger Festspiele produced an extensive staging in cooperation with the Burgtheater.

48. Kraus, "Grimassen über Kultur und Bühne," 12.

49. Edward Timms, *Karl Kraus, Apocalyptic Satirist: Culture and Catastrophe in Habsburg Vienna* (New Haven, CT: Yale University Press, 1986), 417. The article Timms cites is Karl Kraus, "Vorurteile," *Die Fackel* 9, no. 241 (January 15, 1908): 15.

50. Karl Kraus, "Und in Kriegszeiten," *Die Fackel* 14, no. 363–365 (December 1912): 71.

51. The issue of Kraus and Judaism is examined in detail in Paul Reitter, *The Anti-Journalist: Karl Kraus and Jewish Self-Fashioning in Fin-de-Siècle Europe* (Chicago: University of Chicago Press, 2008).

52. Act 1, Scene 1, Kraus, *Die letzten Tage der Menschheit: Tragödie in fünf Akten*.

53. This is analyzed by Gerald Stieg, "'Die letzten Tage der Menschheit': Eine negative Operette?" in *Österreich und der Große Krieg*, ed. Klaus Amann and Hubert Lengauer (Vienna: C. Brandstätter, 1989).

54. Adorno's critique of standardization in popular music is in turn critiqued in Gendron, "Theodor Adorno Meets the Cadillacs," 18–36.

55. The opening depends on the pun of a theater poster that reads "zum erstenmal" (for the first time), a phrase used to advertise premieres. Kraus, *The Last Days of Mankind*, 41. The German appears in Kraus, *Die letzten Tage der Menschheit: Tragödie in fünf Akten*, 83.

56. At one point, Kraus insisted that he understood everything about Heuberger's

Der Opernball without, in Edward Timms's words, "having to endure a complete performance." Timms, *Karl Kraus, Apocalyptic Satirist*, 416.

57. Karl Kraus, "In dieser großen Zeit," *Die Fackel* 16, no. 404 (December 5, 1914): 2.

58. st [Julius Stern], "Theater an der Wien," *FB*.

59. Denscher, *Der Operettenlibrettist Victor Léon*, 394.

60. Beller, "The Tragic Carnival," 157–58.

61. This independence has obvious resonance with later Frankfurt School critical theory. Many Frankfurt School theorists valued Kraus's work highly.

62. Kraus's adoption of anti-Jewish rhetoric is examined in Reitter, *The Anti-Journalist*, 69–106.

63. Marsha L. Rozenblit, *Reconstructing a National Identity: The Jews of Habsburg Austria during World War I* (Oxford: Oxford University Press, 2001), 40.

64. Rozenblit, 44.

65. Béla Jenbach (1871–1943) moved to Vienna with his family in the 1880s and joined the Burgtheater ensemble as an actor in 1907. In the 1920s he cowrote several of Franz Lehár's late works, including *Paganini* (1925) and *Der Zarewitsch* (1927). He died in 1943 of untreated stomach cancer after spending years hiding from the Nazis in a basement in Vienna. See Stefan Frey, "Béla Jenbach," in *Lexikon verfolgter Musiker und Musikerinnen der NS-Zeit*, ed. Claudia Maurer Zenck, Peter Petersen, and Sophie Fetthauer (Hamburg: Universität Hamburg, 2016), https://www.lexm.uni-hamburg.de/object/lexm_lexmperson_00003529.

66. Frey, *Unter Tränen lachen*, 108. The title *Es lebe die Liebe!* can even be found on the libretto in the theater censor's archive, NÖ Reg. Präs Theater TB-672/8, NÖLA.

67. Kálmán's *Gräfin Mariza* (1924) would allude to *Der Zigeunerbaron* even more directly: when the title character is forced to make up the name of a fiancé, she chooses "Koloman Zsupán" from Strauss's operetta—only to have a baron by that name suddenly crash her engagement party.

68. Stein, Jenbach, and Kálmán, *Die Csárdásfürstin: Operette in drei Akten: Soufflier- und Regiebuch*. Subsequent productions have often rearranged the score and sometimes the plot as well, as will be discussed later in this chapter. These changes have often gone unmentioned.

69. Recall Wilhelm Kaczag's possibly apocryphal dismissal of *Die lustige Witwe* as a "vaudeville," presumably fit for a varieté rather than his classier establishment, discussed in chapter 1.

70. Upon the theater's opening, the critic Leopold Jacobson described the interior as white, gold, and red (the standard colors for theaters of this time and the color scheme of the Theater an der Wien as well). bs [Leopold Jacobson], "Die Eröffnung des Johann-Strauß-Theaters," *NWJ*, October 31, 1908.

71. The Bildarchiv Austria also holds another, similar shot (presumably from the same occasion, with a smaller group of people). One of the "unknown men" noted in that photo's caption is librettist Leo Stein (with Austro-Hungarian mustache). It does not provide any other new details. In both photographs, Karl Bachmann (Edwin) is wearing a uniform, suggesting that the photograph was taken after a rehearsal or performance of the finale of Act 1. "Kálmán, Emmerich," November 1915, Bildarchiv Austria, ÖNB Pf 1262 D18, http://www.bildarchivaustria.at/Pages/ImageDetail.aspx?p_iBildID=13769470.

72. The number was inevitably described as a csárdás by Viennese critics. However, it also contains elements of the Romanian *doina*, particularly in its rhythm, a form Kálmán probably knew much better than the Viennese. I am grateful to Jason Roberts of the University of Texas, Austin, for this suggestion.

73. For example, see track 1, Anna Netrebko, *Souvenirs*, Prague Philharmonia, cond. Emmanuel Villaume, recorded 2008, Deutsche Grammophon, 4777639, digital download.

74. Stein, Jenbach, and Kálmán, *Die Csárdásfürstin: Operette in drei Akten: Soufflier- und Regiebuch*.

75. Max Schönherr, "Modelle der Walzerkomposition: Grundlagen zu einer Theorie des Walzers," *Österreichische Musikzeitschrift* 30 (1975): 273–86.

76. Sylva and Edwin sing a third duet as well, the joyful No. 12, "Tanzen möcht' ich," a fast waltz composed in a Viennese style. Unlike the other Viennese numbers, it is not ironic—except that its jubilation would shortly be undercut by the tragic second-act finale, a predictable twist the audience surely anticipated.

77. The operetta's international iterations are considered in Zoltán Imre, "Operetta beyond Borders: The Different Versions of *Die Csárdásfürstin* in Europe and the United States (1915–1921)," *Studies in Musical Theatre* 7, no. 2 (June 2013): 175–205.

78. "r." [Ludwig Hirschfeld], "Die Csádásfürstin," *NFP*, November 18, 1915.

79. a.e. [Alexander Engel], "Johann-Strauss-Theater," *NWJ*, November 18, 1915.

80. ld. [pseud.], "Johann-Strauß-Theater," *Die Zeit*, November 18, 1915.

81. s.t. [pseud.], "Johann-Strauß-Theater," *Wiener Abendpost: Beilage der Wiener Zeitung*, November 18, 1915.

82. a.e. [Alexander Engel], "Johann-Strauss-Theater," *NWJ*.

83. "r." [Ludwig Hirschfeld], "Die Csádásfürstin," *NFP*.

84. st [Julius Stern], "Johann-Strauß-Theater," *FB*, November 18, 1915.

85. rp [Ludwig Karpath], "Die Csárdásfürstin," *NWT*, November 18, 1915.

86. st [Julius Stern], "Johann-Strauß-Theater," *FB*.

87. Rozenblit, *Reconstructing a National Identity*. See particularly chapter 2, "Austrian Jews and the Spirit of 1914," 39–58.

88. Performance of *Die Csárdásfürstin*, Volksoper Wien, April 3, 2011. The video is available as Emmerich Kálmán, *Die Csárdásfürstin*, directed by Miklós Szinetár with Anna Moffo (Sylva Varescu), Rene Kollo (Edwin), filmed 1971 (Hamburg: Deutsche Grammophon, 2006), DVD.

CHAPTER 5. EXOTIC LIAISONS

1. Julius Brammer and Alfred Grünwald, *Die Bajadere: Operette in 3 Akten: Soufflier- und Reigebuch* (Berlin: Drei Masken Verlag, 1922).

2. D.B. [David Josef Bach], "Johann-Strauss-Theater," *AZ*, October 14, 1918. Quoted in Martin Lichtfuss, *Operette im Ausverkauf*, 41. The humanitarian crisis of the late war and immediate postwar years is examined in Healy, *Vienna and the Fall of the Habsburg Empire*.

3. Hugo von Hofmannsthal, *Hugo von Hofmannsthal and the Austrian Idea: Selected Essays and Addresses, 1906–1927*, ed. and trans. David S. Luft (West Lafayette, IN: Purdue

University Press, 2011); Michael P. Steinberg, *The Meaning of the Salzburg Festival: Austria as Theater and Ideology, 1890–1938* (Ithaca, NY: Cornell University Press, 1990).

4. A general account of this period can be found in Birgit Peter, "Between Tradition and a Longing for the Modern: Theater in Interwar Vienna," in *Interwar Vienna*, ed. Deborah Holmes and Lisa Silverman (Rochester, NY: Camden House, 2009), 161–75. A high culture–centric analysis is Robert Pyrah, *The Burgtheater and Austrian Identity: Theatre and Cultural Politics in Vienna, 1918–38* (London: Legenda, 2007).

5. See, for example, "Streik der Operettentheater: Aus Protest gegen die Nichtherabsetzung der Lustbarkeitsteuer," *Illustriertes Wiener Extrablatt*, January 30, 1924. More details on taxes can be found in Yates, *Theatre in Vienna*, 206.

6. The greatest authorities on the theater politics of this era are Stefan Frey and Kevin Clarke. See Kevin Clarke, *"Im Himmel spielt auch schon die Jazzband"*; Stefan Frey, *"Unter Tränen Lachen."* Marischka in particular preserved selective but nonetheless voluminous documentation of his tenure at the theater, which provides a detailed record of this era. Important collections consulted include the Sammlung Marischka (unnumbered, ÖTM), Nachlass Victor Léon (ZPH 906/924/925, WB) and the Alfred Grünwald Papers (*T-Mss 1998-30, NYPL Billy Rose Theatre Division).

7. The rental and press debate is examined in Clarke, *"Im Himmel spielt auch schon die Jazzband,"* 208–30.

8. A reflective consideration of this impulse is Matthew Head, "Musicology on Safari: Orientalism and the Spectre of Postcolonial Theory," *Music Analysis* 22, no. 1/2 (July 2003): 211–30. See also Jonathan Bellman's response to Head in "Musical Voyages and Their Baggage: Orientalism in Music and Critical Musicology," *Musical Quarterly* 94, no. 3 (September 1, 2011): 417–38.

9. Ralph P. Locke, *Musical Exoticism: Images and Reflections* (Cambridge: Cambridge University Press, 2009), 59–63.

10. Robert Lemon, *Imperial Messages: Orientalism as Self-Critique in the Habsburg Fin de Siècle* (Rochester, NY: Camden House, 2011), 1. Some of the works he analyzes, such as Hugo von Hofmannsthal's poem "Der Kaiser von China spricht" (pp. 15–51) trade in transparent metaphors for the author's own empire. Most obviously, Hofmannsthal's poem, written in the years following Crown Prince Rudolf's suicide, prominently features a Chinese imperial succession crisis.

11. An argument along these lines can be found in Lichtfuss, *Operette im Ausverkauf*, 220.

12. In opera, the opposite is far more common. See James Parakilas, "The Soldier and the Exotic: Operatic Variations on a Theme of Racial Encounter: Part I," *Opera Quarterly* 10, no. 2 (December 21, 1993): 33–56.

13. Examples include Franz Carl Endres, *Die Türkei: Bilder und Skizzen von Land und Volk* (Munich: Beck, 1917); Else Marquardsen, *Das Wesen des Osmanen: Ein Berater für Orientfahrer.* (Munich: Roland-Verlag, 1916). The nature of representation in this period is surveyed in Maureen Healy, "In aller 'Freundschaft'?: Österreichische 'Türkenbilder' zwischen Gegnerschaft und 'Freundschaft' vor und während des Ersten Weltkrieges," in *Glanz—Gewalt—Gehorsam: Militär und Gesellschaft in der Habsburgermonarchie (1800 bis 1918)*, ed. Laurence Cole, Christa Hämmerle, and Martin Scheutz (Essen: Klartext, 2011), 269–92.

14. While the subjects of these operettas are provocative, their content is rarely incendiary. For example, *Jung-England* ends with the suffragette firebrand marrying her police chief nemesis. The suffragettes' inappropriately masculine ways and the police's chauvinism are mocked roughly equally throughout. Rudolf Bernauer and Ernst Welitsch, *Jung-England: Operette in drei Akten, Regiebuch* (Berlin: Harmonie, 1914).

15. Alfred Grünwald's life is the subject of a book edited by his son Henry Grunwald, *Ein Walzer muß es sein: Alfred Grünwald und die Wiener Operette*. Alfred Grünwald's papers are preserved in the Billy Rose Theatre Division of the New York Public Library for the Performing Arts (*T-Mss 1998-030 Grunwald, NYPL) and include many drafts and copies of his work, though the collection contains little correspondence dating from before 1930—that is, the period under consideration here.

16. Julius Brammer and Alfred Grünwald, *Die Rose von Stambul: Vollständiges Regiebuch* (Vienna: Karczag, 1916), 8, 22.

17. "Theater an der Wien," *NWJ*, December 3, 1916.

18. "Die Einrichtung sehr luxuriös, wie die Gemächer einer jungen europäischen Dame, und doch muß im ersten Moment ersichtlich sein, daß sich dieser Salon im Orient befindet. Im Hintergrunde einige große quadratförmige Fenster, eventuell eine Aussichtsrampe, die mit Gittern versehen sind, aber trotzdem das herrliche Panorama von Stambul mit seinen Minaretts und Moscheen in feenhafter Sonnenbeleuchtung sehen lassen...das Ganze sehr dezent und geschmackvoll." Brammer and Grünwald, *Die Rose von Stambul: Vollständiges Regiebuch*, 7–8.

19. Reviews consistently refer to Kemal Pascha, the spelling in the final printed libretto. The published score refers to Kamek Pascha, as do earlier versions of the libretto.

20. Frey, Stemprok, and Dosch, *Leo Fall*, 157.

21. Jürgen Osterhammel, *Unfabling the East: The Enlightenment's Encounter with Asia*, trans. Roger Savage (Princeton, NJ: Princeton University Press, 2018). See in particular chapter 12, "Women," pp. 446–79.

22. "Theater an der Wien: Erstaufführung der Operette 'Die Rose von Stambul,'" *Österreichische Volks-Zeitung*, December 3, 1916. Cited in Marcus Pyka, "'Von Reformen ganz enormen träumen wir am Bosporus': Das Osmanische Reich als Vorbild wider Willen in Leo Fall's Erfolgsoperette Die Rose von Stambul," in *Sehrayin: Die Welt der Osmanen, die Osmanen in der Welt: Wahrnehmungen, Begegnungen und Abgrenzungen: Festschrift Hans Georg Majer*, ed. Yavuz Köse (Wiesbaden, Germany: Harrassowitz, 2012), 459.

23. "Theater," *Die Bombe*, December 10, 1916.

24. Beller, "The Tragic Carnival," 156.

25. The draft can be found in the ÖNB MS, catalogued as F88 Leo Fall 365. (This collection contains a number of interesting documents related to this operetta, including a full orchestration of the prelude as F88 Leo Fall 87.) The libretto submitted to the censor is, like all other censor's scripts, in NÖLA, in this case catalogued as Sig 344/15. The official *Regiebuch* was published in 1916 by Karczag Verlag.

26. Julius Brammer and Alfred Grünwald, *Die Rose von Stambul*, typescript draft of Act 1 libretto, F88 Leo Fall 365, ÖNB MS.

27. These can all be found in the libretto first draft (F88 Leo Fall 365, ÖNB MS); see discussion in note 25.

28. The full orchestration of the prelude can be seen in the sketches and drafts collected as F88 Leo Fall 87, ÖNB MS.

29. The sketches contain an early draft of the Act 1 finale in which this theme once again intrudes upon Western-oriented music to indicate a forced conformity to Turkish customs.

30. "Achmed ist ein vollendeter Kavalier in Auftreten und Exterieur. Modern nach der letzten europäischen Mode gekleidet. Sein Gesicht ist interessant, rassig, dunkler Teint, kleiner englischer Schnurrbart, Monocle. Nur der Fez erinnert an den Osmanen." *Die Rose von Stambul,* NÖ Reg. Präs Theater TB-344/15, NÖLA.

31. Brammer and Grünwald, *Die Rose von Stambul: Vollständiges Regiebuch,* 29. This second description is corroborated by actor Hubert Marischka's notes on his costume for the operetta, which make no notes about skin color but describe Act 1's costume as a "brown uniform with brown boots, saber, brown leather belt, cap, ring, wristwatch, brown gloves, monocle, handkerchief." Untitled notebook, Nachlass Hubert Marischka, Box 4, Shelf 15, ÖTM.

32. "Theater an der Wien" *NWJ.*

33. rp [Ludwig Karpath], "Die Rose von Stambul," *NWT,* December 3, 1916.

34. rp [Ludwig Karpath], "Die Rose von Stambul," *NWT.*

35. p.f. [Paul Frank], "Theater an der Wien," *FB,* December 3, 1916.

36. "Theater an der Wien," *NWJ.*

37. rp [Ludwig Karpath], "Die Rose von Stambul," *NWT.*

38. p.f. [Paul Frank], "Theater an der Wien," *FB.*

39. rp [Ludwig Karpath], "Die Rose von Stambul," *NWT*; Pyka, "'Von Reformen ganz enormen träumen wir am Bosporus.'"

40. Kálmán goes on to cite, with creative spelling, "Kippling [*sic*], Claude Ferrard, und ähnliche Werke." "Emmerich Kálmán über Die Bajadere," in "Sonderheft Die Bajadere," *Komödie: Wochenrevue für Bühne und Film,* January 1922, 4.

41. a.e. [Alexander Engel], "Carl-Theater," *NWJ,* December 24, 1921.

42. Additionally, the *Reichspost* critic wrote, "In short order, India has become a trump card in film and operetta." H. [Otto Howorka?], "Carltheater," *RP,* December 24, 1921. More generally, see Meenakshi Shedde and Vinzenz Hediger, "Come On, Baby, Be My Tiger," in *Import/Export: Cultural Transfer between India and Germany,* ed. Angelika Fitz et al. (Berlin: Parthas, 2005).

43. Ludwig Hirschfeld, "Die neue Kalman-Operette Die Bajadere. Erstaufführung im Carl-Theater," *NFP,* December 24, 1921.

44. "Sonderheft Die Bajadere," 4–5.

45. This is Act 1, Scene 8 of Cilea's opera, beginning with Michonnet's "Ecco il monologo." The librettists may have been familiar with the opera or, even more likely, knew Ernst Legouvé and Eugène Scribe's 1849 play on which the opera is based. This and other offstage phenomena are considered in Arman Schwartz, "Rough Music: Tosca and Verismo Reconsidered," *19th-Century Music* 31, no. 3 (Spring 2008): 228–44.

46. Mardayn's singing was universally praised by critics. She may have had a small amount of help singing this number: a footnote in the published score indicates that Odette was "supported" (*unterstützt*) by a solo oboe, also played from backstage. (The score suggests that the oboe doubles the vocal line in much of the song, including several complex

coloratura passages, but it is not indicated in the cadenza.) However, the necessity of this assistance may have had been more related to acoustics and backstage placement than vocal requirements.

47. Compare Radjami's Act 1, Finale I (rehearsal figure 14) invitation, "Tout Paris ist heut' von mir höfflichst eingeladen... O Champagner, sperrst uns auf das Himmelreich" to the opening of *Die Fledermaus's* Act 2 finale ("Im Feuerstrom der Reben"). The situation has obvious parallels to Prince Orlofsky's "Ich lade gern mir Gäste ein."

48. The modern version of the instrument had been developed in the mid-nineteenth century in Hungary and was only occasionally seen outside Budapest, usually playing the role of Wagner's *Holztrompete* in Act 3 of *Tristan und Isolde,* though this seems to have been a short-lived early twentieth-century fad. Zoltán Falvy, "'Tárogató' as a Regional Instrument," *Studia Musicologica Academiae Scientiarum Hungaricae* 38, no. 3/4 (January 1997): 361–70. It is unclear which instrument was used in the premiere. Gertrud Marischka dated the first use of a saxophone in operetta to *Der Orlow* in 1925, several years later, but her memoir should be taken with a grain of salt. See Petersen, "Operetta after the Habsburg Empire," 38.

49. H.T. [Heinrich Reinhardt?], "Johann-Strauß-Theater," *NWT,* December 24, 1921; Hirschfeld, "Die neue Kalman-Operette Die Bajadere. Erstaufführung im Carl-Theater," *NFP*; "Die Bajadere im Carl-Theater," *Illustriertes Wiener Extrablatt,* December 25, 1921.

50. Brammer and Grünwald, *Die Bajadere: Regiebuch.*

51. This commodification is further developed in the figure of Pimprinette, the head of the Théâtre de Chatelêt's claque. Speaking with a journalist named Dr. Cohen, Pimprinette says that after years of experience he is expert in gauging an operetta audience's response and that he believes that the end of the second act of this operetta has provided them great satisfaction. He then undermines this remark by noting, "Wie es zum zweiten Aktschluss kommt und die Operette tragisch wird—schwimmen sie in Tränen, diese Tränenschwimmerei kostet 8 Francs Honorar (Für den dritten Akt hab' ich die Lacher auf meiner Seite – kosten 10 Francs per Stück!)." ("Like when the finale of the second act of the operetta becomes tragic—they swim in tears, this bath of tears costs an 8 franc fee [for the third act I have laughter on my side—it costs 10 francs apiece!].")

52. Brammer and Grünwald, *Die Bajadere: Regiebuch.* The character Napoleon's actual name is Casimir, but he changed it to impress Marietta. King Louis-Philippe was, of course, forced to abdicate the July Monarchy in eventual favor of Napoleon III.

53. Scott, *German Operetta on Broadway and in the West End,* 31–32. Scott points to "Seeräuber Jenny" from *Die Dreigroschenoper* as a later example. The memoir by Robert Stolz and his wife misdates the premiere of *Der Tanz ins Glück* as having taken place on October 28, 1920, an error reproduced in a number of subsequent works. In fact it took place on December 23, 1920. Robert and Einzi Stolz, *Servus Du: Robert Stolz und sein Jahrhundert* (Munich: Blaunvalet, 1980), 527; "Raimund-Theater," *NFP,* Abendblatt, December 24, 1920.

54. Jane Feuer, "The Self-Reflexive Musical and the Myth of Entertainment," *Quarterly Review of Film Studies* 2, no. 3 (1977): 313–26. Reprinted in *Film Genre Reader II,* ed. Barry Keith (Austin, TX: University of Texas Press, 1995), 443.

55. Theodor W. Adorno, "On the Fetish Character in Music and the Regression of Listening," in *The Culture Industry,* ed. J. M. Bernstein (London: Routledge Classics, 1991), 38.

56. Adorno, 30.

57. "Sonderheft Die Bajadere," 7.

58. "Kleider auf der Bühne" in "Sonderheft Die Bajadere," 15.

59. Hirschfeld, "Die neue Kalman-Operette Die Bajadere. Erstaufführung im Carl-Theater," *NFP*.

60. Lehár's career in the 1910s and 1920s had been decidedly uneven. *Wo die Lerche singt* (1918) and *Die blaue Mazur* (1920), both modestly scaled folk-influenced works, were highly successful. But subsequent attempts to adopt the cosmopolitan, modern style of Kálmán and Fall were less successful: among Lehar's flops or succès d'estime we may number *Die Tangokönigin* (1921), *Frasquita* (1922), *Die gelbe Jacke* (1923), *Libellentanz* (1923; a new libretto written to music from *Der Sterngucker* from 1916), and *Clo-Clo* (1924). This period in Lehár's career is described in more detail in Frey, *Was sagt ihr zu diesem Erfolg*, 237–74.

61. Tauber recorded prolifically, and many of his recordings are available on CD. One large collection is Richard Tauber, *Richard Tauber, Superstar*, 10 CDs (Membran, 2009).

62. The encounter is described in Evelyn Steinthaler, *Morgen muss ich fort von hier: Richard Tauber: Die Emigration eines Weltstars* (Vienna: Milena, 2011), 46–47.

63. Norbert Linke, *Franz Lehár* (Reinbek bei Hamburg, Germany: Rowohlt, 2001), 82.

64. Tauber also found that he could earn 500 Kronen a night singing operetta (while he made 1,000 kronen a month as an ensemble member of the Wiener Staatsoper). Frey, *Was sagt ihr zu diesem Erfolg*, 230.

65. Owing to scheduling conflicts, the world premiere in Vienna had been sung by Carl Clewing, a Heldentenor and another operatic sellout. He was not nearly as successful as Tauber.

66. This era in Berlin is examined in Tobias Becker, *Inszenierte Moderne*. Lehár worked primarily under the aegis of the Rotter brothers, Berlin's answer to Wilhelm Karczag. The Rotter dynasty is described in Marline Otte, *Jewish Identities in German Popular Entertainment, 1890–1933*, 251–55.

67. *Paganini* was criticized both for the overblown nature of its score and for its casual relationship with the historical figure whose life it purported to illustrate. *Friederike* was dismissed for the same reasons, but the condemnation was more pointed because the historical figure it depicted was German cultural icon Goethe. *Friederike* was notably protested by the right and the left. One memorable account is Ernst Bloch, "Lehár – Mozart (1928)," in *Literary Essays*, trans. Andrew Joron (Stanford, CA: Stanford University Press, 1974), 11–14. A more general account of its reception can be found in Lichtfuss, *Operette im Ausverkauf*, 282–96.

68. In a 1930 interview upon *Das Land des Lächeln's* Viennese premiere, Lehár said: "Warum ich die *Gelbe Jacke* umarbeitete? Damals, vor acht Jahren, war mein Erfolg als Komponist noch nicht so groß wie heute. Ich musste Konzessionen machen. Heute muß ich das nicht mehr. Durch *Zarewitsch, Paganini, Friederike* bin ich nun in eine ganz bestimmte Richtung geraten. Ich bemühe mich, eine Operette zu schaffen, die nicht bloß einem Tagesbedürfnis genügen soll....Ich kann heute schaffen, wie ich es für richtig und notwendig halte, Konzessionen sind nun mehr überflüssig." "Gespräch mit Lehár," *Wiener Allgemeine Zeitung*, May 29, 1930.

69. Stefan Frey suggests a possible explanation for this confusion over Tauber's health:

the underlying cause may have been an undisclosed venereal disease. Frey, *Franz Lehár oder das schlechte Gewissen der leichten Musik*, 249.

70. Bernard Grun claims Tauber's infirmity as a cause without citing a source. Bernard Grun, *Gold and Silver: The Life and Times of Franz Lehár* (London: W. H. Allen, 1970), 229; Otto Schneidereit, *Richard Tauber: Ein Leben, eine Stimme* (Berlin: Lied der Zeit Musikverlag, 1976), 95.

71. The two most important name changes are the female protagonist, who is Lea in the first version and Lisa in the second, and her Viennese suitor, who is Claudius in *Die gelbe Jacke* and Gustav (Gustl) in *Das Land des Lächelns*. *Das Land des Lächelns* was credited "nach Viktor Léon von Ludwig Herzer und Fritz Löhner," and some later editions of the score leave Léon's name off the title page entirely. Herzer and Löhner had written Lehár's previous operetta, *Friederike*, and the experience had been, by all accounts, positive.

72. Lieutenant Gustl's name (Graf Gustav von Pottenstein, Oberleutenant) seems to be an obvious if not very significant allusion to Arthur Schnitzler's novella of the same title. In the operetta, he is a generic Austro-Hungarian officer type. Sou-Chong's name was inspired by lapsang souchong tea (his first duet with Lisa is sung while they enjoy tea together).

73. Schwarz was a well-known soprano who was a fixture in both Vienna and Berlin, performing roles like Aida, Tosca, and Sieglinde. She frequently sang operetta with Tauber but otherwise remained in the operatic realm. She did not become a star on the level of Tauber or the most popular actresses of the era such as Rita Georg and Fritzi Massary.

74. The plot is, of course, a sort of reverse *Butterfly*. Martin Lichtfuss even writes, "Was die Autoren anstrebten und was auch vom Publikum erwartet wurde, war die Bestätigung eines Japan-China-Klischees, wie es durch Werke wie *Madama Butterfly* oder *Turandot* im Mode gekommen war." Lichtfuss, *Operette im Ausverkauf*, 218. Among critics, the writer of the *Vossische Zeitung* said that Lehár's work could be more productively compared to Puccini or Goldmark (presumably referring to the latter's opera *Die Königin von Saba*) than *The Mikado* or *The Geisha*. The *Neues Wiener Journal* explicitly compared the score to *Butterfly*; in the *BZ am Mittag* Erich Urban also referred to *Samson et Dalila*. E.N. [pseud.], "Der neue Lehár," *Vossische Zeitung*, October 12, 1929; Julius Bistron, "Lehar-Premiere im Theater an der Wien," *NWJ*, September 27, 1930; Erich Urban, "Das Land des Lächelns," *BZ am Mittag*, October 11, 1929.

75. "Die Lehár-Premiere im Metropol-Theater," *NWJ*, October 13, 1929. The review is unsigned, which suggests that the paper probably did not send a critic from Vienna to Berlin but rather used a local freelancer.

76. Oscar Bie, "Metropoltheater: Das Land des Lächelns," *Berliner Börsen-Courier*, October 11, 1929.

77. Hans Tessmer, "Das Land des Lächelns," *Der Tag*, October 12, 1929.

78. Edmund Kühn, "Metropol-Theater," *Germania*, October 12, 1929.

79. Bie, "Metropoltheater: Das Land des Lächelns," *Berliner Börsen-Courier*.

80. Karl Westermeyer, "Franz Lehar; Das Land des Lächelns," *Berliner Tageblatt und Handelzeitung*, October 11, 1929, Abend-Ausgabe edition.

81. A number of early operetta recordings can be heard on the compilation LP Alexander Girardi et al., *Creators of Operetta*, LP (Pearl/Gemm, 1982). A CD accompanies Frey,

Unter Tränen Lachen, but with the exception of Kartousch and Marischka most of the performances date from the 1930s and later.

82. Tessmer, "Das Land des Lächelns."

83. Urban, "Das Land des Lächelns."

84. E.N. [pseud.], "Der neue Lehár."

85. The number appears on pages 120–21 of the *Gelbe Jacke* score, in the middle of the Act 3 finale. It is in the same key and immediately recognizable. Franz Lehár, "Wie entsteht einer Schlager?" *NFP*, April 24, 1932.

86. Richard Tauber, "Wie Schlager entstehen," *Breslauer Neueste Nachrichten*, February 11, 1928. Cited in Frey, *Was sagt ihr zu diesem Erfolg*, 239.

87. Additional examples are "Freunde, das Leben ist Lebenswert," also from *Giuditta*; Tauber's own composition "Du bist die Welt für mich" from *Der singende Traum*; and, less paradigmatically, "Allein, wieder allein" from *Der Zarewitsch*, in which a pastiche of Russian folk songs overpowers some of the usual Tauber-Lieder features.

88. Speed of distribution is often identified by modernist critics as a key breaking point of modern artwork. Oscar Bie discusses this particularly in regard to the Schlager in Oscar Bie, "Ein Schlager reist um die Welt," *Die Woche* 27, no. 3 (1931): 863–64. Bie's essay is analyzed in Brian Currid, *A National Acoustics: Music and Mass Publicity in Weimar and Nazi Germany* (Minneapolis: University of Minnesota Press, 2006), 70–74. See also Walter Benjamin, "The Work of Art in the Age of Its Technological Reproducibility," in *The Work of Art in the Age of Its Technological Reproducibility and Other Writings on Media*, ed. Michael W. Jennings, Brigid Doherty, and Thomas Y. Levin, trans. Edmund Jephcott (Cambridge, MA: Harvard University Press, 2008), 19–55.

89. Peter Wicke, "Schlager," in *Die Musik in Geschichte und Gegenwart*, ed. Ludwig Finscher (Kassel: Bärenreiter, 1998), 1064–65. Key accounts of the Schlager, most enumerating its problems, include Theodor W. Adorno, "Schlageranalyse," in *Gesammelte Schriften*, vol. 18, *Musikalishe Schriften V* (Frankfurt: Suhrkamp, 1984), 778–87; Dietrich Kayser, *Schlager, das Lied als Ware: Untersuchungen zu einer Kategorie der Illusionsindustrie* (Stuttgart: Verlag J.B. Metzler, 1975); Currid, *A National Acoustics*.

90. The history of and conventional interpretation of the Schlager is discussed in Currid, *A National Acoustics*, 65–80. A typical Marxist critique of the Schlager is Kayser, *Schlager, das Lied als Ware*.

91. Ludwig Herzer and Fritz Löhner, *Das Land des Lächelns: Romantische Operette in drei Akten nach Viktor Léon: Vollständiges Regie- und Soufflierbuch* (Vienna: Karczag, 1929), 59.

92. Theodor W. Adorno, *Einleitung in die Musiksoziologie*, Gesammelte Schriften 14 (Frankfurt: Suhrkamp, 2003), 206.

93. Some photos and illustrations can be seen in the Berlin reviews of the operetta—for example, E.N. [pseud.], "Der neue Lehár"; Schrenk [pseud.?], "Das Land des Lächelns. Der neue Lehár im Metropoltheater," *Deutsche allgemeine Zeitung*, October 11, 1929; "Das Land des Lächelns," *Berliner Morgenpost*, October 11, 1929.

94. Herzer and Löhner, *Das Land des Lächelns*, 58–61. The directions are from the perspective of the audience members rather than the stage.

95. "Die Lehár-Premiere im Metropol-Theater," *NWJ*.

96. Bie, "Metropoltheater: Das Land des Lächelns," *Berliner Börsen-Courier*.

97. Kühn, "Metropol-Theater," *Germania*.

98. Benjamin, "The Work of Art in the Age of Its Technological Reproducibility," 24.

99. Bie, "Metropoltheater: Das Land des Lächelns," *Berliner Börsen-Courier*.

100. "Die Lehár-Premiere im Metropol-Theater," *NWJ*.

101. Lichtfuss, *Operette im Ausverkauf*, 220. Lichtfuss does not mention any potential motivations of Fritz Löhner, one of the librettists and an ardent Zionist.

102. Lehár's wife, Sophie, received the rare distinction of being given "honorary Aryan" status from the Nazis. Lehár was very much in favor with the Nazis, and his music was frequently performed for the duration of the war (even works with Jewish librettists, whose names were simply removed from programs), but Lehár and Sophie nonetheless spent part of the war in Switzerland out of concern for her safety. See Stefan Frey, "'Dann kann ich leicht vergessen, das teure Vaterland…': Lehár unterm Hakenkreuz," in *Operette unterm Hakenkreuz: Zwischen hoffähiger Kunst und "Entartung,"* ed. Wolfgang Schaller (Berlin: Metropol, 2003), 91–103.

CHAPTER 6. OPERETTA IN THE PAST TENSE

1. Tourism, nostalgia, and late operetta are examined in detail in Petersen, "Operetta after the Habsburg Empire," chapter 2. These issues are also salient in *Im weissen Rößl*, an operetta that premiered in Berlin and is written in Berlin revue-operetta style but that also creates a nostalgic image of Austria. See Nils Grosch and Carolin Stahrenberg, eds., *"Im weißen Rößl": Kulturgeschichtliche Perspektiven* (Münster: Waxmann, 2016); Ulrich Tadday, ed., *Im weißen Rössl: Zwischen Kunst und Kommerz*, Musik-Konzepte, 133/134 (Munich: edition text + kritik, 2006).

2. One very late example is Lehár's 1938 reworking of *Zigeunerliebe*, which added the csárdás "Hör' ich Cymbalklänge," which subsequently has become a popular encore number. The changes are described in detail in Angerer, "Zorikas Traum von der silbernen Operette: Lehárs originelle Konzeption des Sowohl – Als auch," 115–18.

3. Emphasis in original. Linda Hutcheon and Mario Valdés, "Irony, Nostalgia, and the Postmodern: A Dialogue," *Poligrafías* 3 (2000): 22. The article is written as a dialogue, and this is from Hutcheon's portion.

4. These revivals are examined in Peter Franklin, *Seeing through Music: Gender and Modernism in Classic Hollywood Film Scores* (Oxford: Oxford University Press, 2011), 54–56. See also Kevin Clarke, "'Der Walzer erwacht—die Neger entfliehen': Erich Wolfgang Korngolds Operetten(bearbeitungen) von Eine Nacht in Venedig 1923 bis zur Stummen Serenade 1954," *Frankfurter Zeitschrift für Musikwissenschaft*, 12, no. 1 (2009): 16–95.

5. On Benatzky, see Fritz Hennenberg, *Ralph Benatzky: Operette auf dem Weg zum Musical: Lebensbericht und Werkverzeichnis* (Vienna: Edition Steinbauer, 2009); Ralph Benatzky, *Ralph Benatzky: Triumph und Tristesse: Aus den Tagebüchern von 1919 bis 1946*, ed. Inge Jens and Christian Niklew (Berlin: Parthas, 2002). On Abraham, see Klaus Waller, *Paul Abraham: Der tragische König der Operette* (Norderstedt, Germany: BoD, 2017); Daniel Hirschel, "Paul Abraham," in *Operette unterm Hakenkreuz: Zwischen hoffähiger Kunst und "Entartung,"* ed. Wolfgang Schaller (Berlin: Metropol, 2003), 40–60.

6. Nico Dostal, *Ans Ende deiner Träume kommst du nie: Berichte, Bekenntnisse, Betrachtungen* (Innsbruck: Pinguin-Verlag, 1982), 121. Abraham suffered badly in the war,

moving first to Cuba and then to New York, where he fell into severe mental illness and spent nearly a decade in an institution, eventually returning to Germany.

7. Andrew Lamb, "Paul Abraham [Pál Ábrahám]," *Grove Music Online*, Oxford University Press, http://www.oxfordmusiconline.com/subscriber/article/grove/music/00056.

8. The pioneer in this kind of nostalgia was one of the most successful works of the war period, the Schubert bio-operetta *Das Dreimäderlhaus*, which was literally assembled out of nineteenth-century musical components into a contemporary shape. See Sabine Giesbrecht-Schutte, "'Klagen eines Troubadours': Zur Popularisierung Schuberts im 'Dreimäderlhaus,'" in *Martin Geck: Festschrift zum 65. Geburtstag*, ed. Ares Rolf and Ulrich Tadday (Dortmund: Klangfarben, 2001), 109–33.

9. Richard Traubner calls it "totally predictable." This was, in fact, the point. Traubner, *Operetta*, 297.

10. "Auch ich war einst ein feiner Csárdáskavalier/hab' kommandiert Zigeuner/g'rade so wie ihr." Emmerich Kálmán, Julius Brammer, and Alfred Grünwald, *Gräfin Mariza: Operette in 3 Akten* (Vienna: Karczag, 1924).

11. This line is quoted by Adorno as an example of the false individuality asserted by operetta characters, who display a soulfulness that is, for the resident of a modern city, delusional. Adorno, "Arabesken zur Operette," 516–19. The opposite of this pseudo-individuality is the more legitimately modern "Dingwelt" of the revue. This recalls Siegfried Kracauer's analysis of the Tiller Girls; see Siegfried Kracauer, "The Mass Ornament," in *The Mass Ornament*, ed. and trans. Thomas Y. Levin (Cambridge, MA: Harvard University Press, 1995), 75–88.

12. *Drei Walzer* is analyzed as nostalgia in Zoe Alexis Lang, "'Light' Music and Austrian Identity: The Strauss Family Legacy in Austrian Politics and Culture, 1918–1938" (PhD diss., Harvard University, 2005), 184–229.

13. Mann's Prince Karl Heinrich and Imma Spoelmann become Sandór Boris and Mary Lloyd in the operetta. Mann's imaginary state of Grimmburg, like Flausenthurn in the contemporaneous *Ein Walzertraum*, was located somewhere in Germany and represented a satiric version of Wilhelminan society, while *Die Herzogin von Chicago*'s state of Sylvania is determinedly Austro-Hungarian. Thomas Mann, *Königliche Hoheit* (Frankfurt am Main: Fischer, 2012).

14. Mary's name is borrowed from that of an English music hall star.

15. Julius Brammer, Alfred Grünwald, and Emmerich Kálmán, *Die Herzogin von Chicago: Operette in zwei Abteilungen (zwei Akte mit einem Vor- und Nachspiel): Vollständiges Regie- und Soufflierbuch* (Vienna: W. Karczag, 1928), 155.

16. Its collage recalls Siegfried Kracauer's tour of the UFA film studios in "Calico World," in *The Mass Ornament: Weimar Essays*, ed. and trans. Thomas Y. Levin (Cambridge, MA: Harvard University Press, 1995), 281–90.

17. Sandór's ethnic confusion is explained in the libretto: his father is from Sylvania, but his mother is Hungarian.

18. Clarke, "*Im Himmel spielt auch schon die Jazzband*," 103. Perhaps it is not a coincidence that the two pages detailing his attire for *Die Herzogin von Chicago* are the only missing part of his costume notebook, neatly cut out with a knife. Untitled notebook, Nachlass Hubert Marischka, Box 4, Shelf 15, ÖTM.

19. It can be seen in a souvenir photograph of Rita Georg in the title role, Atelier D'Ora Benda, April 19, 1928, #306735 - 204956-D, ÖNB Bildarchiv.

20. "Hör ich deine Geige wieder/die du einst gespielt hast und gefühlt hast im Mai," Sandor's csárdás seems to be based on Tassilo's lament "Komm, Zigány" from *Gräfin Mariza*.

21. "Choreographie zu *Die Herzogin von Chicago*," directed by Otto Langer. Typescript produced by Dorit Herz-Rosenberg Theater-Verlag und Vertrieb, Vienna. *T-Mss Grunwald Box 7 Folder 7, NYPL.

22. Kai Marcel Sicks, "Charleston, Girls, und Jazztanzbar: Amerikanismus und die Identitätskrise der Operette in den zwanziger Jahren," in *Einschnitte: Identität in der Moderne*, ed. Oliver Kohns and Martin Roussel (Würzburg: Königshausen & Neumann, 2007), 153–65.

23. The jazz heard in Europe in Germany in the 1920s is examined in J. Bradford Robinson, "Jazz Reception in Weimar Germany: In Search of a Shimmy Figure," in *Music and Performance during the Weimar Republic*, ed. Bryan Gilliam (Cambridge: Cambridge University Press, 1994), 107–34.

24. Adorno, "Arabesken zur Operette," 518.

25. Ernst Decsey, "Die neue Kálmán-Operette," *NWT*, April 6, 1928.

26. The 1933 Viennese premiere of Richard Strauss's *Arabella* in fact borrowed sets from a production of Richard Heuberger's *Der Opernball* that had been mounted the previous year. See Josef Reitler, "Richard Strauss' *Arabella* in der Staatsoper," *NFP*, October 22, 1933.

27. Decsey, *Franz Lehár*.

28. Ernst Decsey, "Der Esel Aristoteles," *NWT*, January 27, 1934, Wochenausgabe edition.

29. Compare, for example, to the criticism of Hanslick as described in Gooley, "Hanslick on Johann Strauss Jr.: Genre, Social Class, and Liberalism in Vienna."

30. Decsey, "Der Esel Aristoteles."

31. Petersen, "Operetta after the Habsburg Empire," 59.

32. Petersen, 91–120. See also Kauffmann, *Operette im "Dritten Reich."*

33. Some memoirs and accounts of these exiles: Grunwald, *Ein Walzer muß es sein*; Robert Stolz and Einzi Stolz, *Servus Du: Robert Stolz und sein Jahrhundert* (Munich: Blanvalet, 1985); Vera Kálmán, *Csardas: Der Tanz meines Lebens* (Frankfurt: Ullstein, 1988); Benatzky, *Ralph Benatzky: Triumph und Tristesse*.

34. Many of these artists are profiled in detail in the Lexikon verfolgter Musiker und Musikerinnen der NS-Zeit, ed. Claudia Maurer Zenck, Peter Petersen, and Sophie Fetthauer, Universität Hamburg (http://www.lexm.uni-hamburg.de).

35. Even as some of their works were still performed, many composers and writers, deprived of their customary royalty income, faced poverty in the United States. Unfortunately, Austrian composers and writers were regarded by Americans alternately as too old-fashioned and as too representative of the enemy. Emmerich Kálmán had, as usual, the most success. In 1945 his Vienna-themed Broadway musical *Marinka* was a modest success. *Miss Underground*, however, a musical written with Lorenz Hart for Vivienne Segal about the Parisian resistance, containing numbers such as "Alexander's Blitztime Band," was never produced (it was first canceled, and then its completion was cut short by Hart's sudden death) and remains in manuscript in the ÖNB MS.

36. Rabenalt, *Operette als Aufgabe*, 238.

37. Wilhelm Sinkovicz, "In Bad Ischl ist die Welt in Ordnung," *Die Presse*, August 6, 2011, https://www.diepresse.com/683859/in-bad-ischl-ist-die-welt-in-ordnung.

38. "Operette: hipp oder miefig?," special issue, *Österreichische Musikzeitschrift* 21, no. 3 (2016).

39. Kevin Clarke, "Aspekte der Aufführungspraxis oder: Wie klingt eine historisch informierte Spielweise der Operette?," *Frankfurter Zeitschrift für Musikwissenschaft* [*European Journal of Musicology*], 9 (2006): 22.

40. Bad Ischl is located in the Alpine Salzkammergut and has long been a retreat for Vienna's elite, including Emperor Franz Joseph himself. Besides the Lehár Festival and the villa, Bad Ischl is the home of the Franz Lehár archive. A historical account of Ischl in the summer is Franz Rajna, "Von der Ischler Operettenbörse," *Pester Lloyd*, August 28, 1927.

41. The Bavarian radio station BR-Klassik's ongoing series and yearly prize "Operetten-Frosch" highlights notable productions, many of which never make it to video; in February 2020 the prize was awarded to a production of *Die Csádásfürstin* at the Theater Ulm. "Der Frosch geht an das Theater Ulm für *Die Csárdásfürstin*," February 2, 2013, BR-Klassik (blog), https://www.br-klassik.de/themen/oper/operettenpreis-2020-csardasfuerstin-theater-ulm100.html.

42. The results range from compelling to staid. They are nonetheless valuable for their presentation of full scores in their original orchestrations, including many works otherwise unavailable in recorded form. While it is impossible to know what Lehár would have made of this, of all operetta composers he is the most likely to have approved. A representative, rather lugubrious example is Emmerich Kálmán, *Die Bajadere*, WDR Funkorchester Köln conducted by Richard Bonynge with Heike Susanne Daum (Odette), Rainer Trost (Radjami) et al. Recorded February 2014, cpo 777 982-2, 2016, compact disc.

43. The Budapest Operetta Theater is a particularly noteworthy example. Their glitzy, dance-intensive production style and use of musical theater performers (rather than opera singers) distinguishes them from most German-language theaters and makes them perhaps one of the more genuinely historically conscious of operetta venues.

44. Mörbisch produces one operetta per year, and many recent productions have been released as DVDs by Videoland. For this style, the most relevant period is the intendancy of Harald Serafin, which lasted from 1993 to 2012. In 2013 Dagmar Schellenberger took over and began to move the festival in a somewhat less traditional direction but was abruptly fired in 2016 in favor of a return to conservatism. See Kevin Clarke, "'Brutal Cultural Politics': Dagmar Schellenberger Kicked Out of Mörbisch Festival," *Operetta Research Center* (blog), October 19, 2016, http://operetta-research-center.org/dagmar-schellenberger-kicked-out-off-moerbisch-festival/.

45. David Levin, *Unsettling Opera: Staging Mozart, Verdi, Wagner, and Zemlinsky* (Chicago: University of Chicago Press, 2007), 45–46.

46. Barbara Feldbacher, "Und wär's auch nichts als ein Traum vom Glück," *Applaus*, November 2004, 38. Quoted in Clarke, "Aspekte der Aufführungspraxis oder," 63.

47. Booklet essay by Curt A. Roesler, included in Emmerich Kálmán, *Die Zirkusprinzessin*, Ingeborg Hallstein, Rudolf Schock, directed by Mandred R. Köhler, 1969 (Halle: Arthaus Musik, reissued 2012), DVD. See also Franz Lehár, *Zigeunerliebe*, Janet Perry, Ion

Buzea, directed by Václav Kašlík, 1974 (Halle: Arthaus Musik, reissued 2012), DVD; Emmerich Kálmán, *Die Csárdásfürstin*, Anna Moffo, René Kollo, directed by Miklós Szinetár, 1971 (Hamburg: Deutsche Grammophon, reissued 2006), DVD.

48. Traubner does qualify that he is indisposed to the work because "I am not too fond of circuses." Richard Traubner, "Kálmán: Die Zirkussprinzessin," *Opera News*, July 2012, https://www.operanews.com/Opera_News_Magazine/2012/7/Recordings/KÁLMÁN_Die_Zirkusprinzessin.html.

49. Consider, for example, Erich Wolfgang Korngold's adaptations of operettas by Johann Strauss II, which brought nineteenth-century scores into the musical style of the 1920s. Clarke, "'Der Walzer erwacht—die Neger entfliehen'"; Philip Gossett, *Divas and Scholars: Performing Italian Opera* (Chicago: University of Chicago Press, 2006).

50. Clemens Risi, "Kunst der Oberfläche: Zur Renaissance der Operette im Gegenwartstheater," in *Kunst der Oberfläche: Operette zwischen Bravour und Banalität*, ed. Bettina Brandl-Risi and Clemens Risi (Leipzig: Henschel, 2015), 16. This heritage is also discussed in Koch, "Das NS-Wunschkonzert: Operette als Narkotikum."

51. Clarke, "Aspekte der Aufführungspraxis," 65.

52. The Kosky vision of operetta is examined in detail in Brandl-Risi and Risi, *Kunst der Oberfläche*.

53. Barrie Kosky, "Die uneheliche Schwester: Über die Hybridität der Operette," in "Operette: hipp oder miefig?," special issue, *Österreichische Musikzeitschrift* 71, no. 3 (2016): 55.

54. Several other productions are analyzed in Frieder Reininghaus, "Notärzte oder Vampire? Wernicke, Marthaler und die Operetten-Folgen," in "Operette: hipp oder miefig?," special issue, *Österreichische Musikzeitschrift* 71, no. 3 (2016): 38–45.

55. The production is available on DVD: Johann Strauss II, *Die Fledermaus*, Salzburger Festspiele, directed by Hans Neuenfels and conducted by Marc Minkowski, recorded 2001 (Halle, Germany: Arthaus Musik, 100341). It is discussed in the context of Mortier's intendancy in Manuel Brug, "Nur ein müder Knallfrosch," *Die Welt*, August 20, 2001, https://www.welt.de/print-welt/article468886/Nur-ein-mueder-Knallfrosch.html. See also Claus Spahn, "Das Salzburg-Gespenst," *Die Zeit*, August 23, 2001, http://www.zeit.de/2001/35/200135_opersalzb..xml.

56. Helene Partik-Pable to the BBC, "Racy Strauss Booed in Salzburg," *BBC News*, August 20, 2001, http://news.bbc.co.uk/2/hi/entertainment/1501048.stm.

57. "Urteil im Salzburger 'Fledermaus'-Prozess," *Neue Zürcher Zeitung*, March 31, 2003, https://www.nzz.ch/article8RMTC-1.233846.

58. The description is based on a live performance in July 2017; the production is also available on DVD: Franz Lehár, *Das Land des Lächelns*, Opernhaus Zürich, cond. Fabio Luisi, dir. Andreas Homoki with Piotr Beczala (Sou-Chong), Julia Kleiter (Lisa), et al., recorded June 2017 (Leipzig: Accentus Music, 2018); Piotr Beczala, "Heart's Delight: The Songs of Richard Tauber," recorded October 2012, Deutsche Grammophon 001833702, digital download.

59. I examined this production in more detail (and interviewed Homoki) in Micaela Baranello, "Limits of Perspective: On Franz Lehár's Operetta *The Land of Smiles* in Zürich" *VAN*, July 20, 2017, https://van-us.atavist.com/limits-of-perspective. It is discussed further in Thomas Schacher, "Der Kulturchauvinismus bleibt ohne Widerspruch," *Neue*

Zürcher Zeitung, June 19, 2017, https://www.nzz.ch/feuilleton/das-land-des-laechelns-am
-opernhaus-zuerich-der-kulturchauvinismus-bleibt-ohne-widerspruch-ld.1301772.

60. The most frequently discussed example of this is Stefan Herheim's 2008 production of *Parsifal* at the Bayreuth Festival. Herheim directed a similar but more muddled
production of Offenbach's *Barbe-bleue* (as *Blaubart*) at Kosky's Komische Oper Berlin in
2018, staged as a palimpsest of Komische Oper founder Walter Felsenstein's filmed version
of the opera.

61. The production is not available on video; this description is based on a live performance. *Die lustige Witwe,* music by Franz Lehár, cond. Hartmut Keil, dir. Claus Guth,
Oper Frankfurt, Frankfurt, Germany, December 31, 2018; cast included Kirsten MacKin-
non (Hanna) and Christoph Pohl (Danilo).

62. Manuel Brug, "Frankfurt, Claus Guth und die Operette: 'Kiss me, Hanna' von Cole
Lehár," *Brugs Klassiker* (blog), May 14, 2018, http://klassiker.welt.de/2018/05/14/frankfurt
-claus-guth-und-die-operette-kiss-me-hanna-von-cole-lehar/. The production might also
be compared to Christof Loy's far more spare postwar theater-within-a-theater production
of Strauss's *Die Frau ohne Schatten* from the Salzburger Festspiele.

BIBLIOGRAPHY

Abbate, Carolyn. "Offenbach, Kracauer, and Ethical Frivolity." *Opera Quarterly* 33, no. 1 (Winter 2017): 62–86.

Adorno, Theodor. "Arabesken zur Operette." In *Gesammelte Schriften, 19, Musikalische Schriften VI*, 516–19. Frankfurt: Suhrkamp, 2003.

———. *Einleitung in die Musiksoziologie*. In *Gesammelte Schriften*, 14. Frankfurt: Suhrkamp, 2003.

———. "Lustige Witwe." In *Gesammelte Schriften, 19, Frankfurter Opern- und Konzertkritiken*, 249–51. Frankfurt: Suhrkamp, 1997.

———. "On the Fetish Character in Music and the Regression of Listening." In *The Culture Industry*, edited by J. M. Bernstein. London: Routledge Classics, 1991.

———. "Schlageranalyse." In *Gesammelte Schriften, 18, Musikalishe Schriften V*, 778–87. Frankfurt: Suhrkamp, 1984.

Angerer, Manfred. "Zorikas Traum von der silbernen Operette. Lehárs originelle Konzeption des Sowohl – Als auch." *Studien zur Musikwissenschaft: Beihefte der Denkmäler der Tonkust in Österreich* 36 (1985): 111–22.

Angermüller, Rudolf. "Zigeuner und Zigeunerisches in der Oper des 19. Jahrhunderts." In *Die "Couleur locale" in der Oper des 19. Jahrhunderts*, edited by Heinz Becker, 131–60. Regensburg, Germany: Gustav Bosse Verlag, 1976.

Anzenberger, Friedrich. "Die Strauss-Pflege der 'Hoch- und Deutschmeister' unter Carl Michael Ziehrer: Untersuchungen zur Programmgestaltung einer traditionsreichen Wiener Militärkapelle." In *Straussiana 1999: Studien zu Leben, Werk und Wirkung von Johann Strauss (Sohn)*, edited by Monika Fink and Walter Pass, 1:7–22. Tutzing, Germany: Hans Schneider, 2001.

Arnbom, Marie-Theres, Kevin Clarke, and Thomas Trabitsch, eds. *Welt der Operette: Glamour, Stars und Showbusiness*. Vienna: Brandstätter, 2012.

Baranello, Micaela. "*Arabella*, Operetta, and the Triumph of Gemütlichkeit." *Opera Quarterly* 41, no. 4 (Autumn 2015): 199–222.

———. "The Operetta Factory: Production Systems of Silver-Age Vienna." In *The Cam-*

bridge Companion to Operetta, edited by Derek B. Scott and Anastasia Belina, 189–204. Cambridge: Cambridge University Press, 2019.

———. "'Operettendämmerung': *Die lustigen Nibelungen* and the Failures of Wagnerian Operetta." *Opera Quarterly* 33, no. 1 (Winter 2017): 28–48.

———. "Viennese Blood: Assimilation and Exclusion in Viennese Popular Music." In *Watersheds*, edited by Marijeta Bozovic and Matthew D Miller, 53–69. Brighton, MA: Academic Studies Press, 2016.

Batta, András. *Träume sind Schäume: Die Operette in der Donaumonarchie*. Budapest: Corvina, 1992.

Batta, András, and János Kárpáti, eds. *Music in Hungary: An Illustrated History*. Budapest: Rózsavölgyi, 2011.

Bauer, Anton. *150 Jahre Theater an der Wien*. Zurich: Amalthea-Verlag, 1952.

Baumeister, Martin. *Kriegstheater: Großstadt, Front und Massenkultur 1914–1918*. Essen: Klartext, 2005.

Beaumont, Antony. *Zemlinsky*. London: Faber, 2000.

Becker, Tobias. "Globalizing Operetta before the First World War." *Opera Quarterly* 33, no. 1 (November 11, 2017): 7–27.

———. *Inszenierte Moderne: Populäres Theater in Berlin und London, 1880–1930*. Berlin: De Gruyter, 2014.

Beller, Steven, ed. *Rethinking Vienna 1900*. New York: Berghahn Books, 2001.

———. "The Tragic Carnival." In *European Culture in the Great War: The Arts, Entertainment, and Propaganda, 1914–1918*, edited by Aviel Roshwald and Richard Stites, 126–61. Cambridge: Cambridge University Press, 1999.

———. *Vienna and the Jews, 1867–1938: A Cultural History*. Cambridge: Cambridge University Press, 1989.

Bellman, Jonathan. "Musical Voyages and Their Baggage: Orientalism in Music and Critical Musicology." *Musical Quarterly* 94, no. 3 (September 1, 2011): 417–38.

———. *The Style Hongrois in the Music of Western Europe*. Boston: Northeastern University Press, 1993.

Benatzky, Ralph. *Ralph Benatzky: Triumph und Tristesse: Aus den Tagebüchern von 1919 bis 1946*. Edited by Inge Jens and Christian Niklew. Berlin: Parthas, 2002.

Benjamin, Walter. "The Work of Art in the Age of Its Technological Reproducibility." In *The Work of Art in the Age of Its Technological Reproducibility and Other Writings on Media*, edited by Michael W. Jennings, Brigid Doherty, and Thomas Y. Levin, translated by Edmund Jephcott, 19–55. Cambridge, MA: Harvard University Press, 2008.

Bernauer, Rudolf. *Das Theater meines Lebens: Erinnerungen*. Berlin: L. Blanvalet, 1955.

Bernauer, Rudolf, and Ernst Welitsch. *Jung-England: Operette in drei Akten, Regiebuch*. Berlin: Harmonie, 1914.

Bierbaum, Otto Julius. *Stilpe: Ein Roman aus der Froschperspektive*. Berlin: Schuster & Loeffler, 1897.

Bistron, Julius. *Emmerich Kálmán*. Vienna: Karczag, 1932.

Blaszkiewicz, Jacek. "Writing the City: The Cosmopolitan Realism of Offenbach's *La vie parisienne*." *Current Musicology* 103 (Fall 2018).

Bloch, Ernst. "Lehár – Mozart (1928)." In *Literary Essays*, translated by Andrew Joron, 11–14. Stanford, CA: Stanford University Press, 1974.

Bohlman, Philip. *Jewish Music and Modernity*. Oxford: Oxford University Press, 2008.

Bourdieu, Pierre. *Distinction: A Social Critique of the Judgement of Taste*. Cambridge, MA: Harvard University Press, 1984.

———. *The Field of Cultural Production*. Edited by Randal Johnson. New York: Columbia University Press, 1993.

Boyer, John W. *Culture and Political Crisis in Vienna: Christian Socialism in Power, 1897–1918*. Chicago: University of Chicago Press, 1995.

———. *Political Radicalism in Late Imperial Vienna: Origins of the Christian Social Movement, 1848–1897*. Chicago: University of Chicago Press, 1981.

Brammer, Julius, and Alfred Grünwald. *Die Rose von Stambul: Vollständiges Regiebuch*. Vienna: Karczag, 1916.

Brandl-Risi, Bettina, and Clemens Risi, eds. *Kunst der Oberfläche: Operette zwischen Bravour und Banalität*. Leipzig: Henschel, 2015.

Brixel, Eugen. "Die Ära Wilhelm Karczag im Theater an der Wien." PhD diss., University of Vienna, 1966.

Broch, Hermann. *Hugo von Hofmannsthal and His Time: The European Imagination, 1860–1920*. Edited and translated by Michael P. Steinberg. Chicago: University of Chicago Press, 1984.

Brodbeck, David. *Defining Deutschtum: Political Ideology, German Identity, and Music-Critical Discourse in Liberal Vienna*. Oxford: Oxford University Press, 2014.

Brown, Julie. "Otto Weininger and Musical Discourse in Turn-of-the-Century Vienna." In *Western Music and Race*, edited by Julie Brown, 84–101. Cambridge: Cambridge University Press, 2007.

Cankar, Ivan. *Knjiga za lahkomiselne ljudi*. Ljubljana: L. Schwentner, 1901.

———. "Vor dem Ziel." In *Vor dem Ziel: Literarische Skizzen aus Wien*. Translated by Erwin Köstler. Klangenfurt, Austria: Drava Verlag, 1995.

Cantu, Maya. *American Cinderellas on Broadway Musical Stage: Imagining the Working Girl from Irene to Gypsy*. London: Palgrave Macmillan, 2015.

Chalfa Ruyter, Nancy Lee. "Dvoransko Kolo: From the 1840s to the Twentieth Century." In *Balkan Dance: Essays on Characteristics, Performance and Teaching*, edited by Anthony Shay, 239–49. Jefferson, NC: McFarland, 2008.

Chase, Jefferson S. *Inciting Laughter: The Development of "Jewish Humor" in the 19th Century German Culture*. Berlin: De Gruyter, 1999.

Chowrimootoo, Christopher. *Middlebrow Modernism: Britten's Operas and the Great Divide*. Berkeley: University of California Press, 2018.

Clarke, Kevin. "Aspekte der Aufführungspraxis oder: Wie klingt eine historisch informierte Spielweise der Operette?" *Frankfurter Zeitschrift für Musikwissenschaft* [now called *European Journal of Musicology*] 9 (2006): 21–75.

———. " 'Der Walzer erwacht—die Neger entfliehen': Erich Wolfgang Korngolds Operetten(bearbeitungen) von Eine Nacht in Venedig 1923 bis zur Stummen Serenade 1954." *Frankfurter Zeitschrift für Musikwissenschaft* [*European Journal of Musicology*] 12, no. 1 (2009): 16–95.

———. *"Im Himmel spielt auch schon die Jazzband": Emmerich Kálmán und die transatlantische Operette, 1928–1932*. Hamburg: von Bockel, 2007.

———. "Zurück in die Zukunft: Aspekte der Aufführungspraxis des 'Weissen Rössl.'" In *Im weißen Rössl: Zwischen Kunst und Kommerz*, edited by Ulrich Tadday. Musik-Konzepte 133/134. Munich: edition text + kritik, 2006.

Cole, Laurence. *Military Culture and Popular Patriotism in Late Imperial Austria*. Oxford: Oxford University Press, 2014.

Crittenden, Camille. *Johann Strauss and Vienna: Operetta and the Politics of Popular Culture*. Cambridge: Cambridge University Press, 2000.

Csáky, Moritz. *Ideologie der Operette und Wiener Moderne: Ein Kulturhistorischer Essay zur österreichischen Identität*. Vienna: Böhlau, 1996.

Csendes, Peter, and Ferdinand Opll, eds. *Wien: Geschichte einer Stadt*, Vol. 3, *Von 1790 bis zur Gegenwart*. Vienna: Böhlau, 2006.

Currid, Brian. *A National Acoustics: Music and Mass Publicity in Weimar and Nazi Germany*. Minneapolis: University of Minnesota Press, 2006.

Dahlhaus, Carl. *Nineteenth-Century Music*. Translated by J. Bradford Robinson. Berkeley: University of California Press, 1989.

———. "Zur musikalischen Dramaturgie der Lustigen Witwe." *Österreichische Musikzeitschrift* 12, no. 40 (1985): 657–64.

Dalinger, Brigitte, Kurt Ifkovits, and Andrea Braidt, eds. *"Gute Unterhaltung!": Fritz Grünbaum und die Vergnügungskultur im Wien der 1920er und 1930er Jahre*. Frankfurt: Peter Lang, 2008.

Decsey, Ernst. *Franz Lehár*. Vienna: Drei Masken Verlag, 1924.

———. *Franz Lehár*. 2nd ed. Berlin: Drei Masken Verlag, 1930.

Denscher, Barbara. *Der Operettenlibrettist Victor Léon: Ein Werkbiographie*. Bielefeld, Germany: Transcript, 2017.

Denscher, Barbara, and Helmut Peschina. *Kein Land des Lächelns: Fritz Löhner-Beda, 1883–1942*. Salzburg: Residenz, 2002.

Denscher, Bernhard. *Gold gab ich für Eisen: Österreichische Kriegsplakate 1914–1918*. Vienna: Jugend & Volk, 1987.

Deutsches Bühnen-Jahrbuch. Vols. 15 and 16. Berlin: F. A. Günther & Sohn, 1904 and 1905.

Dompke, Christoph. *Unterhaltungsmusik und NS-Verfolgung*. Neumünster, Germany: von Bockel, 2011.

Dostal, Nico. *Ans Ende deiner Träume kommst du nie: Berichte, Bekenntnisse, Betrachtungen*. Innsbruck: Pinguin-Verlag, 1982.

Dyer, Richard. *Stars*. 2nd ed. London: BFI Publishing, 1998.

Eckertz, Erich. *Heine und sein Witz*. Berlin: Felber, 1908.

Endres, Franz Carl. *Die Türkei: Bilder und Skizzen von Land und Volk*. Munich: Beck, 1917.

Erk, Ludwig, ed. *Deutscher Liederhort: Auswahl der vorzüglichern deutschen Volkslieder aus der Vorzeit und der Gegenwart mit ihren eigenthümlichen Melodien*. Vol. 1. Berlin: Enslin, 1856.

Everett, William A. *Sigmund Romberg*. New Haven, CT: Yale University Press, 2007.

Falvy, Zoltán. "'Tárogató' as a Regional Instrument." *Studia Musicologica Academiae Scientiarum Hungaricae* 38, no. 3/4 (January 1997): 361–70.

Feuer, Jane. "The Self-Reflexive Musical and the Myth of Entertainment." *Quarterly Review of Film Studies* 2, no. 3 (1977): 313–26.

Franklin, Peter. *Seeing through Music: Gender and Modernism in Classic Hollywood Film Scores*. Oxford: Oxford University Press, 2011.

Freeze, Timothy. "Gustav Mahler's Third Symphony: Program, Reception, and Evocations of the Popular." PhD diss., University of Michigan, 2010.

Frey, Stefan. "Béla Jenbach." In *Lexikon verfolgter Musiker und Musikerinnen der NS-Zeit*, edited by Claudia Maurer Zenck, Peter Petersen, and Sophie Fetthauer. Hamburg: Universität Hamburg, 2016. https://www.lexm.uni-hamburg.de/object/lexm_lexmperson _00003529.

———. "'Dann kann ich leicht vergessen, das teure Vaterland...' Lehár unterm Hakenkreuz." In *Operette unterm Hakenkreuz: Zwischen hoffähiger Kunst und "Entartung,"* edited by Wolfgang Schaller, 91–103. Berlin: Metropol, 2003.

———. *Franz Lehár oder das schlechte Gewissen der leichten Musik*. Tübingen: Niemeyer, 1995.

———. "Oscar Straus." In *Lexikon verfolgter Musiker und Musikerinnen der NS-Zeit*, edited by Claudia Maurer Zenck, Peter Petersen, and Sophie Fetthauer. Hamburg: Universität Hamburg, 2017. https://www.lexm.uni-hamburg.de/object/lexm_lexmperson _00002671.

———. *"Unter Tränen Lachen": Emmerich Kálmán: Eine Operettenbiographie*. Berlin: Henschel, 2003.

———. *Was sagt ihr zu diesem Erfolg: Franz Lehár und die Unterhaltungsmusik des 20. Jahrhunderts*. Frankfurt: Insel, 1999.

Frey, Stefan, Christine Stemprok, and Wolfgang Dosch. *Leo Fall: Spöttischer Rebell der Operette*. Vienna: Edition Steinbauer, 2009.

Frigyesi, Judit. *Béla Bartók and Turn-of-the Century Budapest*. Berkeley: University of California Press, 1998.

Gänzl, Kurt, and Andrew Lamb. *Gänzl's Book of the Musical Theatre*. London: Bodley Head, 1988.

Geehr, Richard S. *Adam Müller-Guttenbrunn and the Aryan Theater of Vienna: 1898–1903: The Approach of Cultural Fascism*. Göppingen, Germany: A. Kümmerle, 1973.

Gendron, Bernard. "Theodor Adorno Meets the Cadillacs." In *Studies in Entertainment: Critical Approaches to Mass Culture*, edited by Tania Modleski, 18–36. Bloomington: Indiana University Press, 1986.

Gier, Albert. *Wär' es auch nichts als ein Augenblick: Poetik und Dramaturgie der komischen Operette*. Bamberg, Germany: University of Bamberg Press, 2014.

Giesbrecht-Schutte, Sabine. "'Klagen eines Troubadours': Zur Popularisierung Schuberts im 'Dreimäderlhaus.'" In *Martin Geck: Festschrift zum 65. Geburtstag*, edited by Ares Rolf and Ulrich Tadday, 109–33. Dortmund, Germany: Klangfarben, 2001.

Glanz, Christian. "Das Bild Südosteuropas in der Wiener Operette." PhD diss., Universität Graz, 1988.

Gooley, Dana. "Hanslick on Johann Strauss Jr.: Genre, Social Class, and Liberalism in Vienna." In *Rethinking Hanslick: Music, Formalism, and Expression*, edited by Nicole Grimes, Siobhán Donovan, and Wolfgang Marx, 91–107. Rochester, NY: University of Rochester Press, 2013.

Gossett, Philip. *Divas and Scholars: Performing Italian Opera*. Chicago: University of Chicago Press, 2006.

Grosch, Nils, and Carolin Stahrenberg, eds. *'Im weißen Rößl': Kulturgeschichtliche Perspektiven*. Münster, Germany: Waxmann, 2016.

Grun, Bernard. *Gold and Silver: The Life and Times of Franz Lehár*. London: W. H. Allen, 1970.

——. *Prince of Vienna: The Life, the Times, and the Melodies of Oscar Straus*. New York: G.P. Putnam's Sons, 1957.

Grunsky, Peter. *Richard Heuberger: Der Operettenprofessor*. Vienna: Böhlau, 2002.

Grunwald, Henry. *Ein Walzer muß es sein: Alfred Grünwald und die Wiener Operette*. Vienna: Überreuter, 1991.

Hadamowsky, Franz, and Heinz Otte. *Die Wiener Operette: Ihre Theater- und Wirkungsgeschichte*. Vienna: Bellaria-Verlag, 1947.

Hamann, Brigitte. *Hitler's Vienna: A Dictator's Apprenticeship*. Translated by Thomas Thornton. Oxford: Oxford University Press, 2000.

Hanslick, Eduard. *Am Ende des Jahrhunderts, 1895–1899*. Berlin: Allgemeiner Verein für deutsche Literatur, 1899

Harten, Uwe. "Koessler, Hans von," *Oesterreichisches Musiklexikon*. Vienna: Verlag der Österreichischen Akademie der Wissenschaften, 2003, http://www. musiklexikon.ac.at/ml/musik_K/Koessler_Hans.xml.

Hauenschild, Ute-Christiane. *Rideamus: Die Lebensgeschichte des Fritz Oliven*. Berlin: Hentrich & Hentrich, 2009.

Head, Matthew. "Musicology on Safari: Orientalism and the Spectre of Postcolonial Theory." *Music Analysis* 22, no. 1/2 (July 2003): 211–30.

Healy, Maureen. "In aller 'Freundschaft'?: Österreichische 'Türkenbilder' zwischen Gegnerschaft und 'Freundschaft' vor und während des Ersten Weltkrieges." In *Glanz—Gewalt—Gehorsam: Militär und Gesellschaft in der Habsburgermonarchie (1800 bis 1918)*, edited by Laurence Cole, Christa Hämmerle, and Martin Scheutz, 269–92. Essen, Germany: Klartext, 2011.

——. *Vienna and the Fall of the Habsburg Empire: Total War and Everyday Life in World War I*. Cambridge: Cambridge University Press, 2004.

Hennenberg, Fritz. *Ralph Benatzky: Operette auf dem Weg zum Musical: Lebensbericht und Werkverzeichnis*. Vienna: Edition Steinbauer, 2009.

Herzer, Ludwig, and Fritz Löhner. *Das Land des Lächelns: Romantische Operette in drei Akten nach Viktor Léon: Vollständiges Regie- und Soufflierbuch*. Vienna: Karczag, 1929.

Hirschel, Daniel. "Paul Abraham." In *Operette unterm Hakenkreuz: Zwischen hoffähiger Kunst und "Entartung,"* edited by Wolfgang Schaller, 40–60. Berlin: Metropol, 2003.

Hofmannsthal, Hugo von. *Hugo von Hofmannsthal and the Austrian Idea: Selected Essays and Addresses, 1906–1927*. Edited and translated by David S. Luft. West Lafayette, IN: Purdue University Press, 2011.

Holzer, Rudolf. *Die Wiener Vorstadtbühnen: Alexander Girardi und das Theater an der Wien*. Vienna: Verlag der Österreichischen Staatsdruckerei, 1951.

Hooker, Lynn M. "Hungarians and Hungarianisms in Operetta and Folk Plays in the Late Habsburg and Post-Habsburg Era." In *The Cambridge Companion to Operetta*, edited by Derek B. Scott and Anastasia Belina, 61–75. Cambridge: Cambridge University Press, 2020.

——. *Redefining Hungarian Music from Liszt to Bartók*. Oxford: Oxford University Press, 2013.

Horkheimer, Max, and Theodor W. Adorno. *Dialectic of Enlightenment: Philosophical Fragments*. Edited by Gunzelin Schmid Noerr. Translated by Edmund Jephcott. Stanford, CA: Stanford University Press, 2002.

Hübl, Arthur von. *Die Theorie und Praxis der Farbenphotographie mit Autochromplatten.* Halle, Germany: W. Knapp, 1908.

Hutcheon, Linda, and Mario Valdés. "Irony, Nostalgia, and the Postmodern: A Dialogue." *Poligrafías* 3 (2000): 29–54.

Huyssen, Andreas. *After the Great Divide: Modernism, Mass Culture, Postmodernism.* Bloomington: Indiana University Press, 1986.

Imre, Zoltán. "Operetta beyond Borders: The Different Versions of *Die Csárdásfürstin* in Europe and the United States (1915–1921)." *Studies in Musical Theatre* 7, no. 2 (June 2013): 175–205.

Janik, Allan, and Stephen Toulmin. *Wittgenstein's Vienna.* New York: Simon and Schuster, 1973.

Jelavich, Peter. *Berlin Cabaret.* Cambridge, MA: Harvard University Press, 1993.

John, Eckhard. "Es waren zwei Königskinder." In *Populäre und traditionelle Lieder: Historisch-kritisches Liederlexikon.* Freiburg: Zentrum für Populäre Kultur und Musik, Universität Freiburg, 2013. http://www.liederlexikon.de/lieder/es_waren_zwei_koenigskinder.

Jókai, Maurus. "Gemüthsart und Temperament des magyarischen Volkes," in Crown-Prince Rudolf, ed., *Die Österreichisch-Ungarische Monarchie in Wort und Bild.* Vol. 5, 299–300. Vienna: K.K. Hof- und Staatsdruckerei, 1888.

Judson, Pieter M. *Exclusive Revolutionaries: Liberal Politics, Social Experience, and National Identity in the Austrian Empire, 1848–1914.* Ann Arbor: University of Michigan Press, 1996.

Kálmán, Emmerich, Julius Brammer, and Alfred Grünwald. *Gräfin Mariza: Operette in 3 Akten.* Vienna: Karczag, 1924.

———. *Die Herzogin von Chicago: Operette in zwei Abteilungen (zwei Akte mit einem Vor- und Nachspiel): Vollständiges Regie- und Soufflierbuch.* Vienna: W. Karczag, 1928.

Kálmán, Vera. *Csardas: Der Tanz meines Lebens.* Frankfurt: Ullstein, 1988.

Kauffmann, Matthias. *Operette im "Dritten Reich": Musikalisches Unterhaltungstheater zwischen 1933 und 1945.* Neumünster, Germany: von Bockel Verlag, 2017.

Kaufmann, Dorothea. *"...routinierte Trommlerin gesucht": Musikerin in einer Damenkapelle; zum Bild eines vergessenen Frauenberufes aus der Kaiserzeit.* Karben, Germany: Coda, 1997.

Kayser, Dietrich. *Schlager, das Lied als Ware: Untersuchungen zu einer Kategorie der Illusionsindustrie.* Stuttgart: Verlag J. B. Metzler, 1975.

Keil, Ulrike. "Professionelle Damenkapellen und Frauenorchester um die Jahrhundertwende." In *"Von delectatio bis entertainment": Das Phänomen der Unterhaltung in der Musik: Arbeitstagung der Fachgruppe Soziologie und Sozialgeschichte der Musik in Düsseldorf am 22 und 23. November 1997,* 99–110. Musik-Kultur 7. Essen, Germany: Die blaue Eule, 2000.

Keller, Otto. *Die Operette in ihrer geschichtlichen Entwicklung: Musik, Libretto, Darstellung.* Leipzig: Stein Verlag, 1926.

Klotz, Volker. *Bürgerliches Lachtheater: Komödie, Posse, Schwank, Operette.* 4th ed. Heidelberg: Universitätsverlag Winter, 2007.

———. "Cancan contra Stechschritt: Antimilitarismus mit Rückfällen in der Operette." In *Österreich und der Große Krieg,* edited by Klaus Amann and Hubert Lengauer, 52–60. Vienna: Christian Brandstätter, 1989.

———. *Es lebe: Die Operette: Anläufe, sie neuerlich zu erwecken.* Würzburg, Germany: Königshausen & Neumann, 2014.

———. *Operette: Porträt und Handbuch einer unerhörten Kunst.* Rev. ed. Kassel, Germany: Bärenreiter, 2004.

Knepler, Georg. *Karl Kraus liest Offenbach: Erinnerungen, Kommentare, Dokumentationen.* Vienna: Löcker, 1984.

Koch, Hans-Jörg. "Das NS-Wunschkonzert: Operette als Narkotikum." In *Operette unterm Hakenkreuz: Zwischen hoffähiger Kunst und "Entartung,"* edited by Wolfgang Schaller, 115–31. Berlin: Metropol, 2003.

Kosky, Barrie. "Die uneheliche Schwester: Über die Hybridität der Operette." *Österreichische Musikzeitschrift,* special issue, "Operette: hipp oder miefig?," 71, no. 3: (2016): 54–58.

Kracauer, Siegfried. "Calico World." In *The Mass Ornament: Weimar Essays,* 281–90. Edited and translated by Thomas Y. Levin. Cambridge, MA: Harvard University Press, 1995.

———. *From Caligari to Hitler: A Psychological History of the German Film.* Princeton, NJ: Princeton University Press, 1947.

———. *Jacques Offenbach and the Paris of His Time.* Translated by Gwenda David and Eric Mosbacher. New York: Zone Books, 2002.

———. "The Mass Ornament." In *The Mass Ornament: Weimar Essays,* 75–88. Edited and translated by Thomas Y. Levin, Cambridge, MA: Harvard University Press, 1995.

Kraus, Karl. *Die letzten Tage der Menschheit: Tragödie in fünf Akten.* Edited by Christian Wagenknecht. Karl Kraus Schriften 10. Frankfurt: Suhrkamp, 1986.

———. *In These Great Times: Selected Writings.* Translated by Patrick Healy. Amsterdam: November Editions, 2017.

———. *The Last Days of Mankind: The Complete Text.* Translated by Fred Bridgham and Edward Timms. New Haven, CT: Yale University Press, 2016.

———. *The Last Days of Mankind: A Tragedy in Five Acts with a Prologue and an Epilogue.* Translated by Patrick Healy. Amsterdam: November Editions, 2016.

Krzeszowiak, Tadeusz. *Theater an der Wien: Seine Technik und Geschichte 1801–2001.* Vienna: Böhlau, 2002.

Lamb, Andrew. "Paul Abraham [Pál Ábrahám]." *Grove Music Online,* Oxford University Press, http://www.oxfordmusiconline.com/subscriber/article/grove/music/00056.

Láng, Attila E. *200 Jahre Theater an der Wien: "Spectacles Müssen Seyn."* Vienna: Holzhausen, 2001.

Lang, Zoë Alexis. *The Legacy of Johann Strauss: Political Influence and Twentieth-Century Identity.* Cambridge: Cambridge University Press, 2014.

———. " 'Light' Music and Austrian Identity: The Strauss Family Legacy in Austrian Politics and Culture, 1918–1938." PhD diss., Harvard University, 2005.

Lehár, Franz, Victor Léon, and Leo Stein. *Die lustige Witwe: Vollständiges Soufflierbuch mit Sämtlichen Regiebemerkungen.* Vienna: Doblinger, 1906.

Lemon, Robert. *Imperial Messages: Orientalism as Self-Critique in the Habsburg Fin de Siècle.* Rochester, NY: Camden House, 2011.

Léon, Victor, Karl von Bakonyi, and Emmerich Kálmán. *Der gute Kamerad.* Vienna: Karczag, 1911.

Léon, Victor, and Emmerich Kálmán. *Gold gab ich für Eisen.* Vienna: Karczag, 1914.

Levin, David. *Unsettling Opera: Staging Mozart, Verdi, Wagner, and Zemlinsky*. Chicago: University of Chicago Press, 2007.

Levine, Lawrence W. *Highbrow/Lowbrow: The Emergence of Cultural Hierarchy in America*. Cambridge, MA: Harvard University Press, 1988.

Lichtfuss, Martin. *Operette im Ausverkauf: Studien zum Libretto des Musikalischen Unterhaltungstheaters im Österreich der Zwischenkriegszeit*. Vienna: Böhlau, 1989.

Linder, August, ed. *Deutsche Weisen: Die beliebtesten Volks- und geistlichen Lieder für Klavier (mit Text)*. Stuttgart: Albert Auers Musikverlag, c. 1900.

Linhardt, Marion. "Mobilization and the Creation of Collective Identities: War and Popular Theatre in 1914." Translated by Judith Beniston. *Austrian Studies* 21 (2013): 76–98.

———. *Residenzstadt und Metropole: Zu einer kulturellen Topographie des Wiener Unterhaltungstheaters (1858–1918)*. Tübingen: Niemeyer, 2006.

———, ed. *Stimmen zur Unterhaltung: Operette und Revue in der publizistischen Debatte (1906–1933)*. Vienna: Lehner, 2009.

———, ed. *"Warum es der Operette so schlecht geht": Ideologische Debatten um das musikalische Unterhaltungstheater (1880–1916)*. Special issue of *Maske und Kothurn* 45, no. 1–2 (2001).

———. "'Wer kommt heut' in jedem Theaterstück vor? Ä Jud'!': Bilder des 'Jüdischen' in der Wiener Operette des frühen 20. Jahrhunderts." In *Judenrollen: Darstellungsformen im Europäischen Theater von der Restauration bis zur Zwischenkriegszeit*, edited by Hans Bayerdörfer and Jens Malte Fischer, 191–206. Tübingen, Germany: Niemeyer, 2008.

Linke, Norbert. *Franz Lehár*. Reinbek bei Hamburg, Germany: Rowohlt, 2001.

Locke, Ralph P. *Musical Exoticism: Images and Reflections*. Cambridge: Cambridge University Press, 2009.

Maderthaner, Wolfgang, and Siegfried Mattl. "'... den Straßenexcessen ein Ende machen': Septemberunruhen und Arbeitermassenprozeß 1911." In *Sozialistenprozesse: Politische Justiz in Österreich, 1870–1936*, edited by Karl R. Stadler, 117–50. Vienna: Europaverlag, 1986.

Maderthaner, Wolfgang, and Lutz Musner. *Unruly Masses: The Other Side of Fin-De-Siècle Vienna*. Translated by David Fernbach and Michael Huffmaster. New York: Berghahn Books, 2008.

Maibach, Arthur. "Vergessen und verdrängt." In *Glitter and Be Gay: Die authentische Operette und ihre schwulen Verehrer*, edited by Kevin Clarke, 140–45. Hamburg: Männerschwarm, 2007.

Mailer, Franz. *Weltbürger der Musik: Eine Oscar-Straus-Biographie*. Vienna: Österreichischer Bundesverlag, 1963.

Mann, Thomas. *Königliche Hoheit*. Frankfurt am Main: Fischer, 2012.

Marquardsen, Else. *Das Wesen des Osmanen: Ein Berater für Orientfahrer*. Munich: Roland-Verlag, 1916.

McGrath, William J. *Dionysian Art and Populist Politics in Austria*. New Haven, CT: Yale University Press, 1974.

Meier, John. *Das deutsche Soldatenlied im Felde*. Strassburg, Germany: Verlag von Karl J. Trübner, 1916.

Meilhac, Henri. *L'Attaché d'Ambassade: Comédie en trois actes, en prose*. Paris: Michel Lévy Frères, 1861.

Meilhac, Henri. *Der Gesandtschafts-Attache: Lustspiel in drei Acten*. Translated by Alexander Bergen. Vienna: Anton Schweiger, 1862.

Müller, Hans. *Buch der Abenteuer*. Berlin: E. Fleischel & Co, 1905.

Müller-Guttenbrunn, Adam. *Wien war eine Theaterstadt*. Vienna: Graeser, 1885.

Müsebeck, Ernst. *Gold gab ich für Eisen: Deutschlands Schmach und Erhebung in zeitgenössischen Dokumenten, Briefen, Tagebüchern aus den Jahren 1806–1815*. Berlin: Deutsches Verlagshaus Bong & Co., 1913.

Musil, Robert. *The Man without Qualities*. Edited by Burton Pike. Translated by Sophie Wilkins. 2 vols. London: Picador, 1995.

Müsterberg, Margarete, trans. and ed. *A Harvest of German Verse*. New York: Appleton and Co., 1916.

Myers, Margaret. "Searching for Data about European Ladies' Orchestras, 1870–1950." In *Music and Gender*, edited by Pirkko Moisala and Beverley Diamond, 189–218. Urbana: University of Illinois Press, 2000.

Nischkauer, Norbert. *Edmund Eysler: 12. März 1874 – 4. Oktober 1949*. Vienna: self-published, 2000.

Osterhammel, Jürgen. *Unfabling the East: The Enlightenment's Encounter with Asia*. Translated by Roger Savage. Princeton, NJ: Princeton University Press, 2018.

Otte, Marline. *Jewish Identities in German Popular Entertainment, 1890–1933*. Cambridge: Cambridge University Press, 2006.

Parakilas, James. "The Soldier and the Exotic: Operatic Variations on a Theme of Racial Encounter: Part I." *Opera Quarterly* 10, no. 2 (December 21, 1993): 33–56.

Pesovár, Ernő. "Typen und Entstehung des Csárdás." *Studia Musicologica Academiae Scientiarum Hungaricae* 29, no. 1/4 (January 1, 1987): 137–79.

Peteani, Maria von. *Franz Lehár*. Vienna: Glocken-Verlag, 1950.

Peter, Birgit. "Between Tradition and a Longing for the Modern: Theater in Interwar Vienna." In *Interwar Vienna*, edited by Deborah Holmes and Lisa Silverman, 161–75. Rochester, NY: Camden House, 2009.

Petersen, Ulrike. "Operetta after the Habsburg Empire." PhD diss., University of California, Berkeley, 2013. http://digitalassets.lib.berkeley.edu/etd/ucb/text/Petersen_berkeley_0028E_13191.pdf.

Piotrowska, Anna G. *Gypsy Music in European Culture: From the Late Eighteenth to the Early Twentieth Centuries*. Translated by Guy R. Torr. Boston: Northeastern University Press, 2013.

Platt, Len, Tobias Becker, and David Linton, eds. *Popular Musical Theatre in London and Berlin: 1890 to 1939*. Cambridge: Cambridge University Press, 2014.

Poller, Hugo. "Die ökonomische Bewirtschaftung eines Operettentheaters." PhD diss., University of Würzburg, 1920. Staatsbibliothek zu Berlin (MS 20/1052).

Ponstingl, Michael. *Strassenleben in Wien: Fotografien von 1861 bis 1913*. Vienna: Christian Brandstätter Verlag/Albertina, 2005.

Pyka, Marcus. "'Von Reformen ganz enormen träumen wir am Bosporus': Das Osmanische Reich als Vorbild wider Willen in Leo Fall's Erfolgsoperette *Die Rose von Stambul*." In *Sehrayin: Die Welt der Osmanen, die Osmanen in der Welt: Wahrnehmungen, Begegnungen und Abgrenzungen: Festschrift Hans Georg Majer*, edited by Yavuz Köse, 441–61. Wiesbaden, Germany: Harrassowitz, 2012.

Pyrah, Robert. *The Burgtheater and Austrian Identity: Theatre and Cultural Politics in Vienna, 1918–38*. London: Legenda, 2007.

Quissek, Heike. *Das deutschsprachige Operettenlibretto: Figuren, Stoffe, Dramaturgie*. Stuttgart: Verlag J.B. Metzler, 2012.

Rabenalt, Arthur Maria. *Operette als Aufgabe: Aufsätze zur Operettenkrise*. Berlin: Heinz Menge-Verlag, 1948.

Reininghaus, Frieder. "Notärzte oder Vampire? Wernicke, Marthaler und die Operetten-Folgen." *Österreichische Musikzeitschrift*, special issue, "Operette: hipp oder miefig?," 71, no. 3: (2016): 38–45.

Reitter, Paul. *The Anti-Journalist: Karl Kraus and Jewish Self-Fashioning in Fin-de-Siècle Europe*. Chicago: University of Chicago Press, 2008.

Risi, Clemens. "Kunst der Oberfläche: Zur Renaissance der Operette im Gegenwartstheater." In *Kunst der Oberfläche: Operette zwischen Bravour und Banalität*, edited by Bettina Brandl-Risi and Clemens Risi, 15–25. Leipzig: Henschel, 2015.

Roberts, Elizabeth. *Realm of the Black Mountain: A History of Montenegro*. London: Hurst & Company, 2007.

Robinson, J. Bradford. "Jazz Reception in Weimar Germany: In Search of a Shimmy Figure." In *Music and Performance during the Weimar Republic*, edited by Bryan Gilliam, 107–34. Cambridge: Cambridge University Press, 1994.

Romberg, Sigmund. *Her Soldier Boy* (New York: G. Schirmer, 1916).

Roth, Joseph. "Erinnerung an eine weisse Damenkapelle (Frankfurter Zeitung, 20.6.1931)." In *Werke*. Edited by Klaus Westermann. Vol. 3, 348–50. Cologne: Kiepenheuer & Witsch, 1991.

Rozenblit, Marsha L. "For Fatherland and Jewish People: Jewish Women in Austria during the First World War." In *Authority, Identity, and the Social History of the Great War*, edited by Frans Coetzee and Marilyn Shevin-Coetzee, 199–220. New York: Berghahn Books, 1993.

———. *The Jews of Vienna, 1867–1914: Assimilation and Identity*. Albany, NY: State University of New York Press, 1983.

———. *Reconstructing a National Identity: The Jews of Habsburg Austria during World War I*. Oxford: Oxford University Press, 2001.

Salten, Felix. *Felix Salten—Wurstelprater: Ein Schlüsseltext zur Wiener Moderne*. Edited by Siegfried Mattl, Karl Müller-Richter, and Werner Michael Schwarz. Vienna: Promedia, 2004.

Sárosi, Bálint. *Gypsy Music*. Translated by Fred Macnicol. Budapest: Corvina Pres, 1978.

Saunders, Nicholas J. *Trench Art: Materialities and Memories of War*. Oxford: Berg, 2003.

Schaller, Wolfgang, ed. *Operette unterm Hakenkreuz: Zwischen hoffähiger Kunst und "Entartung."* Berlin: Metropol, 2007.

Schneider, David E. *Bartók, Hungary, and the Renewal of Tradition: Case Studies in the Intersection of Modernity and Nationality*. Berkeley: University of California Press, 2006.

Schneider, Herbert. "Couplet." In *MGG Online*, edited by Laurenz Lütteken. Kassel, Germany: Bärenreiter, 1995. https://www.mgg-online.com/mgg/stable/12453.

Schneidereit, Otto. *Berlin, wie es weint und lacht: Spaziergänge durch Berlins Operettengeschichte*. 2nd ed. Berlin: Lied der Zeit Musikverlag, 1973.

———. *Franz Lehár: Eine Biographie in Zitaten*. Innsbruck: Pinguin-Verlag, 1984.

———. *Richard Tauber: Ein Leben, eine Stimme*. Berlin: Lied der Zeit Musikverlag, 1976.

Schönherr, Max. "Modelle der Walzerkomposition: Grundlagen zu einer Theorie des Walzers." *Österreichische Musikzeitschrift* 30 (1975): 273–86.

Schorske, Carl E. *Fin-de-Siècle Vienna: Politics and Culture*. New York: Knopf, 1979.

Schwartz, Arman. "Rough Music: Tosca and Verismo Reconsidered." *19th-Century Music* 31, no. 3 (Spring 2008): 228–44.

Scott, Derek B. *German Operetta on Broadway and in the West End, 1900–1940*. Cambridge: Cambridge University Press, 2019.

———. *Sounds of the Metropolis: The Nineteenth-Century Popular Music Revolution in London, New York, Paris, and Vienna*. Oxford: Oxford University Press, 2008.

Segel, Harold B. *Turn-of-the-Century Cabaret: Paris, Barcelona, Berlin, Munich, Vienna, Cracow, Moscow, St. Petersburg, Zurich*. New York: Columbia University Press, 1987.

Semrau, Eugen. "Mehr als ein Leben: Konstruktion und Funktion der Robert-Stolz-Legende." In *Operette unterm Hakenkreuz: Zwischen hoffähiger Kunst und "Entartung"*, edited by Wolfgang Schaller, 179–97. Berlin: Metropol, 2007.

Senelick, Laurence. *Jacques Offenbach and the Making of Modern Culture*. Cambridge: Cambridge University Press, 2017.

Shaw, George Bernard. *Shaw's Music: The Complete Musical Criticism in Three Volumes*. New York: Dodd, Mead, 1981.

Shedde, Meenakshi, and Vinzenz Hediger. "Come On, Baby, Be My Tiger." In *Import/Export: Cultural Transfer between India and Germany*, edited by Angelika Fitz, Merle Kröger, Alexandra Schneider, and Dorothee Wenner. Berlin: Parthas, 2005.

Sicks, Kai Marcel. "Charleston, Girls, und Jazztanzbar: Amerikanismus und die Identitätskrise der Operette in den zwanziger Jahren." In *Einschnitte: Identität in der Moderne*, edited by Oliver Kohns and Martin Roussel, 153–65. Würzburg, Germany: Königshausen & Neumann, 2007.

Silcher, Friedrich. *Volkslieder gesammelt und für vier Männerstimmen*. Tübingen: Verlag der H. Laupp'schen Buchhandlung, 1902.

Slavíčkova, Eva. "Militärkapelle und ihre Stellung in dem Musikleben des 19. Jahrhunderts: Einfluss der Militärkapelle auf die Olomoucer Musikkultur bis zum Jahre 1918." *Musicologica Olomucensia* 5 (2000): 144.

Smith, Frank Berkeley. *The City of the Magyars*. London: T. Fisher Unwin, 1903.

Stanley, Jason. *How Propaganda Works*. Princeton, NJ: Princeton University Press, 2015.

Statistische Central-Commission. *Spezialortsrepertorium der österreichischen Länder*. Vienna: Verlag der K. K. Hof- und Staatsdruckerei, 1915.

Stegemann, Thorsten. *Wenn man das Leben durchs Champagnerglas Betrachtet—: Textbücher der Wiener Operette zwischen Provokation und Reaktion*. Frankfurt: Peter Lang, 1995.

Stein, Fritz. *50 Jahre Die Lustige Witwe*. Vienna: Doblinger, 1955.

Stein, Leo, Bela Jenbach, and Emmerich Kálmán. *Die Csárdásfürstin: Operette in drei Akten: Soufflier- und Regiebuch*. Leipzig: Weinberger, 1916.

Steinberg, Michael P. *The Meaning of the Salzburg Festival: Austria as Theater and Ideology, 1890–1938*. Ithaca, NY: Cornell University Press, 1990.

Steinthaler, Evelyn. *Morgen muss ich fort von hier: Richard Tauber: Die Emigration eines Weltstars*. Vienna: Milena, 2011.

Stieg, Gerald. "'Die letzten Tage der Menschheit': Eine negative Operette?" In Österreich und der Große Krieg, edited by Klaus Amann and Hubert Lengauer. Vienna: C. Brandstätter, 1989.

Stolz, Robert, and Einzi Stolz. *Servus Du: Robert Stolz und sein Jahrhundert*. Munich: Blanvalet, 1985.

Tadday, Ulrich, ed. *Im weißen Rössl: Zwischen Kunst und Kommerz*. Musik-Konzepte 133/134. Munich: edition text + kritik, 2006.

Timms, Edward. *Karl Kraus, Apocalyptic Satirist: Culture and Catastrophe in Habsburg Vienna*. New Haven, CT: Yale University Press, 1986.

———. *Karl Kraus, Apocalyptic Satirist: The Post-War Crisis and the Rise of the Swastika.* New Haven, CT: Yale University Press, 2005.

———. "Karl Kraus's Adaptations of Offenbach: The Quest for the Other Sphere." *Austrian Studies* 13 (January 1, 2005): 91–108.

Traubner, Richard. "Kálmán: Die Zirkussprinzessin." *Opera News*, July 2012. https://www.operanews.com/Opera_News_Magazine/2012/7/Recordings/KÁLMÁN__Die_Zirkusprinzessin.html.

———. *Operetta: A Theatrical History*. Rev. ed. New York: Routledge, 2003.

Tucker, Sherrie. *Swing Shift: "All-Girl" Bands of the 1940s*. Durham, NC: Duke University Press, 2000.

Uhland, Ludwig. *Werke*. Edited by Harmut Fröschle and Walter Scheffler. Vol. 1, *Sämtliche Gedichte*. Munich: Winkler Verlag, 1980.

Waller, Klaus. *Paul Abraham: Der tragische König der Operette*. Norderstedt, Germany: BoD, 2017.

Weber, William. *The Great Transformation of Musical Taste: Concert Programming from Haydn to Brahms*. Cambridge: Cambridge University Press, 2008.

Westermeyer, Karl. *Die Operette im Wandel des Zeitgeistes: Von Offenbach bis zur Gegenwart*. Berlin: Drei Masken Verlag, 1931.

Wicke, Peter. "Schlager." In *Die Musik in Geschichte und Gegenwart*, edited by Ludwig Finscher, 8:1063–70. Kassel: Bärenreiter, 1998.

Wildenbruch, Ernst von. *Die Haubenlerche: Schauspiel in vier Akten*. Berlin: Freund & Jeckel, 1897.

Winter, Jay. *Sites of Memory, Sites of Mourning: The Great War in European Cultural History*. Cambridge: Cambridge University Press, 2014.

Wolff, Larry. *Inventing Eastern Europe: The Map of Civilization on the Mind of the Enlightenment*. Stanford, CA: Stanford University Press, 2010.

Wolzogen, Ernst von. *Wie ich mich ums leben brachte: Erinnerungen und Erfahrungen*. Braunschweig: Georg Westermann, 1922.

Yates, W. E. *Theatre in Vienna: A Critical History, 1776–1995*. Cambridge: Cambridge University Press, 1996.

Zimmerman, Hans-Peter. "Der gute Kamerad: Ludwig Uhlands freiheitliche Konzeption des militärischen Totenkults." *Zeitschrift für Volkskunde* 95 (1999): 1–13.

Zweig, Stefan. *The World of Yesterday*. Lincoln: University of Nebraska Press, 1964.

INDEX

Herzer, Ludwig, 146
Herzl, Robert, 121
Herzogin von Chicago, Die (Kálmán), 160–66
Heuberger, Richard, 22, 29, 46, 199–200n56
Hirschfeld, Ludwig, 50, 119
Hofmannsthal, Hugo von, 124, 202n10
Holländer, Victor, 184n37
Homoki, Andreas, 173
Hooker, Lynn, 80, 195n42
Horkheimer, Max, 52
Hungary. *See also* style hongrois
    Kálmán's portrayal of, 74
    Viennese image of, 73, 75–78
Huszka, Jenő, 76–77
Hutcheon, Linda, 159

"Ich hatt' einen Kameraden," 98, 99–100, 101–5, 108
"Immer nur lächeln," 154–55
India, and exoticism of *Die Bajadere*, 134–40

Jacobi, Viktor, 76–77
Jacobson, Leopold, 27, 44, 92, 168, 200n70
Jelavich, Peter, 47
Jenbach, Béla, 110, 168, 200n65
Jews and Judaism, 49–51, 109–10, 120, 189nn20,21,30. *See also* anti-Semitism
Johann-Strauß-Theater, 85, 94, 112, 194n36, 200n70
John, Eckhard, 38
Jókai, Maurus, 75
Jones, Sidney, 21
Jonny spielt auf (Krenek), 162
Judaism. *See* anti-Semitism; Jews and Judaism
Judson, Pieter, 9
Jung-England (Bernauer and Welitsch), 203n14
Juxheirat, Die (Lehár), 26

Kaiserin Josephine (Kálmán), 160
Kálmán, Emmerich
    on Abraham, 159
    Az Obistos, 80, 95
    background of, 77
    Die Bajadere, 122–23, 134–45
    biographies of, 193n12
    Die Csárdásfürstin, 93, 108–9, 110–19, 120–21, 173
    emergence of, 46
    Gold gab ich für Eisen, 94–105, 108–9, 110, 120, 198n39
    Gräfin Mariza, 159–60, 200n67
    Der gute Kamerad, 95
    Ein Herbstmanöver, 84–85

Die Herzogin von Chicago, 160–66
    and incorporation of style hongrois in operetta, 74–75, 80–85
    Kaiserin Josephine, 160
    Miss Underground, 211n35
    and music criticism, 193–94n23
    nostalgic operettas of, 159–60
    Tatárjárás, 78–79, 95
    in United States, 168, 211n35
    Der Zigeunerprimas, 73–74, 85–92, 195n45
Karczag, Wilhelm, 15, 16, 24–25, 26, 41, 72, 78, 94, 184n39, 200n69
Karpath, Ludwig, 42, 119, 134, 186n78
Kartousch, Louise, 79, 80, 97, 109
Kauders, Albert, 25
Kauffman, Mattias, 10, 179n23
Keller, Otto, 10, 22–23, 182n3
Kellerbauer, Walter, 79
Kemal, Mustafa, 128
Klotz, Volker, 61
Koch, Hans-Jörg, 23
Koessler, Hans, 77
kolo, 29, 32, 185n63
Komische Oper Berlin, 171–72
Komödie, 143–44
Konwitschny, Peter, 93, 120–21, 173
Korngold, Erich Wolfgang, 159
Kosky, Barrie, 171–72
Kracauer, Siegfried, 45, 63, 184n36
Kraus, Karl, 11, 42–43, 93–94, 105–10, 120, 173, 196n6, 199–200n56
Krauss, Clemens, 167
Krenek, Ernst, 162, 167
Kühn, Edmund, 150

labor
    Eva and, 65, 70, 71–72
    Ein Walzertraum and, 55–56
ladies' orchestras, 53–56, 57–60
Land des Lächelns, Das (Lehár), 123, 125, 145–57, 173, 207nn71,74
Lang, Georg, 184n39
Langkammer, Karl, 22
Lehár, Franz. *See also lustige Witwe, Die* (Lehár)
    background of, 25
    on broad appeal of operetta, 23
    career of, in 1910s and 1920s, 206n60
    emergence of, 46
    ethnic identity of, 33
    Eva, 64–72
    experimentalism of, 65
    Friederike, 146, 151
    Die gelbe Jacke, 146, 147, 148, 151, 207n71

Founded in 1893,
UNIVERSITY OF CALIFORNIA PRESS
publishes bold, progressive books and journals
on topics in the arts, humanities, social sciences,
and natural sciences—with a focus on social
justice issues—that inspire thought and action
among readers worldwide.

The UC PRESS FOUNDATION
raises funds to uphold the press's vital role
as an independent, nonprofit publisher, and
receives philanthropic support from a wide
range of individuals and institutions—and from
committed readers like you. To learn more, visit
ucpress.edu/supportus.